"The publication of this book is a call to join with the National Institute for Civil Discourse in its mission of improving our spaces for civic dialogue. Fundamentally, I believe that to achieve the aspirations expressed in our founding documents, we must be able to engage in civil public conversations among citizens of the greatest possible diversity all across the country."
    —**Gabrielle Giffords**, former U.S. Representative; from the Foreword

"*A Crisis of Civility?* is vital to our national dialogue on the exigency of civility in our society. In these pages, a network of prominent scholars make a compelling case for civility as the one essential mechanism for distilling the vast diversity of ideologies and opinions in America, so that we can arrive at solutions to our most pressing challenges. Today's forces of division and proliferation of sensationalism have combined as virulent enemies of civility. Fortunately, the National Institute for Civil Discourse is leading the movement to revive civility, compromise, and consensus building. Now, we must all join the cause and remind one another that, as we debate our differences, our use of words is powerful and critically important in setting a constructive tone for the important conversations that will determine America's future."
    —**Olympia Snowe**, Senior Fellow, the Bipartisan
    Policy Senator; former United States Senator

"Americans all along the political spectrum are worried about our ability to get along and develop constructive solutions for our political problems. So many of our country's challenges are made even more difficult by a lack of opportunities to engage in civil discourse, to talk across the boundaries that can too often divide us. The chapters in this book provide clear-eyed discussions of contemporary politics that help us to understand how we got to this point and how we can work together to improve our democracy. This is essential reading for scholars, practitioners, and anyone concerned about our nation's future."

—**Tom Daschle**, Founder and CEO, The Daschle Group;
former Senator and Senate Majority Leader

"As the media continues to cover our increasingly coarsened political, public, and even private discourse, this research will be critically important to our understanding of how words can be weaponized and language can motivate violence. This book will also be invaluable as we revive the democratic norms of civility and respect. I can't wait to share it with my colleagues."

—**Katie Couric**, former anchor and Managing Editor, *CBS Evening News*; former Special Correspondent, *ABC News*

"The best antidote for the bitter partisanship that has overtaken American public life is also the simplest: getting people of diverse viewpoints to know and listen to each other. The thoughtful chapters in this book are an invaluable addition to NICD's effort to keep American democracy vibrant and strong."

—**Mickey Edwards**, Vice President, The Aspen Institute;
former United States Representative

"If we are serious about restoring civility, we need to know how to recognize it and what actions might improve it, how different disciplines approach the challenge, and how past civility crises have ended. This book is a treasure trove of clear thinking and analysis to guide the restoration of civil discourse."

—**Alice M. Rivlin**, founding Director of the Congressional Budget Office and former Vice Chair of the Federal Reserve

"Many Americans perceive a crisis of incivility, yet demanding civility may suppress worthy voices. If you seek insight on these and related issues, *A Crisis of Civility?* is the best available guide, filled with thoughtful, original contributions by scholars who represent diverse perspectives and approaches."

—**Peter Levine**, Lincoln Filene Professor of Citizenship and Public Affairs, Tisch College of Civic Life, Tufts University

"How should the fractious state of politics be understood? And what can be done about it? With contributions from an impressive array of scholars, *A Crisis of Civility?* surveys public perceptions of civility, details contemporary examples of incivility, and mines the past for practical solutions. It is essential reading for a time when common decency no longer seems very common."

—**Keith J. Bybee**, Vice Dean and Paul E. and the Hon. Joanne F. Alper '72 Judiciary Studies Professor, College of Law, Syracuse University

"This first of its kind interdisciplinary, research-based examination of civility in politics sheds light on the importance of improving the current tenor of political discourse to enhance the well-being and safety of our nation. The contributing scholars also underscore the pressing need to promote understanding, tolerance, and respect for the differences among us, which is a guiding principle for the field of psychology. This is a must read not only for those in politics and journalism but also for the public at large."

—**Arthur C. Evans, Jr.**, PhD, Chief Executive
Officer, American Psychological Association

"America has many solvable problems, and because of our dysfunctional politics, we are likely to solve few of them. This collection of essays by some of America's top researchers is therefore essential. It will help readers to understand the various kinds of civility, why most of them are declining, and what we can do—as individuals and in organizations—to bring about better public discourse."

—**Jonathan Haidt**, Professor of Ethical Leadership, New York
University Stern School of Business, and author of *The Righteous
Mind: Why Good People Are Divided by Politics and Religion*

"I don't think a day goes by in the United States when I don't see or read about a fracture in our civil life—whether it be a bully's words, a politician's accusations, or a mass murder. Make no mistake, we have a crisis of civility in this country today. The National Institute for Civil Discourse was founded out of one such tragedy—the attempted assassination of former Congresswoman Gabrielle Giffords in 2010 by a lone shooter. In the years since then, the NICD has become the leading voice on reviving civility in our country and this collection of essays—taken together—is an urgent call to action to seek what binds us rather than what divides us. There is no more important topic to the survival of our democratic experiment."

—**Steven Petrow**, *USA Today* Opinion Columnist;
host, *The Civilist* podcast

A CRISIS OF CIVILITY?

The state of political discourse in the United States today has been a subject of concern for many Americans. Political incivility is not merely a problem for political elites; political conversations between American citizens have also become more difficult and tense. The 2016 presidential elections featured campaign rhetoric designed to inflame the general public. Yet the 2016 election was certainly not the only cause of incivility among citizens. There have been many instances in recent years where reasoned discourse in our universities and other public venues has been threatened.

This book was undertaken as a response to these problems. It presents and develops a more robust discussion of what civility is, why it matters, what factors might contribute to it, and what its consequences are for democratic life. The authors included here pursue three major questions: Is the state of American political discourse today really that bad, compared to prior eras; what lessons about civility can we draw from the 2016 election; and how have changes in technology such as the development of online news and other means of mediated communication changed the nature of our discourse?

This book seeks to develop a coherent, civil conversation between divergent contemporary perspectives in political science, communications, history, sociology, and philosophy. This multidisciplinary approach helps to reflect on challenges to civil discourse, define civility, and identify its consequences for democratic life in a digital age. In this accessible text, an all-star cast of contributors tills the earth in which future discussion on civility will be planted.

Robert G. Boatright is Professor of Political Science at Clark University and the Director of Research at the National Institute for Civil Discourse (NICD) at the University of Arizona.

Timothy J. Shaffer is Assistant Professor of Communication Studies at Kansas State University and Principal Research Specialist for the National Institute for Civil Discourse.

Sarah Sobieraj is Associate Professor of Sociology at Tufts University.

Dannagal Goldthwaite Young is Associate Professor of Communication at the University of Delaware.

A CRISIS OF CIVILITY?

Political Discourse and Its Discontents

Edited by Robert G. Boatright, Timothy J. Shaffer, Sarah Sobieraj, and Dannagal Goldthwaite Young

Routledge
Taylor & Francis Group

NEW YORK AND LONDON

First published 2019
by Routledge
52 Vanderbilt Avenue, New York, NY 10017

and by Routledge
2 Park Square, Milton Park, Abingdon, Oxon, OX14 4RN

Routledge is an imprint of the Taylor & Francis Group, an informa business

Library of Congress Cataloging-in-Publication Data
Names: Boatright, Robert G., editor.
Title: A crisis of civility? : political discourse and its discontents / edited
  by Robert G. Boatright, Timothy J. Shaffer, Sarah Sobieraj,
  and Dannagal Goldthwaite Young.
Description: New York, NY : Routledge, 2019. | Includes bibliographical
  references and index.
Identifiers: LCCN 2018051613 | ISBN 9781138484429 (hardback) |
  ISBN 9781138484450 (pbk.) | ISBN 9781351051965 (epub) |
  ISBN 9781351051958 (mobipocket/kindle) | ISBN 9781351051989
  (master ebook) | ISBN 9781351051972 (web pdf)
Subjects: LCSH: Political culture—United States. | Polarization
  (Social sciences)—Political aspects—United States. | Courtesy—
  Political aspects—United States. | Social media—Political aspects—
  United States. | Mass media—Political aspects—United States. |
  Presidents—United States—Election—2016. | United States—Politics
  and government—21st century—Public opinion.
Classification: LCC JK1764 .C75 2019 | DDC 306.20973—dc23
LC record available at https://lccn.loc.gov/2018051613

ISBN: 978-1-138-48442-9 (hbk)
ISBN: 978-1-138-48445-0 (pbk)
ISBN: 978-1-351-05198-9 (ebk)

Typeset in Bembo
by Apex CoVantage, LLC

CONTENTS

FIGURES

TABLES

CONTRIBUTORS

Editors

Robert G. Boatright is Professor of Political Science at Clark University and Director of Research at the National Institute for Civil Discourse (NICD) at the University of Arizona. His research focuses on the effects of campaign and election laws on the behavior of politicians and interest groups, with a particular focus on primary elections and campaign finance laws and practices. He is the author or editor of seven books, including *Getting Primaried: The Causes and Consequences of Congressional Primary Challenges* (University of Michigan Press, 2013); *Interest Groups and Campaign Finance Reform in the United States and Canada* (University of Michigan Press, 2011); and the edited volume *The Deregulatory Moment? A Comparative Perspective on Changing Campaign Finance Laws* (University of Michigan Press, 2016).

Timothy J. Shaffer is Assistant Professor of Communication Studies at Kansas State University and Principal Research Specialist for the National Institute for Civil Discourse. As a scholar, Shaffer centers his research on the advancement of democratic engagement through deliberative democracy and citizen engagement in higher education and community settings. He has published in journals such as *The Good Society*, *Journal of Public Deliberation*, *Journal of Higher Education Outreach and Engagement*, *Journal of Community Engagement and Scholarship*, and *Rural Sociology*. He has also contributed to edited volumes on environmental leadership and higher education's civic engagement mission. He is the editor of *Deliberative Pedagogy: Teaching and Learning for Democratic Engagement* (Michigan State University Press, 2017). He received a PhD from Cornell University, an MPA and an MA from the University of Dayton, and a BA from St. Bonaventure University.

Sarah Sobieraj is Associate Professor of Sociology at Tufts University. She is the author of *The Outrage Industry: Political Opinion Media and the New Incivility* (Oxford University Press 2014) with Jeff Berry, and *Soundbitten: The Perils of Media-Centered Political Activism* (NYU 2011). Her most recent journal articles can be found in *PS: Political Science & Politics, Poetics, Political Communication, Social Problems, Sociological Theory, Sociological Inquiry, and The Sociological Quarterly*. Her work has also been featured in venues such as the *New York Times, Politico,* CNN, PBS, *The American Prospect, National Review, Pacific Standard,* and *Salon.* She directs the Digital Sexism Project, investigating the impact of gender-based attacks against women online on political discourse. She received her PhD from the State University of New York, Albany, and an MA from American University.

Dannagal Goldthwaite Young is Associate Professor of Communication at the University of Delaware. Her research interests include political media effects, public opinion, political satire, and the psychology of political humor. Her work on the role and effects of late-night comedy in the changing political environment has been published in numerous journals, including *Media Psychology, Political Communication, International Journal of Press/Politics, Journal of Broadcasting and Electronic Media,* and *Mass Media and Society.* She received her PhD from the University of Pennsylvania.

Authors

Steven C. Bullock is Professor of History at Worcester Polytechnic Institute, where he received the Trustees' Award for Outstanding Research and Creative Scholarship. He has also served as a Fulbright Lecturer in Okinawa, Japan. He is the author of *Tea Sets and Tyranny: The Politics of Politeness in Early America, Revolutionary Brotherhood: Freemasonry and the Transformation of the American Social Order, 1730–1840,* and *The American Revolution: A History in Documents.* He has also published in the *Wall Street Journal, Aeon,* and *Newsday,* and appeared on ABC, CNN, and NPR, and in documentaries that have aired on PBS, the History Channel, and elsewhere.

Kevin Coe (PhD, University of Illinois) is Associate Professor in the Department of Communication at the University of Utah. His research and teaching focus on the interaction of American political discourse, news media, and public opinion. His scholarship has appeared in such journals as *Communication Monographs, Communication Research, Journal of Communication,* and *Public Opinion Quarterly.* He is coauthor, with David Domke, of *The God Strategy: How Religion Became a Political Weapon in America* (Oxford).

John Gastil is Professor in the Department of Communication Arts and Sciences and Political Science at the Pennsylvania State University, where he is a senior scholar at the McCourtney Institute for Democracy. His most recent books include *The Jury and Democracy*, *Democracy in Motion*, *The Australian Citizens' Parliament and the Future of Deliberative Democracy*, and a second edition of *Democracy in Small Groups*. His current research focuses on the Citizens' Initiative Review and efforts to create a more integrated system of online tools for civic engagement.

Gabrielle Giffords represented Arizona's 8th Congressional District from 2007 to 2012. She is the third woman in Arizona's history to be elected the U.S. Congress and the youngest woman elected to the Arizona State Senate. As a member of the House, she participated in the Blue Dog Democrat Coalition and the New Democrat Coalition. While in Congress, Giffords voted in favor of raising the minimum wage, endorsing the 9/11 Commission recommendations, new rules for the House of Representatives targeting ethical issues, the repeal of $14 billion of subsidies to big oil reserves, and the enactment of subsidies for renewable energy. She has also worked tirelessly for border control and veteran affairs. Prior to her time as a Congresswoman, she was a member of the Arizona House of Representatives from 2001 to 2003 and the Arizona Senate from 2003 to 2005. Giffords was a victim of the January 8th shooting in Tucson, Arizona. She has made great progress in recovering with the help of friends, family, and supporters. She resigned from the U.S. Congress on January 25, 2012, to focus on further recovery.

Lindsay H. Hoffman (PhD, The Ohio State University) is Associate Professor of Communication and Associate Director of the Center for Political Communication at the University of Delaware.

Kate Kenski (PhD, University of Pennsylvania) is Associate Professor in the Department of Communication at the University of Arizona. She is coauthor, with Bruce W. Hardy and Kathleen Hall Jamieson, of the award-winning book *The Obama Victory: How Media, Money, and Message Shaped the 2008 Election* (2010, Oxford University Press). Her current research focuses on new media in political campaigns, political incivility, and decision making in online spaces.

Anthony Simon Laden is Professor of Philosophy at the University of Illinois at Chicago, and Associate Director of the Center for Ethics and Education. He is the author of *Reasoning: A Social Picture* (Oxford, 2012) and co-editor, with David Owen, of *Multiculturalism and the Politics of Identity* (Cambridge, 2007).

Carolyn J. Lukensmeyer is Executive Director of the National Institute for Civil Discourse, an organization that works to reduce political dysfunction and incivility in our political system. As a leader in the field of deliberative democracy, she works to restore our democracy to reflect the intended vision of our founding fathers. Dr. Lukensmeyer previously served as Founder and President of America*Speaks*, an award-winning nonprofit organization that promoted nonpartisan initiatives to engage citizens and leaders through the development of innovative public policy tools and strategies. During her tenure, America*Speaks* engaged more than 200,000 people and hosted events across all 50 states and throughout the world. Dr. Lukensmeyer formerly served as Consultant to the White House chief of staff from 1993 to 1994 and on the National Performance Review, where she steered internal management and oversaw government-wide reforms. She was Chief of Staff to Ohio governor Richard F. Celeste from 1986 to 1991, becoming the first woman to serve in this capacity. She earned her PhD in Organizational Behavior from Case Western Reserve University and has completed postgraduate training at the Gestalt Institute of Cleveland. In addition to her work at the National Institute for Civil Discourse, she also serves on the American Academy of Arts and Sciences Commission on the Practice of Democratic Citizenship.

Deborah S. Mower is the Mr. and Mrs. Alfred Hume Bryant Chair of Ethics and Associate Professor of Philosophy at the University of Mississippi. She specializes in moral psychology, moral education, and applied ethics. She recently published two co-edited volumes: *Civility in Politics and Education* as well as *Developing Moral Sensitivity*. She also received a grant from the National Endowment for the Humanities to co-direct a 2016 Summer Institute on Moral Psychology and Education. She is current President of the Society for Ethics Across the Curriculum, an international society devoted to the teaching and learning of ethics.

Ashley Muddiman (PhD, University of Texas at Austin) is Assistant Professor in the Department of Communication Studies at the University of Kansas. She also is Faculty Research Associate with the Center for Media Engagement housed at the Moody College of Communication at the University of Texas at Austin. Her research explores political media effects, specifically those related to political incivility and digital news.

Stephen A. Rains (PhD, University of Texas at Austin) is Professor of Communication at the University of Arizona. His research on civility can be found in the *Journal of Communication*, *Communication Research*, and the *Journal of Computer-Mediated Communication*.

Deana A. Rohlinger is Professor of Sociology at Florida State University. She studies mass media, political participation, and politics in America. She is the author of *Abortion Politics, Mass Media, and Social Movements in America* (Cambridge University Press 2015) as well as dozens of book chapters and research articles on political participation and mass media. Her new book, *Digital Media and Society*, will be published in 2018 by New York University Press.

Patrícia Rossini (PhD, Federal University of Minas Gerais) is a postdoctoral researcher in the School of Information Studies at Syracuse University. She is interested in studying the interplay between political communication and digital technologies, with emphasis on political discussion online. Her research is mostly focused on uncivil and intolerant discourse, political campaigns, deliberation, and political participation.

Danielle Roth (MA, University of Delaware) was a graduate student in Communication at the time of the writing of this chapter. She currently works within the advertising industry.

J. Cherie Strachan is Assistant Dean with Special Projects in Student and Civic Engagement for the College of Humanities, Social, and Behavioral Sciences; Director of the School of Public Service and Global Citizenship; and Professor of Political Science at Central Michigan University. She is also Co-founder and Co-director of the Consortium for Inter-Campus SoTL Research (CISR), which facilitates multi-campus data collection to assess civic engagement initiatives and political science pedagogy. Strachan is the author of *High-Tech Grassroots: The Professionalization of Local Elections*, as well as over 30 reviewed and invited articles and book chapters. Her recent publications focus on the effects of partisan polarization on elections, the role of civility in a democratic society, and the effect of college-level civic education interventions intended to enhance students' civic skills and identities.

Emily Sydnor is Assistant Professor of Political Science at Southwestern University. She received her PhD from the University of Virginia and her work has been published in *PS: Political Science & Politics*, *The Journal of Information Technology and Politics*, and *Political Communication*. Her book, *Disrespectful Democracy*, demonstrates that individuals' reactions to incivility are dependent on their orientation toward conflict and is forthcoming from Columbia University Press.

Cynthia Williams is a PhD candidate at Florida State University, where she researches the role of science in society, media, social movements, repression, and environmental sociology.

Michael R. Wolf is Professor and Chair of the Department of Political Science at Purdue University Fort Wayne. His research focuses on comparative and American public opinion and political behavior. He is coauthor (with Lori Poloni-Staudinger) of *American Difference: A Guide to American Politics in Comparative Perspective* (SAGE/CQ Press) and co-editor of *Political Discussion in Modern Democracies* (Routledge), and has co-authored numerous articles or book chapters on political compromise, civility, and political attitudes.

FOREWORD

American politics and public life have always provided space for vigorous disagreement. At times, Americans have allowed our differences to overshadow the many values we hold in common. Yet we have always managed to overcome division, to ensure that our disagreements are resolved in a way that makes us stronger as a country.

Today, we find ourselves at another moment where discord, disagreement, and suspicion have taken center stage in our public life. This is not something that happened overnight. I experienced it myself during my 2010 campaign for reelection to Congress, which was marked by rhetoric and behavior that undermined, rather than contributed to, the healthy exercise of our democratic traditions. The specter of violence also followed me on the campaign trail, whether it was finding my office windows shot through or a handgun being spilled at my feet during a political event. Of course, the next year a lone shooter opened fire on me and a crowd of fellow citizens who had been gathered for a "Congress on Your Corner" event in the parking lot of a local supermarket. As is well known, I was seriously injured, as were 12 other people. Six people died.

As Americans do so well after a crisis, in the days, weeks, and months following the shooting, the Tucson community and the country as a whole rallied around the survivors and the families of victims in powerful ways. The National Institute for Civil Discourse (NICD) was founded out of this tragedy. The Institute was born out of a love of our country and a profound desire to do all that we could to ensure that nothing like this would ever happen again. To this end, NICD has sponsored a wide range of programs designed to encourage Americans to discuss their differences in a civil fashion, as well as establishing a research program that highlights the challenges to and possibilities of civil discourse.

The publication of this book is a call to join with NICD in its mission of improving our spaces for civic dialogue. Fundamentally, I believe that to achieve the aspirations expressed in our founding documents, we must be able to engage in civil public conversations among citizens of the greatest possible diversity all across the country.

Gabrielle Giffords

PREFACE

Amor patriae ("love of country") was praised by the Roman poet Virgil as a high virtue of public office. It can, Virgil warned, be undermined by a greater love of public praise or public applause. Americans live in a nation and at a time when these two impulses clash daily in the public sphere. In a roiling political climate where positions appear more polarized than ever, it is difficult for voices of equanimity and reason to make it through the clamor of Internet-connected devices and jam-packed broadcast programming.

Public officials confront this dilemma daily—to serve their highest aspirations for the nation and their constituents while simultaneously considering the tone, forums, and methods to achieve public awareness and approval. As citizens, the challenge is to advance the causes we care about while being educated about, even empathetic toward, the thinking of citizens whose views differ from our own. More often than not, real issues are trapped between the symbolism that accompanies concepts of patriotism and the sensational "spin" necessary to drive a story through the media.

The result is a clamorous, gridlocked public sphere where loud and extreme voices condition public discourse and too often dominate policy outcomes.

Forces of balance and compromise are mediated in our lives within a 24-hour news cycle, across inescapable streams of social media commentary, and in data derived by a relentless public opinion polling industry. Combined, these tools foster perpetual scrutiny, anxiety, and conflict, which can squeeze out essential spaces for civil discourse. It is hard to be civil and it is hard to dialogue when the dominant sentiment is that *everything is on the line*. Instead, our communication tools amplify the differences in our choices, deepening discord and sowing division among Americans who might otherwise be proud and genuinely grateful to share this nation in common with one another.

This brings us to a root of civic life that is withering—*the love for one another.* This is a patriotic affection for the attributes and the aspirations of our fellow citizens that feeds a healthy sentiment of pride and a culture of public engagement. Instead, political opportunism and conflict-centered media have opened gaps between ordinary citizens that erode trust, break down healthy communication, and foment intolerant attitudes toward one another.

It would not be hyperbole to say that in today's political climate, the idea of truly civil discourse is a radical—even a revolutionary—idea. The National Institute for Civil Discourse (NICD) was founded to pursue this idea, to do all that we can to bring civility and healthy civic engagement back to the public realm.

The Institute's work is based on extensive research with a commitment to innovation and experimentation. NICD's programs are designed for elected officials, journalists, and the public. We create forums for learning and practicing the skills necessary to re-establish the social norms of civility and respect. This is critical to recognizing that we all share a basic love of country, despite our differences. Such recognition is the bedrock on which we will build bridges that repair the divides that threaten our democracy.

Today the United States' centuries-long experiment with democracy faces a crisis of civility in ways Virgil might have predicted, but never imagined. All democracies endure their tests and challenges; but never before have systemic, existential threats been institutionalized as they are today through our use of media and technology. The general civic spirit and civil demeanor that underlay a healthy *amor patriae* have broken down in ways that we have not seen before, resulting in new threats to our institutions, our public servants, and the public as a whole.

We believe that academic institutions and scholarship play a special role in revitalizing democracy. This is why NICD has cultivated a network of scholars from over 30 institutions of higher education and from a range of different perspectives and political affiliations. We work with them in three essential ways. First, we work with faculty and administrators to provide training in tools and processes that cultivate genuine conditions for scholarship on campus: free speech and the ability to engage with ideas without fear of reprisal. Second, we develop curricular materials that assert civic dialogue as an emerging and essential area of academic inquiry. Third, we support colleges and universities in their efforts to cultivate broad community participation through civic engagement and discourse in the communities where they reside.

This work is transformative work. It is revolutionary in spirit and it is essential as a means to reinvigorate and strengthen our democracy.

Civility is a core attribute of democratic life; it is the fundamental orientation through which compromise solutions are derived. Without the capacity of citizens and public servants to approach any issue through the lens of *amor patriae* and an authentic love of fellow citizens, it is exceedingly difficult to discern meaningful public choices for the good of all. Without generally acceptable compromises, it is unlikely we will ever define and pass into law the decisions we must make to grow and thrive at a time of profound global transformation. To paraphrase Benjamin Franklin at the Constitutional Convention, we must hang together or we will hang separately.

This book is developed from scholarship in the fields of communication, philosophy, history, psychology, sociology, public engagement, public policy, and political science. It is intended to be useful as a guide to further research, and as a curriculum resource for engagement in the classroom. The three sections in this book—"How Americans Think About Civility in Politics," "Instances of Civility and Incivility in Contemporary American Political Discourse," and "Learning From the Past"—point to an essential fork in the road of American democracy. We have in front of us two paths: one where intolerance, incivility, and political and media interests divide Americans in our politics and civic life, and the other where civil and healthy discourse transforms the polarization that has come to define American politics today.

To avoid the path of intolerance and division, a new practice of civic discourse must become an essential, persistent feature of modern democratic life. We hope that students of democracy at every level will see in this book a collection of urgent calls to action. We hope that readers will find a spark of inspiration to join with us on this journey to strengthen our democracy through improved civic discourse and a rekindled love of country.

Carolyn J. Lukensmeyer

INTRODUCTION

A Crisis of Civility?

Robert G. Boatright

Calls for civility have proliferated since the 2016 election. Some of the calls have been eloquent, well reasoned, and quite serious. Former president George W. Bush delivered a speech on October 19, 2017, in which he called upon American politicians to serve as role models of civility. In their book *One Nation After Trump*, political columnists E. J. Dionne, Norman J. Ornstein, and Thomas Mann (2017) elaborate on the steps they believe will be needed to restore civility to American politics. Such sentiments are nothing new; before 2016, Bush, Barack Obama, and Dionne and his colleagues were all actively calling for a renewed emphasis on civility as a means of overcoming political divisions. These calls may have become more urgent since the bitter 2016 campaign and its aftermath, but they are certainly not without precedent.

Other recent calls for civility have been more casual. "Civility" bumper stickers are on their way to becoming as ubiquitous as the "coexist" bumper stickers that have adorned cars for years. In my home state of Massachusetts—a state whose residents are known for their rude driving habits—it is not uncommon to find one's self in traffic with vehicles sporting civility bumper stickers. Are these statements of a political agenda, or merely a polite and completely apolitical plea to treat our fellow citizens with respect? Rude drivers, as well, were with us well before the 2016 election. But to the extent that this election has made calls for civility seem more momentous, or more connected to a national sense of purpose, it is hard to argue that they should not be welcomed.

And it would seem that the public is paying attention. According to a recent Marist Poll, over 70% of Americans believe the level of civility in American politics declined between 2016 and 2017, and merely 6% feel it has improved. In prior surveys, over 20% of Americans reported that civility increased in the year following the election (Taylor 2017). Weber Shandwick, an organization that has conducted a survey of Americans' perceptions of civility, reported in December 2016 that 75% of Americans agreed that there is a "crisis" of civility, and over half of respondents claimed that they were not interested in following politics or engaging in public affairs because of incivility. And when given a choice of who to blame for increases in incivility, Americans overwhelmingly blamed politicians. The problem, then, has existed for some time, but there is evidence that it has gotten worse recently.

These essays were chosen to provide insights into the nature of this problem. They were gathered under the auspices of the National Institute for Civil Discourse (NICD). NICD was founded at the University of Arizona in May 2011, following the tragic assassination attempt on Representative Gabrielle Giffords. NICD has engaged in a number of projects aimed at restoring civility in American life. Among these was the formation of the NICD Research Network, which has drawn together over 50 different academics from a wide range of college and universities, and from a wide range of academic disciplines and points of view. These essays represent just a small portion of the research conducted by NICD Research Network members.

The concept of civility is not "owned" by any particular academic discipline. While the chapters in this book are not intended to provide a comprehensive survey of everything there is to say about civility, they have been selected to show the diverse array of approaches to civility. Social scientists—including political scientists, sociologists, and psychologists—have sought to measure what people think civility is. They have explored the particular behaviors that citizens believe are civil or uncivil, and the effects of civility and incivility on political discourse. Communication scholars and students of the media have explored the relationship between changes in communication technology and norms about civil discourse. Psychologists have studied the correlates of civility in interpersonal communication—who is civil, and what sort of effects civility can have on our emotional well-being. Philosophers have asked about the moral import of civility: should we be civil? And what is the relationship between civility and justice or empathy for others? Can a shared goal of civility hamper our effort to explain ourselves to others or to allow for dissenting voices? And historians have studied changes in norms of civility over time: have citizens and political elites in the past adopted the same norms of discourse in the past, or dealt with incivility in the same way that we do now?

Just as the concept of civility is not the province of any one sort of disciplinary methodology, so it is not easily reconciled with one political ideology or set of beliefs. In today's politics, calls for moderation are also common. It is easy to equate moderation with a sort of political centrism—an effort to seek a middle ground between welfare state liberalism and free market conservatism. There is perhaps some equivalence here—scholars who bemoan the polarization of American politics often reminisce about a bygone era in America when centrists sought compromise between rival factions, or sought to create legislation that could generate bipartisan support. Yet it is entirely possible to be civil in discourse yet firmly committed to an ideological agenda. Senator Jeff Flake's eloquent plea for civility—delivered in the same speech in which he announced his intention to retire from the Senate—was all the more striking because Flake has been a doctrinaire conservative throughout his career in Congress. Flake was not arguing that politicians should abandon their goals or compromise their beliefs; rather, he argued that they should pursue these goals through reasoned argument and through agreed-upon institutional channels.

Moderation, thus, need not be equated with the pursuit of compromise at all costs, nor should it be assumed to be an unprincipled urge to have things both ways. Some contemporary studies of moderation have recognized this. The political philosopher Aurelian Craiutu (2016) has recently sought to elevate moderation not as an ideology but as a disposition—a willingness to pursue a pragmatic politics that accepts the humanity of one's opponents, that abandons the assumption that there is an ultimate goal for human endeavors, and that seeks to place the goal of fostering an inclusive political community above the goal of dictating what the community is or should do. In this sense, civility would seem to be a necessary component of moderation. Civility assumes that we speak to each other—whether in political debate or in our interpersonal relations—in a manner that respects our shared status as citizens, or more broadly, as humans. It means that we should always maintain a certain level of humility when we discuss our rights or our aims.

An interdisciplinary, non-ideological approach to civility such as this suggests that we should not automatically assume that civility should be a paramount goal. It also suggests that the concerns we have in today's politics—our concern about a coarsening of political language, a demonization of one's opponents, or a refusal to engage with opposing points of view—are only a small piece of the problem. Some studies of civility have contended that civil behavior is essentially an agreement to restrain one's self—to seek compromise or to avoid matters where compromise is not possible and conflict is inevitable (e.g., Carter 1998). Such an approach might be beneficial in some social circumstances, but it seems ill-equipped to solve persistent social problems or to address long-simmering grievances. To speak of civility, then, we must speak of more than just avoiding conflict.

Perhaps the best way to illustrate this approach is to consider the meaning of the term "civil society." As philosopher Lawrence Cahoone (2000) notes, in drawing upon Michael Oakeshott's (1975) work, we do not often think today about what is "civil" when we refer to civil society. It is, for the most part, a term that academics use to talk about some amorphous group that we belong to, a grouping that doesn't necessarily have anything to do with politics. Yet we assume that there is something we have in common that precedes the establishment of political institutions. It assumes that when we define ourselves as a people, we do so by granting others within our group a certain level of respect—a presumption that we will interact in a civil fashion. If our politics, then, become uncivil, it can mean either that the bonds that link us together as a people have frayed, or that the link between our community and our political leaders has been severed. In either instance, a decline in civility among our political elites has troubling implications for our ability to treat each other in a civil fashion.

Thinking about the civility in civil society, then, suggests that civility is more than simply good manners, or more than an agreement not to hurt each other's feelings. It suggests that any healthy society should set civility as a goal, even while it debates what civility means for us today. Perhaps we can survive as a society even while agreeing to shrug off a certain amount of rude language or blunt assertion of our goals. But setting civility as a goal requires that we deliberate, that we have, at a minimum, a shared agreement that we are in this together—that we are a society. It suggests, as well, that we should not use calls for civility as a means of silencing others. Perhaps paradoxically, having a civil society may well mean that we must tolerate a certain amount of incivility, or that we not respond to incivility in a tit for tat fashion.

It is evident, then, that we need to address what civility and incivility are, how we measure civility in different political and social contexts, and how we can think constructively about tools to address the prospect of changes in the level of civility. Accordingly, the chapters in this book are grouped into three sections. First, we consider the ways in which civility is defined. Anthony Simon Laden distinguishes between two different definitions of civility in Chapter 1, arguing that civility can be understood either as politeness or as responsiveness. These two definitions derive from different philosophical traditions and can be associated with different ends on the part of citizens or speakers, and violations of these two types of civility require different types of solutions. While civility as responsiveness may be a richer and more normatively appealing concept, it also requires much greater effort to maintain.

In Chapter 2, Ashley Muddiman discusses the actions and statements made by politicians that citizens deem to be uncivil. She makes a distinction between personal incivility—name-calling and such—and public incivility, which entails a rejection of norms of deliberative discourse or a rejection of fact-based argument. Muddiman describes a general agreement on what personal civility and incivility entail but partisan differences in understandings of public civility. In the subsequent chapter, Kate Kenski, Kevin Coe, and Stephen A. Rains compare academic definitions of civility to those held by citizens; they also explore variations in citizens' views on civility and incivility according to age and gender. And in Chapter 4, Emily Sydnor argues that we understand violations of civility norms differently based on characteristics of the speaker and the style of speech, and in the substance of what is being said.

Second, we consider various instances of civility and incivility in contemporary American social and political discourse. Problems in the quality of political discourse do not necessarily originate among our politicians, nor were the most objectionable features of the 2016 election entirely without precedent. In Chapter 5, Dannagal Goldthwaite Young, Lindsay H. Hoffman, and Danielle Roth consider the ways in which media coverage of politics can encourage incivility. Chapters 6 through 8 consider the role of social media in encouraging or discouraging civil discourse. In Chapter 6, Deana A. Rohlinger and Cynthia Williams compare the rhetoric of Twitter users in responding to campus shootings at Florida State University and Ohio State University. Chapter 7, by J. Cherie Strachan and Michael R. Wolf, considers the language used in describing Muslim Americans. In Chapter 8, Patrícia Rossini provides a counterpoint to the predominantly American material in this book by exploring online political rhetoric in Brazil. She argues that incivility tends to be used more as a means of emphasizing the strength of one's political opinions than as an effort to demean or attack opponents. Each of these chapters seeks to draw broader lessons about the quality of American political discourse from events of the past few years.

Third, we draw upon historical accounts of civility in order to understand two things. What is the nature of the problem we confront today? Are things really that much worse than they ever were? It is hard to believe that America is really that much less civil today than in the past. Second, we are interested in how Americans confronted instances of incivility in the past. Are there lessons we can learn today about how discourse was improved upon, or how a sense of shared goals was restored? Chapter 9, by John Gastil, explores contemporary arguments against civility; he seeks to counter these by describing the language surrounding Quakers' pacifist response to World War II. This example shows, he argues, how civility can be an integral and effective part of articulating disagreements with the political status quo. Chapter 10, by Steven C. Bullock, discusses norms of civility in the era of the Revolutionary War. In his discussion of Benjamin Franklin, Bullock contends that Franklin can serve as an American "patron saint of civility," an inspiration to improve the quality of our discourse. In Chapter 11, Timothy J. Shaffer explores the role the U.S. government has played in encouraging civil discourse and in educating Americans on techniques for deliberation. Shaffer describes the little-known program undertaken by the U.S. Department of Agriculture during the New Deal era to provide guidance for public deliberation, and he underscores the importance of this program for enabling rural Americans to communicate with each other and with their government. While such projects are uncommon today, Shaffer argues that they are a model for future government policies.

As this book began with an articulation of how philosophical treatments of the importance of civility can clarify contemporary political debates, so we end in the concluding chapter with a description of the importance of civility as an "orienting attitude." Deborah S. Mower explores the way in which John Stuart Mill emphasized the role of civility. Although Mill is best known for his arguments in favor of liberty, Mower points out that Mill found civil discourse to be an indispensable part of political liberty. Only by committing to civility can we fully tolerate others and engage in free speech. Mower closes with an explanation of how important education and academic research on civility are if we are to realize these values.

The contributors to this book share an interest in civility. This does not mean that all share a definition of what civility is, nor that the book should be seen as a tool to police bad behavior, whatever that is. Instead, the goal of this book is to contribute to establishing the study of civility as a coherent, interdisciplinary endeavor—to raise questions that can inform debates about when and where civility should be a goal, and why it should be a goal. The contributors to this book share, as well, a belief that a civil society is a healthy society—a society in which there is a shared purpose, and in which citizens are capable of seeing their politics as a reflection of the people that have brought that politics into being. In this regard, moments of heightened incivility in our politics—including, perhaps, the moment in which we find ourselves today—can serve as a reminder to us to pay closer attention to who we are as a people and to develop an inclusive, shared language about how we might solve our problems together.

Many of the chapters in this book are based on presentations given at the Second NICD Research Convening, held March 23–25, 2017, in Tucson, Arizona. We thank the Hewlett Foundation's Madison Initiative for providing financial support for the event. We also thank the other participants in the research convening and the members of the NICD Research Network for providing commentary on these chapters, and we thank the NICD staff, and in particular, Raquel Goodrich, Adriana Kelly, Eve Hady, and Tracey Todd for help with the convening and with publicizing the research presented here. Thank you as well to the University of Arizona for its support for NICD; we owe a particular thank you to J. P. Jones, Dean of the College of Social and Behavioral Sciences, and H. Brinton Milward, Chair of the Department of Government and Public Policy, for the support they have given to NICD since its inception. Finally, we thank Jennifer Knerr and the staff at Routledge for their enthusiasm and guidance in steering this book toward publication.

Bibliography

Cahoone, Lawrence. 2000. "Civic Meetings, Cultural Meanings." In Leroy S. Rouner (Ed.), *Civility*. South Bend, IN: Notre Dame University Press, 40–64.

Carter, Stephen L. 1998. *Civility: Manners, Morals, and the Etiquette of Democracy*. New York: Harper.

Craiutu, Aurelian. 2016. *Faces of Moderation: The Art of Balance in an Age of Extremes*. Philadelphia: University of Pennsylvania Press.

Dionne, E. J., Norman Ornstein, and Thomas E. Mann. 2017. *One Nation, After Trump*. New York: St. Martin's Press.

Oakeshott, Michael. 1975. *On Human Conduct*. Oxford: Clarendon Press.

Taylor, Jessica. 2017. "Americans Say Civility Has Worsened Under Trump." *National Public Radio*, July 3. Retrieved from www.npr.org/2017/07/03/535044005/americans-say-civility-has-worsened-under-trump-trust-in-institutions-down.

Weber Shandwick. 2016. *Civility in America VII: The State of Civility*. Retrieved from www.webershandwick.com/uploads/news/files/Civility_in_America_the_State_of_Civility.pdf.

PART I

How Americans Think
About Civility in Politics

1

TWO CONCEPTS OF CIVILITY

Anthony Simon Laden

What breaks when civility breaks down? That, of course, depends on what civility is and what it does. Unfortunately, there is not much in the way of scholarly or popular consensus on that question, and so it can be hard to tell whether those who express the most concern about the breakdown of civility are raising an alarm that is worth heeding, or merely decrying the passing of certain fashions, like men's hats, that won't ultimately be missed. In this chapter, I do some preparatory work toward answering these questions by trying to map two distinct concepts of civility. The first concept takes civility to be a set of manners, a form of politeness: civility involves not insulting those with whom you disagree, subjecting them to *ad hominem* arguments, or otherwise treating them rudely. According to this concept of civility, civility characterizes the surface features of certain kinds of public actions and pronouncements. It is concerned with how we act and speak. Call this the concept of civility as politeness. The second concept takes civility to be a form of engagement in a shared political activity characterized by a certain kind of openness and a disposition to cooperate. In particular, those who conceive of civility this way describe it as a civic virtue that shapes the nature of our interactions with one another, and to what degree those interactions involve genuine responsiveness to one another. According to this concept of civility, civility characterizes what we are doing when we act. Here, the difference between civil and uncivil actions (including forms of speech) involves what we do and not merely how we do it. Call this the concept of civility as responsiveness.

   It turns out that treating civility in one of these ways rather than the other is not merely a matter of choosing how to define a term in one's theoretical arsenal, or focusing on observable behavior vs. attitudes and subjective states. Instead, each concept of civility fits most comfortably within a rather different underlying picture of action and interaction. This means that one's commitments elsewhere about the nature of agency and action, commitments that may be driven by one's disciplinary approach or general theoretical outlook, are likely to drive how one treats civility. That our concepts of civility are situated in this way makes it both easier to talk past one another and harder to see either that this is what is going on or where the miscommunication lies. It can also lead us to take up positions that are inconsistent or don't hold up well to reflective scrutiny. We might, for instance, take evidence of a breakdown in civility as politeness to signal consequences that would be the result of a breakdown of civility as responsiveness. We might try to respond to a breakdown in civility as responsiveness with the arsenal of techniques available to us from a conception of action that is more suited to thinking about civility as politeness. If we fail to notice what anchors our concepts of civility, it may also be harder to appreciate each of them fully or move between them, or understand disagreements we are having about what counts as civility and whether it is in short supply. We may fail to grasp how our different reactions to and solutions for the breakdown of civility respond to very different kinds of situations. By beginning to map these differences, then, I hope to contribute not only to our understanding of civility but also to our ability to talk about it productively.

Philosophy's Contribution: Conceptual Optometry

The kind of conceptual excavation and clarification I propose in this chapter is one of the main contributions philosophy can offer both the social sciences and ordinary life. It is, however, not a practice that many non-philosophers either engage in or always understand. Philosophy, on this approach, is a form of conceptual optometry (or more precisely, lens-grinding). Just as an optometrist diagnoses which corrective lenses adjust your vision in ways that allow you to see certain things more clearly, philosophers examine and evaluate the concepts we use to make sense of the world, showing how they disclose certain things more clearly while possibly obscuring others. I take the value of this kind of work to be pragmatic in the following sense: like corrective lenses, the value of particular concepts is tied to what we want to use them for. Just as I may need one set of lenses for reading and another for seeing into the distance, we may find certain concepts better suited for certain kinds of investigations and others for others, in large part based on what they bring into relief. Moreover, if we are to use our concepts well, we also need to be aware of their limitations: what they obscure or make hard to appreciate.

Various concepts can work together and support one another when they compose what might be called a picture. This is not a matter of strict entailment or any other firm logical relation. A particular picture of some piece of the world can render certain features or details of that corner of the world significant and coherent. But pictures can, as Wittgenstein put it, "hold us captive" (Wittgenstein 1991, 48) because once we have adopted a given picture, it can be hard to change out just a single conceptual piece: the others with which it hangs together may provide a certain resistance to doing so or even prevent us seeing the possibility of doing so. The conceptual optometry that philosophy provides, then, comes through not only analyzing variants of a given concept but also laying out how these variants fit within different pictures and how those pictures might be helpful for certain kinds of projects while nevertheless obscuring details that might be of importance for other ones. My contention in what follows is that discussions of civility run into just this problem: those drawn to one concept of civility sometimes have trouble seeing the other concept as a viable alternative (either as viable or as a genuinely different alternative) because they fail to appreciate how it is situated within a very different picture, one that ties a concept of civility to a concept of action.

Very roughly, conceiving of civility as politeness fits easily within a picture that takes action to be essentially the making of choices. In contrast, civility as responsiveness fits within a picture that takes action to be the exercise of skills. The first picture is common in the empirical social sciences, whereas the second picture is more common in some areas of normative political philosophy and theory. It is thus perhaps not surprising that one finds civility treated as politeness more often in empirical fields and it treated as responsiveness in more normative ones. The two pictures are not, however, competitors in any direct sense. As with most such concepts and pictures, the pictures of action and their associated concepts of civility are conceptual outlooks on the world, each of which discloses certain of the world's features and obscures others. Each thus makes certain forms of reflection and analysis easier and other ones harder. Thus, which picture we adopt should depend on what we are trying to do or understand.

Civility as Politeness

Even among those who go on to offer a different account, it is commonplace to acknowledge that at least one meaning of the term "civility" is a form of politeness or good manners, perhaps the manners that are called for in public, or in a public world of equal citizens (e.g., Bybee 2016; Calhoun 2000). So understood, civility provides us a code of conduct or "mode of behavioral management" (Bybee 2016, 7). For some theorists, however, politeness forms the essential core of civility. What is distinctive about such accounts is that they focus our attention on surface features of an action, rather than the motivation for the action or the nature of the action itself. This focus on surface features is suggested by the term "manners" (the *ways* we do things), and in the etymological link, often pointed out in these contexts, between "polite" and "polish"; politeness involves being polished: altering rough surfaces to make them smooth. On this concept of civility, incivility is entirely a matter of being rude: of insulting others, either directly, or by using inappropriate tones of voice (OR ALL CAPS AND LOTS OF EXCLAMATION POINTS!!!). It can be seen in the difference between yelling "You lie!" to a speaker who is still speaking, and waiting until the speaker has finished to say, "I respectfully submit that my esteemed colleague, the gentleman from Illinois, is in error."

One attraction of this concept of civility is that it is easy to observe, count, and quantify. After all, it is precisely the surface features of action that are out in the open, easy to see. Knowing whether someone's behavior is civil, on this conception, does not require us to interpret her motives or intentions or subjective attitudes. We don't have to decide if she is sincere or well-meaning, or why she is being civil: whether it comes from a genuine commitment to the value of civility or a purely instrumental calculation that being civil will avoid certain costs she wishes not to bear.

Assessing civility as politeness may not even require us to evaluate the substance of the claims someone is making: calling someone a liar is rude, it might be claimed, regardless of whether it is an accurate statement. Yelling truths at someone who is insisting on falsehoods is just as impolite as yelling falsehoods at someone who is insisting on truth. This concept of civility thus has a certain value for those trying to do quantitative work on civility, and those who hold that scholarly objectivity requires being neutral on the sorts of controversial questions that are most likely to incite incivility.

Civility, so conceived, clearly matters to the quality of our public interactions. Regardless of whether incivility understood as rudeness plays a causal role in gridlock and governmental dysfunction, it coarsens public life and makes daily public interactions more stressful and less pleasant. When politicians resort to insulting each other or referring to their opponents by demeaning nicknames, it can be argued, they undermine the dignity and seriousness of politics. Such behavior may feed on itself and ultimately make violence more prevalent. If this form of incivility is on the rise, it is important to figure out why and what to do about it. And it can be plausibly argued that what we do and should care about in our public discussions is just this outer surface of politeness: perhaps it is or should be more important to each of us that strangers with whom we disagree follow basic rules of civil behavior than that they genuinely respect and value us. The importance of rules and social norms is that they work for, as Kant said, a "race of devils" (Kant 1991, 112), not that they convert us into sages or angels.

Finally, understanding demands for civility as demands for a certain form of politeness makes sense of a certain line of criticism of such calls. While politeness can take the rough edges off of social interaction and thus make it easier, requirements of politeness can also serve to exclude members of certain groups from full participation in social life by setting out elaborate codes of conduct to which only some people are privy or by ruling out of court certain kinds of challenges to the status quo based purely on their manner of delivery. It is a common criticism of protests, social movements, and various forms of extra-electoral direct political action that the activists who engage in them are not playing by the rules or following the norms of proper behavior. Those who insist on the "civil" in "civil disobedience" are often responding to such charges. Since what counts as polished behavior and speech in a given society will be contingent and often determined by a dominant or ruling group or class, this can turn demands for civility into a means of safe-guarding privilege. Appreciating this dynamic and the downsides of calls for civility may be easier insofar as we are treating civility as politeness.

Civility as Responsiveness

As with civility as politeness, there are a number of different theories of civility that fit under the concept of civility as responsiveness (e.g., Kingwell 1995; Rawls 1996; Gutmann and Thompson 1998). We can uncover some of its essential features by looking at John Rawls's remarks about what he calls the "duty of civility" and its connection to certain ideals of citizenship and democratic legitimacy. Rawls claims that

> the ideal of citizenship imposes a moral, not a legal, duty—the duty of civility—to be able to explain to one another on those fundamental questions how the principles and policies they advocate and vote for can be supported by the political values of public reason. This duty also involves a willingness to listen to others and a fair-mindedness in deciding when accommodations to their views should reasonably be made.
>
> *(Rawls 1996, 217)*

Elsewhere, Rawls describes the disposition to honor the duty of civility as "one of the cooperative virtues of political life" (Rawls 2001, 117). He goes on to say that

> the duty of public civility goes with the idea that the political discussion of constitutional essentials should aim at free agreement reached on the basis of shared political values, and that the same holds for other questions bordering on those essentials, especially when they become divisive. In the way that a just war aims at a just peace and thus restricts the use of those means of warfare that make achieving a just peace more difficult, so, when we aim for free agreement in political discussion, we are to use arguments and appeal to reasons that others are able to accept.
>
> *(Rawls 2001, 117–18)*

Though some of Rawls's characterization here is tied to his specific ideas of political liberalism and public reason, it shares with several other versions of civility as responsiveness the following three features: (1) the basic idea that civility is a cooperative virtue of political life, and that it involves both (2) the willingness to listen to others and (3) a fair-mindedness in considering their views and when one should adjust one's own position in response to theirs (Kingwell 1995; Gutmann and Thompson 1998). Civility in this second sense is manifested when we engage in genuine dialogue with our fellow citizens, when we make room for their voices to be heard, and make an effort to understand and appreciate what they say. Arguably, the attraction of genuine bipartisanship and government by a "team of rivals" lies here. Civility as responsiveness involves striving to hear those with whom we live together as reasonable, even when they take positions that are unfamiliar or uncongenial, or express them in ways we do not initially recognize as reasonable or even polite. Moreover, it involves not only listening to them but also being open to being moved by them. That is, it is not enough to patiently listen to those with whom one disagrees without any real possibility that what they say might make a difference to what you think or how you hold your position. If we are genuinely engaged in the cooperative activities of political life in a civil fashion, according to this concept of civility, we need to allow ourselves to be vulnerable to what others say. This does not mean always moving to the middle or abandoning our firm convictions in the face of opposition: I can be open to being moved by what another says and yet not, after hearing them, end up in a different position. But it means being fully engaged in the process of jointly figuring out where we can stand together, and that may mean not merely figuring out ways to politely bring everyone to stand where I already do. Finally, it may involve being imaginative and creative in finding alternatives that we can all support. Think here about the difference between legislation that emerges, perhaps transformed, after genuine debate and hearings and the public discussion that these generate, and legislation that is crafted behind closed doors by a single party or faction and thereafter tweaked solely to hold together the narrowest of majorities needed to pass it before such public discussion might erupt.

If the slogan for civility as politeness is "we can disagree without being disagreeable," then the slogan for civility as responsiveness might be "we can agree to disagree" or perhaps better, "disagreement is no reason to stop talking with one another." Those concerned with defending and protecting civility as politeness worry that in a political environment of deep and persistent disagreements, we will lose our manners, and this will have further effects over the quality of our political and social lives. They may see incivility as an unfortunate outgrowth of ideological polarization and perhaps a spur and symptom of increased partisanship. In contrast, those concerned primarily with civility as responsiveness worry that a political environment characterized by strategic thinking that sees politics as a form of conflict and confrontation will lead citizens, whatever their positions and disagreements, to give up on politics as a cooperative activity.

Civility as responsiveness is thus less concerned with the outward manners of action than with the nature of the actions themselves. One can uphold all the norms of civility as politeness without engaging civilly with others in this second sense. Congressional leaders who make it clear as they pursue a legislative agenda that they are not interested in finding a path that involves the opposition party, or they are interested only in opposing and obstructing the majority party, come what may, can do all of this while being polite about it. And while it might be argued that politeness is one way that one manifests an attitude toward others

that is essential to being responsive toward them, it is that attitude and its mani-
festation and not the outward formal signs of it that will be the essential mark of
responsiveness.

Action as Choice vs. Action as the Exercise of Skill

At this point, we need a detour into the philosophy of action and social science
to draw a contrast between two different pictures of action. On the first, commonly found in the empirical and especially quantitative social sciences, actions
are reducible to choices. According to this picture, people's observable actions are
a result of their choosing among available options according to some relatively
simple function or algorithm: we act when we choose how to vote from a list of
candidates or proposals, what to buy or produce from a range of bundles of goods,
or what path to pursue from a set of possible options. In the simplest case, people
act by choosing the option from a given choice set that maximizes their preference or the satisfaction of their desires or their utility. In more complex versions,
the descriptions of the choice options can be made richer, the choice function
more complex, and the metric it uses (e.g., utility, preference-satisfaction) can be
more carefully defined. What interests me about this picture of action, however, is
its reduction of action to choice, rather than the particular features of its theory of
how choices are identified or made.

Contrast this picture with a picture of action as the exercise of various skills
and abilities. On this picture, action is not a matter of making a choice but of
doing something that is potentially complex, extended, and embodied: playing the
violin, engaging in a political discussion or debate, participating in a campaign.
Though we might try to reduce these actions to a series of simpler actions, each
of which requires less in the way of skill, it is still hard to see that we will capture
them well by describing them as a series of choices. The violin player plays the
violin by playing a particular piece, which in turn consists of a series of phrases
and even notes. If playing the violin amounted to merely choosing to play this
note and then that, however, it is hard to see how one could accurately play a
series of notes, but do it badly, or how practice or coaching could help one to
play better.

Each of these pictures of action carries with it further features. Picturing action
as choice tends to involve thinking of the agents making the choices as similar
to one another in their basic motivational structure and also basically fixed. That
is, even if we accept that different people faced with the same choice sets will
choose differently, this picture will push us to explain that difference not through
differences in each agent's mechanism of choice but through other differences. We
ascribe to each agent the same function or algorithm for making choices and then
explain differences in choices made by pointing to the differences in the inputs
to those functions: different preferences or desires or ideologies. For example,
imagine that when faced with a menu featuring pizza and fish, you choose the

fish and I choose the pizza. We explain this discrepancy by saying that we have the same choice function (we choose to maximize the satisfaction of our preferences) but different preferences: you prefer fish and I prefer pizza. We do not, for instance, say that you are choosing alphabetically and I am choosing in order to practice pronouncing Americanized Italian words, or that we both prefer the fish, but I am less adept at choosing in accord with my preferences or translating my interior choices with the act of ordering. One implication of this feature of the picture of action as choice is that those looking to change what people do will look to change the choice sets they face or the values attached to those choices, rather than changing the agents themselves.

In contrast, thinking of action as the exercise of skill focuses our attention on what agents do rather than merely the choices they face. We can't improve the quality of violin playing of a group of people by changing the choice sets they face, by, for instance, incentivizing good violin playing or even practice time. In the absence of some mechanism to develop and improve a skill, one can't just choose to exercise it at a higher level.[1] More generally, thinking of action as the exercise of skill directs our attention to individual agents and opens the possibility that we could change actions by changing agents—by, for instance, teaching them.

Second, picturing action as choice involves thinking of action as something that takes place in an instant. Whatever extended reflection may precede a choice, and whatever extended plan may be necessary to carry out that choice, the essential piece of the action—the choice—is an affair of the moment. Of course, we can pay attention not just to single choices but to series of choices, and doing so will allow for various meta-choices to be the objects of study. Doing this provides a way to think about not only how agents choose in one-off cases but also how they choose strategies (which involve a series of choices or even of conditional choices and choice trees). And it may turn out that we can affect individual choices by changing the environment in which whole strategies are chosen. Nevertheless, picturing action as choice will lead us to think about actions that are essentially momentary, even if repeated.

Exercises of skill, on the other hand, take place over extended periods of time and at least make it possible to think about actions that are ongoing rather than episodic. Playing a particular piece on the violin does not happen in a moment and while playing a piece on the violin will be a temporally bounded episode, playing the violin may not be. (Think, for instance, of the way I can say, "I have been playing the violin for 30 years.") If I pick up my violin to play it, rather than to perform a piece, whether in order to practice or just fiddle around, nothing internal to the action of playing the violin dictates when I am done. Once we begin to think about actions as either temporally extended or ongoing, it turns out that we need to pay attention to features of how we engage in those activities that are less salient on a view of action as punctual or episodic. In particular, we need to pay attention to whether our engagement in those activities is sustainable (Laden forthcoming).

Third, on the picture of action as choice, action becomes something the essentials of which happen in the heads of individuals. Making a choice is basically an intellectual act, whatever physical efforts might be required to implement it. It is also something each of us does on our own. Though groups can make choices, they do so by in some way or other aggregating the choices of individuals or delegating the group's choice to some individual's choice. This is not true of the exercise of skill. While the skill of violin playing is something I exercise alone, it is embedded in a number of social relations tied to teaching, learning, and working within a community of practice (Small 2014). Moreover, some skills are properly the skills of a group rather than of the individuals who make it up. For instance, a board or legislative body or academic department might be good at making collective decisions, and this is not merely a matter of it having a set of wise members, or good choice-aggregating procedures, but something about the quality of their deliberations. Many of the individuals in such an organization will have to have and deploy a set of deliberative skills for this to be true, but they are importantly different skills than those required for good individual decision making. And in an important sense, we can make sense of these skills of teamwork only by understanding them as contributions to the collective skill and not the other way around.

Finally, if we picture action as essentially choice, then we are led to see everything about the action not captured by the choice as accidental, merely a surface feature. For instance, consider the act of voting on this picture: voting is essentially a choice among a list of candidates or proposals or options. We can embed a particular vote within a series of votes and thus account for strategic voting, and we can see a vote as one among a set of means for pursuing some further policy objective, so that we can also think about the relation of particular votes to other actions taken to advance a given goal, and thus examine the choice among different means to a given goal. But beyond such expansions of our sense of what choices a voter faces, the rest of the mechanics of voting will look to be merely surface features. So, whether a voter votes by raising her right hand or her left, by pulling a lever or punching out a chad, with a smile on her face or a scowl, with enthusiasm or a visible show of reluctance, or after extensive open discussion and deliberation with those who disagree with her or in an attempt to settle the matter before debate breaks out will count as nothing more than the style or mechanism with which she enacts her choice. None of it will appear to matter to describing and classifying the action she takes unless it can be broken out as one of the things among which she was choosing.

When, however, we picture actions as the exercise of skills, a different set of dimensions opens up for describing and classifying the action. In particular, exercises of skill involve not only the deployment of various complex techniques but also what we might call the conception of the action being done under which the agent acts. Skills are not the automatic performance of sub-routines: exercising a skill generally involves a kind of reflective and reflexive understanding of what one is doing, which is to say, one exercises a given skill under a description of what one is doing. Practicing is different than performing. Teaching someone how to play chess by playing with them is different than playing against them in a tournament or for fun. Debating with someone to win the argument is different from debating with them to figure something out. Playing pool to win is different from playing pool to win money.[2] And while we can distinguish the members of each foregoing pair by pointing to their different goals, doing so will miss important features that differentiate them.

On this picture, then, two actions might be distinguished by the different descriptions under which they are done, even if they are not easily distinguishable in terms of the choices made in enacting them or their results or consequences. Practicing a piece I know well may produce the same set of movements and sounds as performing it, but we distinguish them as different actions, not in terms of whether I do it alone or in front of an audience but in my understanding of what it is I am doing. Moreover, having a skill involves not only the capacity to exercise it on call but also often the further skill of knowing when it is called for. The violinist who can execute a particular technique or play a line with a certain kind of feeling but who doesn't know when in a piece that technique is called for is a less skilled violin player than the one who also knows this. The importance of these points for our purposes is that this gives us another dimension on which to characterize actions beyond their consequences, means, and physical manifestations without relegating these features of actions to being merely surface features.

Though it is easiest to see the difference between these two pictures of action by thinking about very different types of actions (voting vs. violin playing), the contrast is not between classes of action but between how we conceive of action. We can try to break down violin playing into a series of choices, and we can conceive of voting as part of exercising a skill of engaging in politics or making judgments about political matters. Moreover, there may be all sorts of good reasons to prefer one picture to the other for certain purposes. That is, I don't want to claim that one is the correct way of thinking about action, a description of what action really is. Rather, each is a lens through which we think about action, and each illuminates certain features and obscures others. Which lens we use will depend on what we are trying to see, and the important point will be to be mindful as well of what each obscures. There is no shame in trying to understand only one thing well. The problem comes when one loses sight of the potential importance of the things you don't have in view.

The picture of action as choice has a great advantage for doing quantitative empirical work in the social sciences. It allows us to characterize large numbers of actions undertaken by large numbers of people in ways that then make it possible to subject them to formal models and other techniques to reveal otherwise obscure patterns. Moreover, if we are interested in thinking about how to affect the behavior of large numbers of people, thinking about their actions this way points to a set of policy levers that are easier to activate at scale. If we want to study the effects of institutions, laws, and other social forms on the actions of individuals, it will be easier to see and measure this effect if we picture those actions as choices.

On the other hand, this approach to action, as we have seen, can obscure the possible routes to change that focus on changing individuals, and not merely their choice environments, whether this involves education or other ways of calling forth different actions. It also makes it harder to see the value of certain kinds of action, such as action that contributes to sustaining an ongoing activity. It may also reduce activity that is the exercise of skill to something less skill-dependent, and thus lose track of the features of that action that require training, practice, and the development of that skill.

Seeing Action as Choice Obscures Civility as Responsiveness

There are clear affinities between the concept of civility as politeness and the picture of action as choice on the one hand and the concept of civility as responsiveness and the picture of action as the exercise of skill on the other. The picture of action as choice has a clear place for surface features of action, and thus civility as politeness, whereas it seems that responsiveness will be well characterized as a skill. That might help to explain why empirical social scientists seem to favor the concept of civility as politeness while political philosophers and theorists interested in citizenship and civic virtue are drawn to a concept of civility as responsiveness.

As we have seen, civility as responsiveness is manifested not in a set of outcomes or particular goals but in a way of interacting with others that goes beyond the mere surface features of what we do. This makes it hard to fit into the parameters of a picture of action as choice. It is not well captured as itself a choice of outcome or even a different choice function. The best hope for seeing this kind of civility within a picture of action as choice is as a distinct kind of strategy. On this interpretation, what would distinguish the civil and uncivil courses of action would be the path they chart. Can we bring civility as responsiveness fully into view this way?

To do so, we would need to characterize the end or outcome pursued by the strategy of civility and what distinguishes this strategy from ones that are uncivil. Since civility seems to be called for most clearly when we face disagreements, it seems reasonable to think of civility and incivility as rival strategies for achieving our ends in such situations. In the world of politics, we can then think of this in terms of winning arguments. The sense of winning here is not the philosopher's sense of finding arguments most likely to reveal the truth but the politician's sense of attracting more adherents or getting one's opponents to concede the debate. Since winning an argument is not a matter of having the best arguments, we can ask what strategies of argumentation are effective and what, if any, their collateral costs would be.[3]

Here, it appears that there is room for both civility as politeness and civility as responsiveness to play a role. Ultimately, however, I think that it is hard to fully see the contours of civility as responsiveness from this vantage point, and it is helpful to see why not. First, notice that there are two ways we might understand winning political arguments in the sense at issue. Winning an argument might involve attracting more people to one's side: this is the main way that arguments function in campaigns. But winning an argument might involve moving a final decision about an issue closer to one's own position: this is the main way that arguments function in legislative debates. Each of these seems to make a different form of incivility a tempting strategy to adopt. In the course of a campaign, one way to attract people to my side is to get them to abandon that of my opponent, and I can do that by belittling or showing contempt for her positions or her person. So, here, it looks like rudeness might be an effective strategy for winning arguments. Whether it is in fact effective is going to be an empirical matter. My point here is that the sense of civility that is going to be at issue if we want to think about the temptations of that strategy is civility as politeness.

In the case of the legislative argument, though rude contempt might do some work, it looks like it is going to be a lot less effective in moving the final decision point than a different kind of uncivil strategy: being stubborn and obstinate. That is, to the extent that legislative debates boil down to bargaining sessions and thus a kind of elaborate tug-of-war between competing positions, it can turn out to be an effective strategy to be less accommodating to one's opponent's views, to dig in one's heels, and to not listen to the appeal of the other side or take them seriously. One can do all of this, and probably do it more effectively, without resorting to insult and invective. Thus, it appears as if the sort of incivility that comes into view as a tempting strategy in legislative argument is tied to civility as responsiveness. This seems to suggest that the two concepts of civility can find a place within a picture of action as choice.

Where I think that thought goes wrong, however, is in how it winds up characterizing civility as responsiveness. The contrast to digging in one's heels in negotiation is to be accommodating, to be willing to compromise in the sense of moving to some middle ground. There are two basic forms this strategy takes. In the first, it is still a strategy for winning arguments in the sense at issue here: winding up with decisions that are closer to one's initial position than would otherwise be possible. One might argue that compromising in this way, rather than always holding out for the best deal in negotiations, is a long-term maximizing strategy: it is what game theorists call a strategy of constrained maximization (Kingwell 2012; Gauthier 1986).[4] Alternatively, one might claim that those who adopt this strategy turn out to have a different end altogether: they are not trying to win arguments, but reach agreements. On this view, we might characterize the difference between those drawn to civility and those drawn to incivility in terms of their different aims: the uncivil are trying to win arguments, and the civil are trying to reach agreements. No matter which option we take, however,

I think we end up mischaracterizing important aspects of civility as responsiveness as described at the beginning of the chapter. The responsive citizen is neither putting on a kind of show for the sake of the long-term maximization of her particular interests, nor valuing agreement over her own positions to the point of being willing to bear all sorts of costs to reach agreement. Her end is neither winning arguments nor reaching agreements, and so neither of these accounts of the strategy of civility will capture what is distinctive about civility as responsiveness. A responsive citizen has as her end to continue to engage in a certain kind of shared activity. Since her end is not what the activity leads to or produces but the engagement in the activity itself, it is hard to see clearly what she is trying to do if we are characterizing actions as choices or the mechanical carrying out of strategies that bring about or carry out those choices. That is to say, being responsive involves understanding the activity of politics differently than it is understood in these models. We might say that those models picture politics as a matter of bargaining or negotiation, whereas the responsive citizen sees it as a matter of ongoing deliberation or conversation (for the contrast, see Laden 2007, and more generally, Laden 2012). And this points us, finally, away from the picture of action as choice toward that of action as the exercise of skill.

Civility as a Cooperative Skill

Whereas the picture of action as choice tends to obscure civility as responsiveness from view, the picture of action as the exercise of skill illuminates some of its features in helpful ways. In part, this picture leads us to ask what sorts of skills do we exercise in being civil, and what is the action we thus engage in?[5] Seeing this terrain clearly will help to answer my initial question about what is lost when civility breaks down. Among the skills that comprise civility are those necessary to fully engage in certain kinds of cooperative activities. It is precisely because the picture of action as the exercise of skill provides a way of grasping the nature of truly cooperative activities that it can also help us to see clearly the concept of civility as responsiveness and both its potential value and its distinctness from civility as politeness.

Recall that Rawls describes civility as one of the "cooperative virtues of political life" (Rawls 2001, 117). The implication here is that political life, and in particular, democratic life, is a cooperative activity, and one that admits of being done better or worse (and thus of excellences—virtues). That is to say, living as a democratic citizen is an ongoing cooperative activity that requires the exercise of certain skills. Let me try to unpack that thought a bit. Cooperative activity is activity we do together, rather than merely activity where we interact or each pull causal levers on a common field. In an ideal democratic society, the cooperative activity of citizens comprises four distinct levels: citizens (1) share a commitment to the (2) shared activity of finding (3) shared rules to govern (4) their living together. They do this by exercising the skills necessary to both living together and working out, together, the rules and principles that govern that living together. We can see how each of these levels shapes the activity of democratic life by examining the difference, at each level, between something that is truly shared and a set of individual activities that are merely intertwined.

Start, then, from the idea of living together, and contrast it with living side-by-side. Living side-by-side involves coordinating our otherwise individual and independent activities. It can thus involve an awareness of what others are doing and a commitment to adjust what I do in light of what others are doing or I expect them to do. What is lacking in merely living side-by-side is a more robust form of sharing, where not only is each of our actions coordinated but also there is something that *we* do that is not reducible to what each of us does. This happens when our actions are governed by a shared set of norms or rules or goals that not only coordinates what we each do but also makes our action mutually intelligible to us as our action. The easiest way to grasp the contrast is to distinguish what happens when each of these projects fails. As I have elsewhere put the point,

> If and when we fail to live side-by-side, we bump into one another, and do harm and find it more difficult to each pursue our individual goals. At some point, life becomes nasty, brutish and short. . . . When we fail to live together, we find ourselves alone, unable to reach out to others around us, to make ourselves intelligible to them, to interact with them as fellow subjects. The isolation that failure to reason together creates is not a matter of a failure of coordination. It is the sense that no one understands what you say or do, or who you are.
>
> *(Laden 2012, 22)*

That we describe a shared political life as living together rather than side-by-side need not mean that we are thinking of political society as a community, as having a set of thick shared values or common goals. But it does mean that even where our political lives involve giving one another space to be left alone, and where we do not share any set of final substantive ends, we agree *together* to give each other that space and pursue our individual projects. In order to imagine politics as the project of living together, we already have to imagine citizens as more robustly and irreducibly social than is easy to do if we picture actions as choices. We need to think of ourselves as creatures who can be and wish to be intelligible to one another, who can adopt shared projects and shared ends.

Moving out one step, we get to the idea that democratic citizens not only live together but also do so according to shared rules or principles. That is to say that the basic rules and principles that govern our living together are not imposed on us by an external force or by nature. Sharing governing principles suggests that those principles are ours, not only because they govern us but also because we are their authors: among the activities we engage in together are those of both collective self-government and collective self-constitution. Moreover, the rules that we adopt at least aim to be not merely the results of hard-fought bargains but also genuinely ours. This does not mean that in actual cases we can never resort to such means as majority voting to decide which rules to adopt. But it does require that in doing so, we have already reached a position where whichever side finds itself in the minority can accept the eventual results as not only procedurally legitimate but also substantively so. And that suggests the third level: politics is, then, a further cooperative activity we engage in.

Seeing democratic politics as a cooperative activity, something we do together, is to contrast it with seeing it as a strategic one: an activity each of us engages in as a means to some individual end. Seeing politics as strategic is to see one's fellow citizens as making up the perhaps dynamic environment one has to navigate on the way to one's goals. This is the view of politics that emerges in the previous section. Seeing politics as a cooperative activity, in contrast, involves seeing one's fellow citizens as partners in something we are doing together. Note that in this case, what is as important as the policies that emerge from this activity is the nature of the activity itself: it is something we are genuinely doing together and not just a means of confrontation. Recall here that one aspect of action that emerges when we picture action as the exercise of skill is the importance of the description under which we act. It is this aspect that comes to the fore here.

Though this cooperative activity has a point, it is not so clearly directed at a final goal: it is not a means of winning arguments or even finding consensus. It is thus an ongoing task: it is not something we engage in and then are finished with. This aspect of the activity is also obscured if we think of politics as a series, possibly infinite, of discrete strategic activities, each with their own end. Note that if we think of democratic politics as an ongoing, cooperative activity, it turns out that the adoption of both the civil and uncivil strategies we examined in the previous section fail in similar ways. Insofar as politicians and citizens adopt the goal of winning arguments, they engage in politics as a strategic rather than a cooperative activity regardless of whether they behave politely. Shifting to a conception of politics as a cooperative activity, then, requires not more civility as politeness but a fundamental shift in how we understand the activity of politics itself: from winning arguments to working out with others the rules we are to live by.

The activities of working things out with others, and of living together, however, are much more like playing the violin than choosing a candidate or policy platform. That is to say, they involve the exercise of various skills. We can thus see civility as responsiveness as among the skills we must exercise to engage in these activities well.

Recall that civility as responsiveness casts civility as involving an openness to being moved by what others say, which involves both a willingness to listen and take seriously what others say, even if it at first seems unfamiliar or inscrutable or obviously wrong, and a fair-mindedness in being willing to accommodate their positions. Part of what supports and grounds those attitudes and the activities that express them is a commitment not to individually adopt or pursue ends that are not allowed or supported by the results of our joint deliberations. In that case, I will have reason to reject a "compromise" that is overly one-sided, even if it is in my favor. Think here, for instance, of the person who holds that her tax rate should be lower and who argues for her position in the political arena, but who would not consider withholding her taxes as determined by a fair democratic practice, and not only because she is afraid of the legal consequences. Or consider the person who sacrifices her moral right to retaliate for various wrongs in order to secure the civil peace.[6] In these cases, their commitment to something like democratic deliberation and legitimacy is given precedence over their more particular ends—that is, their fundamental commitment to engaging in a certain cooperative activity in a certain way, rather than to achieving some outcome to which the activity is a means.

As with the person who sacrifices some individual benefit to maintain the civil peace, the civilly responsive citizen sacrifices certain kinds of political advantages in the name of sustaining the possibility of a certain kind of deliberative environment, a certain picture of democratic living together. Civility as responsiveness is a shared commitment to privilege the results of fair deliberation, and to honor the basic rules of such deliberation. It will involve, for instance, not taking all legal means to winning an argument or a political fight but sometimes sacrificing one's advantage in the interest of fairness. It is, as Rawls says, a cooperative virtue of political life.

Whither Politeness?

Although the outward forms of politeness may not be essential to the civil skill of responsiveness, the value of politeness is not so much obscured as transformed by this perspective. Here it helps to distinguish two features of politeness: the outer behavior and the attitude that it is meant to express. Insofar as we think of politeness in terms of the attitude of respect that it is meant to express, it is not difficult to see why polite behavior will be an outgrowth of engaging in responsive politics. What I want to suggest here, however, is that the outward behavior itself also plays an important role in civility as responsiveness, though not precisely the one it plays if we think of it as the essential feature of civility. To understand this transformation, we can return briefly to our violin player and think about the differences between practicing and performing. Among the outward differences between practicing and performing might be the clothes one wears and whether one bows before or after playing. Neither of these features is essential to the difference between performing and practicing: one can perform in sweatpants and one can bow before and after practicing a piece. And yet, wearing proper attire and bowing seem to play some role in marking a particular piece of violin playing as a performance. Let me suggest that we think of these outward displays as rituals, which, like many rituals, are meant to signal to others what one is doing. It isn't only that walking onstage in tails or a long dress and bowing before an audience are a conventional way of saying, "Hey, out there, I am about to perform some music." They also express something about the activity: that it involves a certain compact between performer and audience, that it has a certain kind of formality or solemnity, that each has a role to play and the performer is playing hers. One advantage of having such a socially recognized ritual is that it can be called on in unconventional moments: a performer can call forth an audience from a crowd of passers-by at a subway station through such gestures and their reciprocation. But one can't just turn a piece of playing into a performance by enacting its associated rituals.

Similarly, the norms of politeness might be thought of as rituals that establish certain relations of mutual respect and signal our engagement in an activity that should be governed by them. Of course, if we mistake the rituals for the activity itself, we will only be playing at respect, being merely polite, and will thus fail to engage well in the skill of civility as responsiveness even if we manage to follow the rules of civility as politeness. But in other cases, and especially when we aren't engaged in the normal modes of political conversation and debate, enacting various rituals of politeness can signal to our fellow citizens what we are, in fact, up to, and how it involves relating to them on and equal and respectful footing. It is interesting to note in this regard the emphasis that figures like Gandhi and Martin Luther King Jr. placed on certain norms of politeness in the course of non-violent forms of direct action. Gandhi, for instance, took it to be an essential step in non-violent action that one inform the authorities ahead of time (Gregg Forthcoming, orig. 1934, 1944, 1959; see also King 1963). He famously called off various campaigns against British rule in India when the timing was inconvenient for the British, and always wrote to the viceroy and other British officials as "Dear Friend" (see, e.g., Gandhi 1930). Note that these are precisely moments and activities that, while they are meant to be actions of democratic politics, are easily mistaken for something else: insurrection, mob rule, or the outbreak of violence. In these moments, beyond being the outgrowth of an attitude of respect for one's adversaries, obeying the dictates of civility as politeness serves to announce to others that one's actions are political and to call forth in one's fellow citizens a civic, and civil, response. It may also serve, as it no doubt did for Gandhi and King and their followers, to help them establish a truly responsive frame of mind.[7]

Conclusion: Some Further Lessons

The argument so far has been primarily an exercise in mapping, in showing how these two concepts of civility differ from one another, and how they are easier to see and appreciate within very different pictures of action and thus democratic politics. One consequence of seeing these connections is that they can help us to more fully appreciate the difference between the two concepts of civility and to begin to see more clearly the one that our other theoretical commitments and habits might obscure from view. That, I take it, can only have helpful consequences for studying the forms of civility and incivility in our society and the various causal levers that might curb incivility or foster civility. But there is another kind of lesson we can draw from this mapping, and in particular, its portrayal of civility as responsiveness as a paradigmatic democratic skill, and this will return us to my initial question: what happens when civility breaks down?

Civility as politeness can make our social interactions more pleasant and less stressful and this can oil the gears of social interaction in all sorts of ways. To the extent that this form of civility also keeps us off a slippery slope of bad behavior, preserving civil discourse in this sense may help to keep our more violent tendencies in check, and may make it easier for people to show concern for others who might be harmed or hampered by their favored policies. While these are all important effects, they are all, in a sense, incidental to the well-functioning of a democracy. For one thing, the links between these forms of incivility and various social harms are suppositions about causal effects and it may turn out that the links are not as strong as suggested here. Maybe the seeming increase in rude language is not a sign of breakdowns of social norms against genuine respect, but merely the passing away of outmoded styles. Some may have thought civilization was crashing down when the upper classes stopped dressing in white tie for dinner or stopped knowing the proper use of six different types of forks. Very few of us would look back at their concerns and think they were correct. Perhaps an increase in rude language in casual interactions is like the passing of the fish fork, a sign of the democratization of manners. Perhaps an insistence on politeness is a way for certain dominant groups not to take seriously the substance of the demands of those who challenge them (by ruling them out based only on the manner in which those challenges are articulated). And perhaps, as with the fish fork, concern over the passing of certain norms of comportment and politeness is a distraction from the deeper crises our democracies face: the influence of concentrated wealth, the alienation of large segments of the population, and the increasing divide between the lives of financial and cultural elites and the rest of us. All of these may contribute to the sense that an insistence on the importance of civility is at best a sort of prissy concern with appearances and at worst a veiled attempt to reinforce the position of various dominant groups.

Moreover, from within the perspectives offered by the picture of action as choice, democratic politics and democratic life do not appear as ongoing activities, but a series of discrete actions and choices within a possibly evolving institutional, legal, and social framework. Since we are not then conceiving of our activity as ongoing, we are less likely to be attentive to what is needed to sustain it. It can appear as if institutions, laws, and even social norms are just more or less fixed backgrounds against which we act, and this means we can lose sight of the efforts and sacrifices necessary to keep them working. Winning this legislative battle, passing this law, winning that election are all that matters, and as long as our means are effective, there is nothing more to be said about them unless we have an idiosyncratic concern with style and manners.

Things, however, look different if we adopt the picture of agency and action as the exercise of skill that brings into view the concept of civility as responsiveness. Within this picture of action and the picture of democratic living together it allows us to describe, civility plays a more vital and fundamental role: it is among the central skills we exercise in the ongoing shared activity of democratic politics and democratic life. Its loss is not incidentally related to the breakdown of that activity: it is the breakdown of that activity. Breakdowns of civility as responsiveness, then, are to the possibility of genuinely democratic politics what failure to properly draw a bow across the strings is to genuine violin playing.

Note, then, three implications of this shift in view. First, the connection here between loss of civility and loss of democracy is not incidental or causal: it is conceptual. That does not mean that it is necessarily correct: I may be importantly mischaracterizing any or all of the concepts involved. But it does mean that to the extent these descriptions are correct, and to the extent we value the concept of democracy as the shared activity of working out the shared terms of living together, the breakdown of civility just is the breakdown of democracy.

Second, it opens up a different set of possible responses. The picture of action as choice draws our attention to institutional fixes to changing behavior. If we think of agents as basically reacting in predictable ways to given choice environments, then the obvious place to intervene to change behavior is to change the choice environment those agents face. Much of the work on problems of partisanship, polarization, and gridlock that takes up this picture of action also takes up an institutionalist outlook: it aims to alter what it takes to be destructive patterns of action by changing the incentives agents face or the pathways of action available to them. Norms of civility then enter the picture as a form of sanction: if we reinforce social norms governing civility, this will create penalties for acting uncivilly, and that will change the calculations agents make (see, e.g., Mann and Ornstein 2012, 180–181). What is left out of such reform agendas are the various actions we might take to convince each other to act differently, whether through education, exhortation, or acting in ways that call forth different responses.

These other avenues come more fully into view if we take up the picture of action as the exercise of skill and ask why citizens engaged in the shared activity of democratic politics might fail to deploy the skills that it calls for. Here we might think of three kinds of reasons we fail to deploy a necessary skill. First, we might lack the skill. If I do not know how to play the violin, then no amount of incentivizing will, at least in the short run, and without a means of learning this skill, get me to play the violin, let alone to play it well. If increases in incivility are the result of a lack of skill, then this suggests that we need to increase and improve the avenues for civic education that train us in the skills of responsiveness.

A second reason not to deploy a skill is that I do not see that it is called for here and now. I might be able to play the violin perfectly well, but I will elect to play it only when the time is right. I don't need to exercise my skills of violin playing while cooking dinner or talking with friends. Similarly, I may be perfectly capable of engaging in fully responsive interaction, but not see politics as the place for it. I might view politics as war by other means, or as an activity of confrontations among opposing ideologies or parties. Bringing people to see the need for responsive civility in the moments when it is called for is also not a matter of changing incentive structures or pathways of action: it is an exercise in re-conceptualizing what we are doing. If this is the root of rising incivility, then what we need is something more like political philosophy: not so much the academic discipline but a general public attentiveness to how we understand what we are doing together when we engage in democratic politics.

Finally, I may have the skills and know that this is a time that calls for them, and yet refuse to employ them: perhaps they are difficult or costly, or will prevent me from pursuing some other ends I have. This choice to privilege one's private aims and interests over those demanded by our collective activity is what civic republican thinkers going back to Machiavelli have called "corruption." Think of it as the civic vice that is the opposite of the civic virtue of civility as responsiveness. If an excess of civic vice is the root of an increase in incivility and unresponsiveness in our society, then we may need to call on the various methods for controlling vice developed throughout the centuries: sanctions, education, exhortation, and arguments about the benefits of virtue and the costs of vice. In closing, let me point to the final one on this list. This involves showing what is lost when we choose unresponsive incivility over responsive civility, and how this loss is fundamentally different from the losses we bear when mere politeness declines.

From the vantage point of the concept of civility as responsiveness, democratic politics is an ongoing activity, and like all activity, involves the exercise of skill. Among the work we must do to sustain that activity as something we do together is the constant employment, but also fostering, development, and reproduction, of the skills of civility as responsiveness. As with all sustaining activities, engaging in politics civilly carries costs: in lost arguments, sacrifice of ends realized and advantages gained, and even of what appears to one to be genuinely better policy. If we fail to appreciate how such activities nevertheless sustain something of value, we will become less and less willing to sustain those costs. But as I hope to have shown, what we would lose in a world of unresponsive politics, what we are arguably losing now, is not merely the smooth and comfortable surfaces of our political and social lives but their genuinely democratic character.[8]

Notes

1 Put this way, the point may seem obvious and trivial, but it is one that many policy debates entirely fail to appreciate. One clear example is the discussion of improving teacher quality in education by such mechanisms as rewarding good teaching, as if teachers are choosing to teach badly because there is not enough in it for them to teach well (see Cohen and Moffitt 2009).
2 A point that is the theme of the film *The Hustler* and more directly its sequel, *The Color of Money*.

3 Though Kingwell (1995) defends a form of civility as responsiveness, Kingwell (2012) explores this strategy. He argues there that while incivility can be an effective strategy for winning arguments, it will generate collective action problems in the forms of arms races: ever-escalating levels of incivility that ultimately undermine the very point of conducting politics via argument.

4 Constrained maximization is a strategy whereby an agent chooses the best option within a constrained set, where the constraints come from something like moral permissibility. Gauthier (1983) argues, for instance, that though choosing only among options that honor commitments to others you have made may forgo certain benefits in the short run, agents who choose according to this strategy avail themselves of much greater benefits over the long run by opening up various cooperative possibilities.

5 I am using the term "skill" here and throughout in a broad sense, meant to encompass not only narrow technical skills but also the less narrowly defined practical abilities that play a role in the arts, politics, and the activity of living a human life.

6 This is roughly the description Danielle Allen provides of blacks in the pre-civil rights era South, whose behavior was brought to widespread public awareness in the aftermath of the so-called Battle of Little Rock (Allen 2004).

7 I am grateful to Dennis Dalton for pushing me to see the value of politeness even within the conception of civility as responsiveness, as well as its central importance to Gandhi and King. The attempt to account for its value in terms of rituals here, however, is my own.

8 This chapter grew out of conversations at the second research convening of the National Institute for Civil Discourse. I am grateful to Robert Boatright for the invitation to participate in the convening and contribute to this volume, as well as for many subsequent exchanges about the treatment of civility within political science, and for comments on earlier drafts. I have also benefitted from comments from Dennis Dalton, James Tully, and Antje Weiner.

Bibliography

Allen, Danielle. 2004. *Talking to Strangers*. Chicago: University of Chicago Press.

Bybee, Keith. 2016. *How Civility Works*. Stanford, CA: Stanford University Press.

Calhoun, Chesire. 2000. "The Virtue of Civility." *Philosophy and Public Affairs* 29 (3): 251–275.

Cohen, David K., and Susan L. Moffitt. 2009. *The Ordeal of Equality: Did Federal Regulation Fix the Schools?* Cambridge, MA: Harvard University Press.

Gandhi, Mohandas K. 1930. Letter to Lord Irwin, British Viceroy, 2 March 1930. Retrieved January 3, 2018, from www.bl.uk/reshelp/findhelpregion/asia/india/indianindependence/indiannat/source3/index.html.

Gauthier, David. 1986. *Morals by Agreement*. Oxford: Oxford University Press.

Gregg, Richard. Forthcoming, orig. 1934, 1944, 1959. *The Power of Non-violence*. Edited by James Tully. Cambridge, MA: Cambridge University Press.

Gutmann, Amy, and Dennis Thompson. 1998. *Democracy and Disagreement*. Cambridge, MA: Harvard University Press.

Kant, Immanuel. 1991. "Perpetual Peace." In H. S. Reiss (Ed.) and H. B. Nisbet (Trans.), *Kant: Political Writings*. Cambridge, MA: Cambridge University Press, 93–130.

King Jr., Martin Luther. 1963. "Letter From Birmingham Jail."

Kingwell, Mark. 1995. *A Civil Tongue: Justice, Dialogue and the Politics of Pluralism*. University Park, PA: Pennsylvania State University Press.

Kingwell, Mark. 2012. "'Fuck You' and Other Salutations: Incivility as a Collective Action Problem." In Mark Kingwell, *Unruly Voices*. Toronto: Biblioasis, 149–168.

Laden, Anthony Simon. 2007. "Negotiation, Deliberation and the Claims of Politics." In Anthony Simon Laden and David Owen (Eds.), *Multiculturalism and Political Theory*. Cambridge, MA: Cambridge University Press, 198–217.

——. 2012. *Reasoning: A Social Picture*. Oxford: Oxford University Press.

Laden, Anthony Simon. Forthcoming. "The Value of Sustainability and the Sustainability of Value." In Akeel Bilgrami (Ed.), *Nature and Values*. New York: Columbia University Press.

Mann, Thomas E., and Norman J. Ornstein. 2012. *It's Even Worse Than It Was*. New York: Basic Books.

Rawls, John. 1996. *Political Liberalism*. Paperback edition. New York: Columbia University Press.

Rawls, John. 2001. *Justice as Fairness: A Restatement*. Edited by Erin Kelly. Cambridge, MA: Harvard University Press.

Small, Will. 2014. "The Transmission of Skill." *Philosophical Topics* 42: 85–111.

Wittgenstein, Ludwig. 1991. *Philosophical Investigations*. Translated by G. E. M. Anscombe. Oxford: Wiley-Blackwell.

2

HOW PEOPLE PERCEIVE POLITICAL INCIVILITY

Ashley Muddiman[1]

Calls for political civility have become regular occurrences in recent years. President Barack Obama asked for civility after U.S. representative Gabby Giffords was shot in 2009 (Obama 2011) and during the tumultuous 2016 presidential primaries (Obama 2016). Citizens' letters to the editor plead for civility (Johnson 2016). News has decried the lack of civility from both the Republicans (Nuño 2016) and Democrats (Geier 2016) during the 2016 campaign. Interest in civility—or, more accurately, incivility and violations of civility norms—has seeped into the academic world as well. Studies have examined the effects of political incivility on trust in government and argument legitimacy (Mutz 2015), interest in politics (Brooks and Geer 2007), and openness to alternative political positions (Borah 2014). Researchers have investigated the prevalence of incivility in media content (Sobieraj and Berry 2011), including comment sections (Coe, Kenski, and Rains 2014). Clearly, civility and incivility have captured the attention of politicians, journalists, citizens, and scholars.

Yet this may be where consensus about incivility ends. In just one of President Obama's speeches, he defined incivility as lying, "ignoring science," and using "insulting" language (Obama 2016). In academic research, Maisel (2012) has suggested that scholars ought to rely on a definition of incivility as something that people know when they see it, or, in metaphorical terms, "if it swims like a duck, waddles like a duck, and quacks like a duck, it is probably a duck" (406). Although many researchers agree that disrespect for others is at the center of incivility (e.g., Coe et al. 2014; Maisel 2012; Sobieraj and Berry 2011), beyond the notion of disrespect, definitions vary widely. Some, for instance, define incivility as interpersonal impoliteness (e.g., Mutz 2015), while others emphasize discrimination and threats to democracy (e.g., Papacharissi 2004).

In comparison to scholars, it appears—at first glance—that the American public is much more consistent in its understanding of civility. In national studies, 95% of Americans have reported that civility is important for a healthy democracy (Shea and Steadman 2010), while over 90% of people think that there is a problem with civility in America today ("Civility in America VII: The State of Civility" 2017). These statistics hide a more divided public, however; once citizens are asked to evaluate specific people and behaviors they consider to be uncivil, disagreements begin to appear.

This chapter digs deeper into divides in perceptions of incivility within the context of the behaviors of elite political figures. It does so by discussing messages and behaviors of American political figures that some might consider to be in violation of norms of civility. The chapter provides an overview of how the personal or public nature of incivility might influence how "uncivil" the public might perceive it. Then, it discusses how political partisanship can affect our perceptions of incivility. Next, the chapter covers some topics that scholars may be missing in their investigations of incivility. Finally, the chapter considers the implications of approaching incivility from a perceptions perspective.

Personal v. Public Levels of Incivility

At its foundation, incivility involves a violation of cultural norms about how to act in various contexts (Mutz 2015; Jamieson and Hardy 2012). But in the context of U.S. politics, what cultural norms are politicians expected to follow? Are they expected to be polite to political opponents (Mutz 2015)? Are they expected to argue fairly and reasonably (Jamieson and Hardy 2012)? Are they expected to treat opposing political parties with an attitude of reciprocity (Uslaner 1996)? This is where things become quite tricky in trying to articulate exactly what our civility norms *are*.

Personal-Level Incivility: Rooted in Politeness

Theoretically, there are at least two levels of political incivility (Muddiman 2017). A first level—personal-level incivility—relates closely to interpersonal impoliteness. A number of media and advertising effects studies emphasize rude and impolite interactions as the foundation of incivility (e.g., Brooks and Geer 2007; Mutz 2015). Mutz (2015) describes this approach to incivility most clearly: incivility is something "that violates the norms of politeness" (6). Name-calling, interruptions, yelling, heightened emotion, and the like are considered uncivil and have effects even when people view these behaviors in mediated messages (Borah 2014; Brooks and Geer 2007; Mutz 2015). Importantly, this approach is related to politeness theory, an explanation of what happens when people in face-to-face discussions do or do not threaten the self-esteem of their conversation partners

(Brown and Levinson 1987). Thus, personal-level incivility focuses on individual interactions and violations of interpersonal interaction norms.

Public-Level Incivility: Rooted in Deliberative Theory

A second level of incivility—public-level incivility—relates more closely to political processes and deliberative norms than to politeness norms. Theorists who advocate for this approach call back to the roots of the word "civility," which is related to "citizen" and "city" (Davetian 2009; Orwin 1992). In this conceptualization of civility, rather than striving merely for politeness, citizens are expected to argue using civil, or public, reasons to support their claims (Rawls 1993). Rather than name-calling and interrupting being considered uncivil, in this more deliberative conceptualization of civility, violations like racism and democratic threats (Papacharissi 2004) as well as disorderly and misinformed political discussion (e.g., Entman 2011) are the main concern. Uslaner's (1996) concept of comity is helpful with respect to public-level incivility. He defined comity as a reciprocity of ideas even among people who may not always agree on policy. Deliberative theory, rather than politeness theory, seems a better theoretical fit for public-level incivility than politeness theory. Deliberation emphasizes a fair, open, and process-based discussion that promotes the exchange of multiple viewpoints (Fishkin and Luskin 2005). By refusing to work with each other, framing opposition leaders as treasonous, disregarding the facts, discriminating against citizens, and the like, public-level incivility involves threats to the democratic process rather than threats to an individual's self-esteem.

What Does the Public Think?

To this point, the distinctions between personal- and public-level incivility have been largely theoretical. Is there any evidence to suggest that individuals—members of the public—consider these types of behaviors as uncivil as well? A two-part study I conducted with about 1,000 U.S. residents in May of 2015 is helpful in answering this question.[2] In the first part of the study, I asked participants to evaluate a series of statements describing behaviors of political leaders. Some of the statements described personal-level civility infractions while others described public-level civility infractions. Statements describing personal-level civility infractions included a statement describing inflammatory partisan criticism of congressional legislation, another included a politician calling a lawmaker from the opposing party "delusional," and still another described a politician *damning* the political opposition. Meanwhile, the statements describing *public*-level civility violations included statements such as one explaining that Congress is deadlocked because many members of Congress will not pass a bill supported by their political opponents, or describing House of Representatives members' refusal to compromise with members of the opposing party. Still others included civility *descriptions*. One statement explained that a bill could pass because of bipartisan support and another statement paraphrased a senator saying that there are reasonable, moderate politicians from the opposing party. There were 24 statements in all. Individuals read the statements and rated each one as to whether they considered the behaviors described extremely civil, extremely uncivil, or somewhere in between.

Overall, people recognized civil activities when they saw them. Efforts to work together and create bipartisan policy, as well as instances of political partisans saying respectful, kind things about their opponents, were consistently rated as more civil than the other behaviors (see Figure 2.1).

Compared to civility, both public-level and personal-level examples of *incivility* were perceived as substantially more uncivil. Interestingly, though, personal-level incivility and public-level incivility were perceived to be different from each other (see Figure 2.1). Name-calling, profanity, and personal attacks emblematic of personal-level incivility were perceived as most uncivil, whereas partisan conflict and refusal to compromise and work toward bipartisan legislation were considered uncivil, but less so than personal-level incivility.

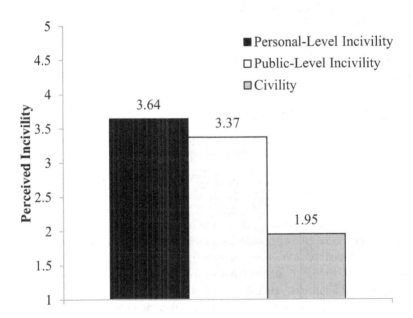

FIGURE 2.1 Average perception of personal-level incivility, public-level incivility, and civility.

Note: All groups are significantly different at $p < .05$.

Source: Author's survey.

Based on this study, it appears that insulting another politician may be considered a worse offense than stalling or undermining political legislative processes, even though both can have serious consequences. Personal-level incivility, for instance, makes it less likely for people to believe that the arguments of a political candidate from an out-group political party are legitimate (Mutz 2015) and more likely for people to become steadfast in their attitudes about political issues (Borah 2014). Unfortunately, public-level incivility's effects on individual citizens have not received much attention from scholars. However, lack of reciprocity toward members of all political parties could halt progress in solving problems facing our communities (Uslaner 1996; Entman 2011). Despite these potential effects, the public seems to have fewer concerns with disordered political processes than they do with impoliteness.

In the second part of the 2015 study, I simply asked individuals to provide one example of what they considered to be uncivil behavior by a politician. The results largely align with how individuals rated examples of incivility provided to them, but with some unexpected twists. People offered many examples of both personal-level incivility and public-level incivility (see Table 2.1). Personal-level incivility examples largely matched what I included in the study described earlier—name-calling, profanities, and emotional exchanges in political settings.

Interestingly, however, the public-level incivility examples were broader than the partisan dysfunction, political disorder, and lack of compromise in the examples I had provided in the previous study. When given the opportunity to provide their own examples, individuals did mention congressional gridlock and lack of

TABLE 2.1 Examples of personal- and public-level incivility

Personal-level incivility examples 21% of sample	Public-level incivility examples 61% of sample
Personal attacks	Lying about President Obama's birthplace
Harry Reid calling ranchers terrorists	Empty promises
Swearing in public	Hillary Clinton email deletion
Screaming and yelling at one another in (*sic*) television	Treason
	Demagogic language
John Boehner being disrespectful to the president	Gridlock by Republican House members and senators
	Paying people for votes
	Backstabbing minorities
	To use the race card to push forward their agenda
	Protesting
	The mayor of a city inciting riots

Note: Two coders coded respondents' open-ended responses to ensure reliability.

Source: Author's survey.

compromise, but they also made note of politicians who spread misinformation, threaten the Constitution in some way, keep information from the public, abuse money, discriminate against groups of people, or, alternatively, use the "race card" or "gender card" to get support for a policy. Some participants even mentioned collective political actions like protesting. While certainly broader than my original conceptualization, all of these behaviors are consistent with the concept of public-level incivility, in that the respondents are indicating the kinds of acts *they* feel would violate norms of political policy, process, and action, rather than just impoliteness. Further, some of these behaviors, like discrimination (Papacharissi 2004) and distorted facts (Entman 2011), have been categorized as uncivil by previous researchers, though their consideration as incivility has not been widespread. Even more intriguingly, while people seem to perceive personal-level incivility as more uncivil than public-level incivility when *rating* examples, in this study respondents were substantially more likely to *provide* examples of public-level incivility than personal-level incivility. Just under a third of the sample provided at least one example of personal-level incivility, but nearly two-thirds of the sample provided at least one example of public-level incivility. So, when given the choice from a list of uncivil behaviors, they see acts of "impoliteness" as the most uncivil. Yet, when asked to come up with examples on their own, they are far more likely to cite uncivil acts that directly relate to broader aspects of democratic health.

In sum, theoretically, there are at least two approaches to incivility: a personal-level and a public-level approach. Diving into individuals' own reactions to and thoughts about incivility supports this distinction. While both personal-level and public-level incivility acts are perceived as uncivil, people tend to react more strongly to personal-level incivility when they see it, but public-level incivility is top-of-mind when they offer their own examples of incivility.

Partisan Reactions to Incivility: It's Okay When *My* Party Does It

As discussed earlier, in studies where people are asked to provide their thoughts about civility, questions are typically asked out of context, without details relating to a specific political party or politician. However, what happens when people know a bit more information about the political figure who is violating a political norm? Are partisans more willing to excuse incivility from a member of their own political party? Some data suggests this may be the case. When asked a follow-up question, a plurality of the same participants in Shea and Steadman's (2010, 23) study who supported civility also reported a preference for a politician's "willingness to stand firm in support of principles." Such findings indicate that some element of partisan group identity might play a role in understanding political incivility.

There are a number of theoretical approaches that would suggest that partisans will not agree about the severity of uncivil acts. Motivated reasoning, a psychological theory that suggests people process information in a biased manner, explains that individuals are often motivated to "arrive at a particular, directional conclusion" when thinking about information (Kunda 1990, 480). In the political world, this can manifest by Republicans and Democrats looking at the exact same information, and focusing only on the parts of the message that support their own beliefs (Lord, Ross, and Lepper 1979). Applied to incivility, it seems plausible that people from different parties will view the same behavior enacted by a political figure and make motivated judgments about how "civil" they find the behavior based on the political figure's political party.

Social identity theory also supports this prediction. Mounting research suggests that, in political settings, individuals think of political parties as in-groups and out-groups (Tajfel and Turner 1979). Over the past few decades, Democrats and Republicans have begun to feel more negatively toward the other political party, even when they did not disagree substantially on political issues (Iyengar, Sood, and Lelkes 2012). When a member of a political out-group behaves badly, people may recognize the violation of a norm, whereas when a member of a political in-group behaves in the same way, people may be less likely to think negatively about that behavior and that person.

Beyond the theoretical evidence, there is empirical data from both parts of the 2015 study mentioned earlier in this chapter that suggests people approach incivility in partisan ways. Part 1 of that study also included an experiment in which individuals were exposed to personal- and public-level incivility from either out-group partisans, in-group partisans, or political figures whose partisanship was not mentioned (Muddiman 2017). Some Democrats, for instance, read statements about Republican politicians violating political norms (out-group incivility), Democratic politicians violating political norms (in-group incivility), or politicians of unknown partisanship violating political norms (unknown incivility). Participants then were asked to report how much incivility they perceived in each description. Like the theory predicted, people perceived politicians from their own political party to be significantly less uncivil than politicians from an opposing political party (see Figure 2.2). This pattern occurred for both personal-level and public-level incivility. Notably, however, insults, name-calling, and other types of personal-level incivility were perceived as uncivil for both in-group and out-group politicians. Contrastingly, refusal to compromise, heightened partisan conflict, and other types of public-level incivility were perceived as uncivil for out-group partisans, but not for in-group partisans. Instead, public-level incivility was considered relatively neutral—not necessarily civil, but not uncivil either.

Even when providing their own examples of what they consider to be uncivil behavior, it is important to note that some respondents gravitate toward partisan incivility. In the second part of my study described earlier, in which participants were asked to come up with examples of politicians' behaviors they would consider to be "uncivil," about 17% of individuals provided examples of incivility that specifically mentioned a partisan political figure. Several respondents mentioned

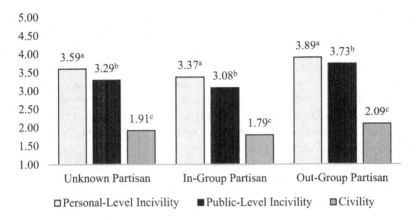

FIGURE 2.2 Average incivility rating by partisan condition and type of incivility.

Note: Lowercase letters that differ within each partisan condition indicate that there was a significant difference between the types of incivility at the $p < .05$ level.

Source: Author's survey.

Hillary Clinton's emails and her response to a deadly attack in Benghazi, Libya, as being uncivil. Another participant explained, "Joe Wilson when he told Obama u [*sic*] lie." Some even listed only a politician or political party in response to "what they considered to be uncivil behavior by a politician." Some participants, for instance, provided responses like "Ted Cruz," "John Boehner," "Obama," or "Democrat," without providing an example of what made that person uncivil. Even without being prompted by researchers to think about political partisanship, many people automatically linked incivility with well-known partisans.

Finally, there is evidence that individuals react to partisan incivility in their behaviors as well, especially when that incivility originates with a member of an opposing political party. Televised incivility increases arousal and draws viewers' attention (Mutz 2015). Comments posted to the *New York Times* website, for instance, received more recommendations from site visitors when they included uncivil language *and* partisan language than they received with either type of language alone (Muddiman and Stroud 2017). Additionally, an experiment examining participation on an online message board found that people were more likely to criticize a commenter if that commenter used incivility in the original post *and* that commenter posted a statement that was disagreeable to them (Gervais 2015). Thus not only do people vary in their perceptions of incivility when the incivility comes from an in-group versus out-group politician, but also they behave differently when partisanship and incivility are combined.

The partisan group perceptions of incivility may have significant effects in real-world politics. Partisan figures tend to use incivility strategically by *calling out* their opponents' incivility at some times while also *engaging* in incivility at other times when they believe it will best rally their supporters (Herbst 2010). Given that partisans react more negatively to incivility from the other side than from their own side, it is clear such rhetorical strategies could work to widen partisan divides even further.

Academics and the Public: Competing Visions of Incivility

Both personal- and public-level norm violations, as well as partisan loyalties, affect the public's considerations of what is perceived to be uncivil, but questions remain. Most notably, does incivility research capture all important forms of political norm violations or are there other types that scholars should explore in the future?

Some previous findings hint that people might have quite broad perceptions of incivility. When political scientists Shea and Steadman (2010, 41) asked people to rate behaviors that, in the words of the survey, should be "against the rules" of civility in politics, many of the responses aligned with the types of incivility this chapter has already covered—for instance, "belittling or insulting someone" and "shouting over someone you disagree with during an argument." Yet some of the people surveyed believed that democratically beneficial acts, such as non-disruptive protest (28%) and "phoning legislators to express your views" (16%), violated norms of civility as well (16). Further, politeness theorists Brown and Levinson (1987) offer many types of interactions that can threaten norms of conversation. Yes, heightened emotion and name-calling are included in their theory, but so are other types of behaviors, like disagreements, promises, and requests. Since these latter types of behaviors are often *required* in a political realm, how should political communication researchers reconcile these competing visions of what civility actually is?

The evidence I collected when asking U.S. residents for examples of incivility suggests that the public takes a much broader approach to incivility than do political and communication researchers. When individuals were able to provide their own examples of incivility among politicians, individuals provided a range of behaviors that fall outside of current incivility definitions. These behaviors were generally related to immorality, illegality, and violence. Both Bill Clinton's affair with Monica Lewinsky and Anthony Weiner's decision to send "lewd photos" to women over text message made appearances in individuals' examples of incivility, as did statements about politicians generally "being inhumane." Related to illegality, participants mentioned that "graft," "stealing," "drunk driving," and "breaking laws that he/she made" all counted as uncivil political behavior. And some examples moved even a step further, linking incivility to violence by providing examples like "selling guns and ammunition to the enemy," "assault," and "shooting someone." Approximately 17% of participants' examples related in some way to these topics, demonstrating the need for us to further explore where academic definitions and public definitions of incivility conflict.

Conclusion

Clearly, incivility is to some extent "in the eye of the beholder" (Muddiman and Stroud 2017, 592). People tend to perceive name-calling and impoliteness as uncivil, as well as lack of reciprocity and political disorder, though perhaps to a lesser extent. They think that their in-group partisans are behaving less badly than out-group partisans, even when the norm violations are the same. And they add to researchers' understanding of political incivility by providing examples of immorality, illegality, and violence to the list of uncivil behaviors.

So why should academics and citizens care what people think about incivility? From an academic perspective, these details should make researchers reconsider how to ask people about civility in U.S. politics. Some previous studies have simply asked whether civility is important—and the response to this question has been a resounding yes. But what can we take from this response if what violates norms of civility varies depending on the situation or type of behavior? Some people answering broad questions about civility and incivility may think that politicians need to stop throwing insults around. Other people may have in mind elected members of Congress who need to learn how to solve problems together rather than refuse to work with another political party. Still others may consider that politicians must start following the law. And everyone, likely, is thinking that the other political party (not their own) needs to fall in line. Essentially, these questions can tell us that citizens think politicians should behave civilly, but asking such broad questions does not tell us *what* behaving civilly means. In the future, researchers should get more specific, examining whether different types of behaviors, contexts, and personality traits affect perceptions of incivility, and whether those *perceptions* affect citizens' approach to politics. Some research has begun investigating these topics (e.g., Kenski, Coe, and Rains 2017), and other scholars should continue this trend.

Further, this chapter addresses the differences between personal- and public-level incivility. It also would be fruitful for researchers to explore the ways in which these two forms of incivility intersect. For instance, the chapter does not address the consequences of these norm violations. Both personal- and public-level incivility may have personal- and public-level effects: perhaps obstinacy from one caucus in Congress (public-level) leads the other party's lawmakers to feel frustrated and lash out interpersonally (personal-level), prompting the original caucus to refuse to ever work with that party ever again (back to public-level). These norm violations are likely related in complex ways, but, as this chapter lays out, researchers should hesitate to paint all incivility with one broad brush.

Citizens should pay attention to these findings as well. Politicians use civility and incivility strategically, engaging in behaviors that they believe will rally the base behind them (Herbst 2010). As we see in this chapter, citizens' reactions to incivility suggest that strategic behaviors such as these may work since people are less likely to consider that members of their own political party are behaving uncivilly compared to members of an opposing party. Although everyone tends to agree that calling a politician a Nazi is uncivil, even then political figures from one's own political party get more of a pass than those from the opposing party. And this difference is especially prominent when partisans accept their own side's refusal to compromise. Citizens need to be aware that their in-group mentalities may be giving the politicians they support a pass to behave in ways that are not necessarily ideal for democratic outcomes.

To conclude this chapter, I ask one final question: are there ways to encourage people to think more similarly about what behavior is politically out of bounds? There are a few appealing options at an educational level. Reaching out to the public to provide definitions of incivility, as the National Institute for Civil Discourse is doing, is one way forward. Similarly, formal debate training could help individuals not only by improving their ability to focus on policy but also by familiarizing them with conflict that does and does not follow what Jamieson and Hardy (2012) call the norms of civil engaged argument. Additionally, formal deliberative processes, like the Oregon Citizen's Initiative Review Commission, designed to help citizens gather evidence and discuss important issues with the goal of publically sharing their conclusions may provide the structure necessary to decrease the likelihood of uncivil political discussion. Civics and educational outreach could help the public learn that behaviors like peaceful protests are constitutionally protected and democratically beneficial whereas impoliteness and absolute refusal to compromise are less acceptable in most situations.

But education and formal debate alone won't necessarily solve the problem of varying incivility reactions in everyday life, particularly when in-group/out-group biases are involved. On a mediated level, journalists may be able to make some changes. Since most people engage with politics through mediated means (Hart 1999), finding a useful way to cover incivility could be helpful. Journalists could, for instance, attempt to cover political incivility less frequently in instances where politicians appear to be strategically using incivility to draw attention to themselves and rally their base (e.g., tweeting derogatory campaign attacks at their opponents). This is a challenging suggestion given journalists' tendency to cover conflict and normative deviance (Shoemaker and Reese 1996). However, there is some evidence emerging that online news audiences may be slightly more attracted to civil rather than uncivil news (Muddiman, Pond-Cobb, and Matson 2017). If this pattern of behavior holds with future research, journalists and news organizations may be persuaded to give less space to incivility in their news coverage.

From a psychological perspective, challenging citizens to "consider the opposite" may also be productive (Lord, Lepper, and Preston 1984). Psychologists have found that if one asks people to think about how they would evaluate an empirical study that supported their opinion about a topic if that study had actually produced the opposite results, they are more likely to reconsider their own opinions. Citizens could be encouraged to do the same with political behaviors, either by information in a news article or by friends, neighbors, or acquaintances with whom they discuss politics. If a Republican sees a Republican politician behaving badly, a conversation partner could ask how she would feel if a Democratic politician were doing the same thing. Or a journalist could implicitly encourage a similar thought process by providing an example of a member of a different party engaging in a behavior at a previous time. When covering a "rowdy town hall" of Democrats challenging the 2017 repeal of the Affordable Care Act (Lowry 2017), for example, journalists could also mention the similar 2009 healthcare protests that largely were made up of Republicans. These journalistic and psychological tactics need more research to determine whether they are successful in the context of political incivility, but they offer potential ways to encourage people to view incivility and civility through a less partisan lens.

Although more research needs to be done to determine whether various individual traits, characteristics of politicians, and political contexts affect perceptions of incivility, this chapter provides a starting point for expanding the definition of incivility to include behaviors *perceived* as uncivil. If U.S. politicians and citizens cannot agree on the baseline norms of behavior in our political sphere, it is difficult to expect that the problems facing the country will be solved.

Notes

1 The author would like to thank Michael Kearney for his help coding the data presented in this chapter, as well as the University of Wyoming College of Arts and Sciences for funding the study overviewed in this chapter.
2 Participants were gathered online in May 2015 using Survey Sampling International. Demographics largely matched those of the Internet using the population of the U.S. They were asked to provide an open-ended response to the following statement: "Many politicians, media figures, academics, and others have talked about incivility lately. Please provide one example of what you considered to be uncivil behavior by a politician." Once they provided a response, they were asked to provide a second example. Two coders coded the open-ended responses to generate the categories of responses overviewed in this chapter. Later in the study, they read 24 statements that included personal-level norm violations, public-level norm violations, or no norm violations. One group of participants viewed behaviors originating from in-group political party figures, another group of participants viewed behaviors originating from out-group political party figures, and a third group of participants viewed behaviors that were not attributed to any specific political party.

Bibliography

Borah, Porismita. 2014. "Does It Matter Where You Read the News Story? Interaction of Incivility and News Frames in the Political Blogosphere." *Communication Research* 41 (6): 809–827. doi: 10.1177/0093650212449353.
Brooks, Deborah Jordan, and John G. Geer. 2007. "Beyond Negativity: The Effects of Incivility on the Electorate." *American Journal of Political Science* 51 (1): 1–16. doi: 10.1111/j.1540–5907.2007.00233.x.

Brown, Penelope, and Stephen Levinson. 1987. *Politeness: Some Universals in Language Use.* Cambridge, MA: Cambridge University Press.

"Civility in America VII: The State of Civility." 2017. Weber Shandwick. Retrieved from www.webershandwick.com/uploads/news/files/Civility_in_America_the_State_of_Civility.pdf.

Coe, Kevin, Kate Kenski, and Stephen A. Rains. 2014. "Patterns and Determinants of Incivility in Newspaper Website Comments." *Journal of Communication* 64: 658–679. doi: 10.1111/jcom.12104.

Davetian, Benet. 2009. *Civility: A Cultural History.* Buffalo, NY: University of Toronto Press.

Entman, Robert M. 2011. "Incivility and Asymmetrical Partisan Warfare." *In the Name of Democracy: Political Communication Research and Practice in a Polarized Media Environment.* Retrieved from www.lsu.edu/reillycenter.

Fishkin, James S., and Robert C. Luskin. 2005. "Experimenting With a Democratic Ideal: Deliberative Polling and Public Opinion." *Acta Politica* 40 (3): 284–298. doi: 10.1057/palgrave.ap.5500121.

Geier, Ben. 2016. "Invective and Violence in American Politics Is Nothing New." *Fortune.* Retrieved from http://fortune.com/2016/05/19/invective-and-violence-in-american-politics-is-nothing-new/

Gervais, Bryan T. 2015. "Incivility Online: Affective and Behavioral Reactions to Uncivil Political Posts in a Web-Based Experiment." *Journal of Information Technology & Politics* 12: 167–185. doi: 10.1080/19331681.2014.997416.

Hart, Roderick P. 1999. *Seducing America: How Television Charms the Modern Voter.* Thousand Oaks, CA: Sage Publications.

Herbst, Susan. 2010. *Rude Democracy.* Philadelphia: Temple University Press.

Iyengar, Shanto, Gaurav Sood, and Yphtach Lelkes. 2012. "Affect, Not Ideology: A Social Identity Perspective on Polarization." *Public Opinion Quarterly* 76 (3): 405–431. doi: 10.1093/poq/nfs038.

Jamieson, Kathleen Hall, and Bruce W. Hardy. "What Is Civil Engaged Argument and Why Does Aspiring to It Matter?" *Political Science & Politics* 45 (3): 412–415. doi: 10.1017/S1049096512000479.

Johnson, Tom. 2016, August 16. "A Plea for Civility in Politics." *The New York Times.* Retrieved from www.nytimes.com/2016/08/17/opinion/a-plea-for-civility-in-politics.html.

Kenski, Kate, Kevin Coe, and Stephen A. Rains. 2017. "Perceptions of Uncivil Discourse Online: An Examination of Types and Predictors." *Communication Research* 9365021769993. doi: 10.1177/0093650217699933.

Kunda, Ziva. 1990. "The Case for Motivated Reasoning." *Psychological Bulletin* 108 (3): 480–498. doi: 10.1037/0033-2909.108.3.480.

Lord, Charles G., Mark R. Lepper, and Elizabeth P. Preston. 1984. "Considering the Opposite: A Corrective Strategy for Social Judgment." *Journal of Personality and Social Psychology* 47 (6): 1231–1243. Retrieved from www.ncbi.nlm.nih.gov/pubmed/6527215.

Lord, Charles G., Lee Ross, and Mark R. Lepper. 1979. "Biased Assimilation and Attitude Polarization: The Effects of Prior Theories on Subsequently Considered Evidence." *Journal of Personality and Social Psychology* 37 (11): 2098–2109. doi: 10.1037/0022-3514.37.11.2098.

Lowry, Bryan. 2017. "Moran Weighs in on Health Care Bill at Rowdy Town Hall in Lenexa." *The Kansas City Star.* Retrieved from www.kansascity.com/news/politics-government/article155675004.html.

Maisel, L. Sandy. 2012. "The Negative Consequences of Uncivil Political Discourse." *Political Science & Politics* 42 (3): 405–411. doi: 10.1017/S1049096512000467.

Muddiman, Ashley. 2017. "Personal and Public Levels of Political Incivility." *International Journal of Communication* 11: 3182–3202.

Muddiman, Ashley, Jamie Pond-Cobb, and Jamie E. Matson. 2017. "Negativity Bias or Backlash: Interaction With Civil and Uncivil Online Political News Content." *Communication Research* 9365021668562. doi: 10.1177/0093650216685625.

Muddiman, Ashley, and Natalie Jomini Stroud. 2017. "News Values, Cognitive Biases, and Partisan Incivility in Comment Sections." *Journal of Communication* 67: 586–609. doi: 10.1111/jcom.12312.

Mutz, Diana C. 2015. *In-Your-Face Politics: The Consequences of Uncivil Media*. Princeton, NJ: Princeton University Press.

Nuño, Stephen A. 2016. "Debate Takeaway: Incivility Rules, GOP Will Support Trump." *NBC Nightly News*. Retrieved from www.nbcnews.com/news/latino/debate-takeaway-incivility-rules-gop-will-support-trump-n531621.

Obama, Barack. 2011. "Remarks by the President at a Memorial Service for the Victims of the Shooting in Tucson, Arizona." *The White House*. Retrieved from www.whitehouse.gov/the-press-office/2011/01/12/remarks-president-barack-obama-memorial-service-victims-shooting-tucson.

Obama, Barack. 2016. "Remarks by the President in Address to the Illinois General Assembly." *The White House*. Retrieved from www.whitehouse.gov/the-press-office/2016/02/10/remarks-president-address-illinois-general-assembly.

Orwin, Clifford. 1992. "Citizenship and Civility as Components of Liberal Democracy." In Edward C. Banfield (Ed.), *Civility and Citizenship in Liberal Democratic Societies*. New York: Paragon House, 75–94.

Papacharissi, Zizi. 2004. "Democracy Online: Civility, Politeness, and the Democratic Potential of Online Political Discussion Groups." *New Media & Society* 6 (2): 259–283. doi: 10.1177/1461444804041444.

Rawls, John. 1993. *Political Liberalism*. New York: Columbia University Press.

Shea, Daniel M., and Barbara Steadman. 2010. *Nastiness, Name-Calling & Negativity*. Allegheny, NY: Allegheny College.

Shoemaker, Pamela J., and Stephen D. Reese. 1996. *Mediating the Message: Theories of Influences on Mass Media Content*. 2nd ed. White Plains, NY: Longman Publishers USA. Retrieved from https://books.google.com.my/books/about/Mediating_the_Message.html?id=E_HtAAAAMAAJ&pgis=1.

Sobieraj, Sarah, and Jeffrey M. Berry. 2011. "From Incivility to Outrage: Political Discourse in Blogs, Talk Radio, and Cable News." *Political Communication* 28 (1): 19–41. doi: 10.1080/10584609.2010.542360.

Tajfel, Henri, and John Turner. 1979. "An Integrative Theory of Intergroup Conflict." In Michael A. Hogg and Dominic Abrams (Eds.), *Intergroup Relations: Essential Readings*. New York: Psychology Press, 33–47.

Uslaner, Eric M. 1996. *The Decline of Comity in Congress*. Ann Arbor, MI: The University of Michigan Press.

3

PERCEPTIONS OF INCIVILITY IN PUBLIC DISCOURSE

Kate Kenski, Kevin Coe, and Stephen A. Rains

Incivility is widespread—from political elites (e.g., Jamieson 1997, 2011; Kenski, Filer, and Conway-Silva 2018) to citizens (e.g., Rains, Kenski, Coe, and Harwood 2017), in news coverage (e.g., Sobieraj and Berry 2011) and online spaces (e.g., Coe, Kenski, and Rains 2014; da Silva 2013; Muddiman and Stroud 2017). In recent years, Americans have expressed concerns about the changing tone of political discourse. Nineteen out of twenty American adults report that incivility is a problem (Weber Shandwick 2016), with nearly 74% contending that civility has declined in the past few years. Adding to the negative outlook, technology experts, scholars, corporate practitioners, and government leaders project that future public online discourse will continue to be shaped by bad actors, harassment, trolls, griping, and distrust (Rainie, Anderson, and Albright 2017). Despite the general agreement that there is a significant problem, there is no consensus about what constitutes incivility, let alone ways to address it.

In this chapter, we focus on the definitional aspects of incivility. In particular, we are interested in whether scholarly definitions of incivility—at both the conceptual and operational level—are consistent with public perceptions of incivility. After all, it is one thing for scholars to debate and parse the concept of incivility in the literature, and potentially quite another for citizens to perceive it in the course of daily life. To explore this relationship, we first provide an overview of how scholars have defined civility and incivility. We then present findings from two studies showing that adults in the U.S. consistently evaluate certain types of online comments as uncivil, disrespectful, unnecessary, and rude. Digging deeper into the types of online comments that garner such reactions, we observe that name-calling and vulgarity result in higher perceptions of incivility than do other forms of speech. We also observe that gender significantly shapes incivility perceptions.

Specifically, men are less likely to perceive messages as uncivil than are women. The implications of these findings are discussed.

Our interest in investigating people's perceptions of everyday incivility is anchored in the possibility that such perceptions influence the extent to which citizens are motivated to participate in political exchanges and explore other forms of political involvement. As Papacharissi (2004) has noted, "Conversations on the meaning of citizenship, democracy, and public discourse highlight civility as a virtue, the lack of which carries detrimental implications for a democratic society" (260). Gervais's research (2015) shows that "uncivil messages increase feelings of aversion and decrease satisfaction among those exposed to disagreeable incivility" (168), suggesting that attention should be paid to how incivility is perceived. Additional evidence of incivility resulting in aversion is offered by Muddiman, Pond-Cobb, and Matson (2017), who found that people are less attracted to uncivil headlines, especially when the uncivil headlines contain "both impoliteness and an unwillingness to compromise" (10). To be fair, some studies suggest that incivility has the capacity to prompt participation and engagement (Borah 2014; Brooks and Geer 2007). It may be the case that not all incivility is bad for the health of democracy. It is unclear, however, whether such increases in participation benefit all types of people equally. Another problematic effect of incivility is the potential for polarization of citizen perceptions about public policy (Anderson, Brossard, Scheufele, Xenos, and Ladwig 2014). Incivility may not be a major cause of polarization, but it can add to it (see Pew Research Center 2014 for polarization levels present in society). With these concerns in mind, we grapple with how incivility has been conceptualized by scholars and consider how such conceptions compare to public reactions to the kinds of statements that are posted online by other adults.

Defining Incivility

The term *incivility* resonates with those who hear it, but settled definitions of the concept are elusive (Jamieson, Volinsky, Weitz, and Kenski 2017; Massaro and Stryker 2012). Jamieson and colleagues (2017) observe that as "scholars have shifted to a constructionist perspective, civility has been less likely to be defined in terms of use of specific words or practice and more likely to be cast as a mode to interaction and a perception" (206). Time, situation, and location may contribute to what people see as civil or uncivil. The same content can be perceived differently depending on the channel or structure of the media platform on which the messages are received (Sydnor 2018). In a concurring opinion in *Jacobellis v. Ohio* (378 US 184 (1964)), Supreme Court Justice Potter Stewart famously wrote of "hard core pornography" that while he did not attempt to define it and "perhaps I could never succeed in intelligibly doing so. But I know it when I see it." Similarly, individuals often feel that they know "incivility" when they see it, but do not necessarily recognize that their fellow citizens may not share the same interpretations. "Claims that incivility can be defined also have been met with a certain amount of derision," contend Massaro and Stryker (2012, 406). "The real issue, though, is whether there is sufficient consensus on the meaning of political incivility in various modern contexts that promoting political-civility norms is reasonable and practicable."

Studies of incivility are often focused on norm violations, but scholars do not necessarily agree on which norms are of concern (Muddiman 2017). Scholars have defined civility through different orientations, with some focusing on interpersonal politeness and etiquette, or what Muddiman (2017) calls personal-level incivility, and others arguing that civility implies much more in the democratic context, such as political process and deliberative norms, or what Muddiman (2017) calls public-level incivility. As Strachan and Wolf (2012) explain, both "public civility and interpersonal politeness sustain social harmony and allow people who disagree with one another to maintain ongoing relationships" (402). According to Papacharissi (2004), "polite manners are a condition necessary, but not sufficient, for civility" (260) and she sees the focus on interpersonal politeness as limiting. She contends that "[c]ivility standards should promote respect for the other, enhance democracy, but also allow human uniqueness and unpredictability" (266) and embraces an understanding of "civility as collective politeness with consideration for the democratic consequences of impolite behavior" (267).

While recognizing the differences that exist in definitions of civility, our review nonetheless suggests that two themes often found in definitions of civility (or incivility) revolve around notions of respect (or disrespect) and necessity (or lack of necessity). Most definitions appear to have respect, broadly conceived, implicitly or explicitly embedded in the concept of civility. Uncivil actions connote a sense of disrespect to others. That is concerning in the deliberative context, in which disrespect may halt productive conversation and exchange. Several scholars have conceived of incivility as encompassing an element of disrespect (e.g., Anderson et al. 2014; Borah 2014; Papacharissi 2004; Santana 2014). Brooks and Geer (2007) maintain that civility involves a sense of "mutual respect" (4), while also suggesting that incivility appears to be "superfluous" (5), adding little substance to the exchange. As explained by Massaro and Stryker (2012, 410), civility has included "an eye toward . . . relevance."

Taking these perspectives into account, we adopt a conceptual definition of incivility as *"features of discussion that convey an unnecessarily disrespectful tone toward the discussion forum, its participants, or its topics"* (Coe et al. 2014, 660). This definition underscores the notion that incivility is both disrespectful and nonessential to discussions and guides our measurement of the public's incivility perceptions. We now turn our attention to data from adults in the U.S. to verify whether their understanding of incivility encompasses the elements of this academic definition.

How the Public Perceives Incivility

Civility scholars have examined individual perceptions about behaviors as well as types of speech in their studies of incivility (e.g., Muddiman 2017; Stryker, Conway, and Danielson 2016). We complement this past work by asking people to evaluate real public discourse (i.e., potentially uncivil statements posted to an actual newspaper website's comment section). Although we acknowledge that behaviors are also an important part of civic norms, our interest is in speech rather than behaviors (e.g., "Rolling one's eyes while a political opponent is speaking," from Stryker et al. 2016, 34) because many public interactions happen online, where text-based speech acts are the dominant form of engagement. Notably, our approach to examining perceptions of potentially uncivil speech is different from other incivility perception studies in the kinds of stimuli we employ. Past research as generally relied on descriptive accounts of hypothetical messages, such as asking people to evaluate possibilities like "A candidate's Senate campaign aired phony television ads using paid out-of-state actors to spread rumors about his political opponent" (Muddiman 2017, 3188) or "Use of obscene or vulgar language in political discourse" (Stryker et al. 2016, 34). In contrast, we ask people react to actual messages produced by members of the lay public in discussing news online. These messages have not been described or framed by the researchers in the evaluation material.

Here, we present the results from two studies. The first study included adults between 40 and 65 years of age (N = 399; March 12–22, 2014). The second study was of college students at a Southwestern university (N = 309, November 16–December 8, 2014). Participants rated ten statements containing one of five types of incivility that have been demonstrated in prior research to meet the criteria of an uncivil speech act following the operational definition of incivility given by Coe et al. (2014). Two control statements that did not contain incivility were also evaluated. Participants read the series of 12 statements and, after each statement, completed four items used evaluate their perceptions of the relative civility of each statement. The four items were rated on seven-point scales with the following adjective anchors: civil/uncivil, rude/polite (reverse coded), necessary/unnecessary, and disrespectful/respectful (reverse coded). These items were randomly rotated, and the valence of the anchors was mixed to avoid negativity or positivity response bias. The items were designed to capture our conceptual definition of incivility as well as the definitions of those scholars who have linked civility and politeness (e.g., Papacharissi 2004). Examining politeness in relation to other characteristics of incivility will help clarify the extent to which citizens connect these constructs when confronted with real-world instances of incivility.

If the conceptual definitions of incivility based on these characteristics have merit, then people should generally evaluate messages that they perceive to be uncivil as also being disrespectful, unnecessary, and rude. Accordingly, they should evaluate messages that they perceive to be civil as also being respectful, necessary, and polite. Our empirical findings suggest that this is indeed the case. Table 3.1 presents each of the 12 statements evaluated and the correlation of the statement's

TABLE 3.1 Statement incivility ratings correlated with being disrespectful, unnecessary, and rude

Statements	40–65-year-olds sample			College-student sample		
	Disrespectful	Unnecessary	Rude	Disrespectful	Unnecessary	Rude
Just because something is not popular with the beer swilling Texas drawling NASCAR crowd here does not mean that the rest of the world agrees that it is worthless.	0.67	0.73	0.74	0.70	0.69	0.72
At least the morons in the state capital no longer have control of this process!	0.74	0.68	0.73	0.58	0.59	0.63
I hope the voters will kick that politician out on his pompous ass next election.	0.73	0.66	0.73	0.62	0.56	0.65
That person said not one damn word in that article. All BS just like the politicians—the same crap.	0.70	0.78	0.70	0.58	0.64	0.62
Americans have been screaming at the top of their lungs that this government is wrong, is corrupt, is lying, is deceiving the people, and is violating our constitution.	0.75	0.75	0.74	0.63	0.62	0.50
We need to get everyone out of office and start fresh. Make it so that lawyers cannot run for office in the executive or legislative branches of government. They lie and should not be trusted.	0.68	0.68	0.70	0.57	0.56	0.61
Quit crying over spilled milk.	0.68	0.72	0.71	0.51	0.43	0.48
I am sick and tired of people throwing tantrums.	0.68	0.71	0.77	0.52	0.47	0.53
Our justice system is just as corrupt and lousy as any in the world.	0.69	0.70	0.72	0.54	0.57	0.57
Texting while driving is stupid.	0.72	0.67	0.76	0.48	0.48	0.46
95% of our students qualify for free or reduced lunches???? What in the world does that have to do with being able to pass a test. (sic) "Poor" is no excuse.	0.79	0.76	0.80	0.69	0.69	0.71
The article was not correct with regard to the personnel required to fly and maintain the unmanned aerial vehicles. The article stated that three individuals were required to fly each UAV. The real number is two (Pilot and Sensor Operator).	0.80	0.76	0.81	0.78	0.63	0.75

Note: $p < .001$ for all correlations.

Source: Authors' surveys.

incivility rating with the other three items. Pearson correlations are statistics that range from -1 to $+1$, where negative correlations mean that the items have the opposite ratings and positive correlations mean that the items yield similar ratings. A zero correlation means that the items are not associated with each other. As shown in Table 3.1, all of the associations between perceptions of a statement's incivility and its evaluations as being disrespectful, unnecessary, and rude were statistically significant and positive across both samples for all 12 statements. For those in the 40- to 65-year-old sample, incivility was associated with being disrespectful ($r = 0.67$ to 0.80), unnecessary ($r = 0.66$ to 0.78), and rude ($r = 0.70$ to 0.81). For those in the college-student sample, incivility was associated with being disrespectful ($r = 0.48$ to 0.78), unnecessary ($r = 0.43$ to 0.69), and rude ($r = 0.46$ to 0.75). The findings provide evidence that people tend to see these items as coming from the same place or influenced by the same overarching principles.

Next, we looked at whether the four items were unidimensional or whether there were patterns in the data suggesting that different concepts ran through the group of items. For both studies, the results suggested that the four items worked well as a unidimensional, collective set.[1] Then, a statistic called Cronbach's alpha was computed to examine the internal consistency of the four items used to assess perceived incivility for each of the five types of incivility examined—name-calling, vulgarity, lying accusation, pejorative for speech, and aspersion. This statistic looks at how well the items cohere, ultimately determining whether the items are reliable when used as a group. When values for alpha approach 1, the grouping is believed to work very well as a measurement of the construct of interest—incivility, in our case. If the four items did not yield consistent responses, that lack of consistency would be reflected in the alpha statistic. As shown in Table 3.2, the alphas were above 0.75 for all five types of incivility. In the middle-aged sample, Cronbach's alpha ranged from 0.80 to 0.93. In the college sample, Cronbach's alpha ranged from 0.76 to 0.91. The findings suggest that the approach taken for measuring perceived incivility was reliable.

Broadly, these findings indicate that the public does not necessarily make the same fine-grained distinctions as scholars. To the public, being disrespectful, unnecessary, and rude is part of how incivility is perceived.

Incivility Perceptions by Types of Speech

Different types of speech may prompt perceptions of incivility. Based on previous research (Coe et al. 2014), we focused on five types of incivility—name-calling, vulgarity, lying accusations, pejoratives for speech, and aspersions—although it is important to acknowledge that there are other types of incivility as well, such as mockery/sarcasm and exaggeration (e.g., Sobieraj and Berry 2011). Name-calling involves making ad hominem attacks. Vulgarities are defined as curse words, including words such as "damn" or using symbols to replace letters (e.g., f#ck). Lying accusations are charges that someone has been intentionally dishonest.

TABLE 3.2 Mean ratings for the five different types of incivility

Type of incivility	α	Overall mean (SD)	Female mean (SD)	Male mean (SD)	Gender gap (female–male)
Name-calling					
Middle-aged sample	.88	5.05 (1.24)	5.36 (1.21)	4.80 (1.22)	0.56
College sample	.82	5.12 (0.93)	5.22 (0.87)	4.91 (1.02)	0.31
Vulgarity					
Middle-aged sample	.90	5.00 (1.33)	5.35 (1.37)	4.74 (1.24)	0.61
College sample	.88	5.45 (0.97)	5.61 (0.94)	5.10 (0.95)	0.51
Lying accusation					
Middle-aged sample	.86	3.99 (1.30)	4.16 (1.38)	3.85 (1.22)	0.31
College sample	.84	4.11 (0.94)	4.23 (0.95)	3.86 (0.86)	0.37
Pejorative for speech					
Middle-aged sample	.86	3.92 (1.16)	4.07 (1.19)	3.80 (1.13)	0.27
College sample	.81	4.01 (0.86)	4.08 (0.83)	3.88 (0.89)	0.20
Aspersion					
Middle-aged sample	.80	3.74 (1.23)	3.76 (1.18)	3.72 (1.28)	0.04
College sample	.76	3.88 (0.87)	3.94 (0.88)	3.76 (0.85)	0.18
Control statement 1					
Middle-aged sample	.93	4.77 (1.76)	4.89 (1.80)	4.66 (1.72)	0.23
College sample	.91	5.15 (1.37)	5.30 (1.33)	4.83 (1.41)	0.41
Control statement 2					
Middle-aged sample	.93	2.69 (1.42)	2.52 (1.45)	2.82 (1.38)	−0.30
College sample	.91	2.77 (1.27)	2.78 (1.27)	2.75 (1.26)	0.03

Source: Authors' surveys.

Pejoratives for speech involve mocking the way that someone has expressed her-/ himself. Aspersions are similar to name-calling but are derisive attacks on ideas rather than attacks directed at individuals.

We took the mean ratings on the four incivility items—civil/uncivil, rude/ polite (reverse scored), necessary/unnecessary, and disrespectful/respectful (reverse scored)—and averaged them together to form an incivility perception scale for each statement. The mean scores ranged from 1 to 7, where 1 meant the statement was *civil* and 7 meant that the statement was *uncivil*. A mean rating of 4 was the midpoint. Ratings above 4 constituted *uncivil* evaluations. We then averaged the statements for each type of incivility; there were two statements for each of the five incivility categories.

As shown in Table 3.2, there were patterns to the incivility ratings of the various types of speech. Looking at the means across the categories, middle-aged adults and college students rated the name-calling and vulgarity statements at least a point higher than the other categories on the seven-point incivility perception scale. Name-calling is the most prevalent form of incivility found in online forums (Coe et al. 2014) and consequently was anticipated to be a form that people would readily identify as uncivil, which was borne out in the data. By definition, vulgarities are understood as breaks in speech norms.

Mean scores for lying accusations were just under the midpoint at 3.99 for the middle-aged sample and just over the midpoint at 4.11 for the college sample, suggesting that lying accusations were not considered to be particularly uncivil. This is noteworthy because lying accusations are considered breaches of conduct in congressional discourse. Impugning someone's integrity, "even if their actions invite it" (Jamieson and Hardy 2012, 412), is considered unconducive to deliberation because "central to the ability to deliberate is a rhetoric of mutual respect." Yet, it appears that at the citizen level, these same concerns are not evident.

Pejoratives for speech and aspersion were also at the midpoint or below it for both samples. Deriding someone's expression and attacking ideas were not considered to be in the same evaluative category as attacking the person.

We also compared reactions to these types of incivility with two different types of civil controls—one based on a sentiment that had strong public consensus around it and one based on factual but unemotive material. These controls were selected because they presented clear points of view. One concern about assessing incivility is that people may consider things to be uncivil merely because they are not views that the perceivers hold. The first control statement yielded a relatively high incivility rating (4.77 for the middle-aged and 5.15 for college students). The statement read, "95% of our students qualify for free or reduced lunches???? What in the world does that have to do with being able to pass a test. (sic) 'Poor' is no excuse." We suspect that the reactions had to do with either disagreement with the assessment or concerns that a vulnerable group was the target. Technically, nothing in the statement met our definitions of name-calling, vulgarity, lying accusations, pejoratives for speech, or aspersion, although the author of the comment clearly had taken a strong position. It is also worth noting that the statement contained repeated punctuation ("????") that might have triggered format reactions similar to those of perceived written "shouting" via the use of capitalization of all letters in a word.

The second control statement read, "The article was not correct with regard to the personnel required to fly and maintain the unmanned aerial vehicles. The article stated that three individuals were required to fly each UAV. The real number is two (Pilot and Sensor Operator)." The commenter had a clear point of view expressed in the first five words of the post. The commenter did not blame a particular person or group, however, and was specific in explaining which claim in the article was viewed as incorrect. This statement was given the lowest incivility ratings of the 12 statements analyzed, with means of 2.69 (middle-aged sample) and 2.77 (college sample).

Taken together, the reactions to these statements show that certain types of speech appear to elicit stronger evaluations of incivility than do others. Further, the fact that one of the two control statements also elicited strong incivility reactions suggests that agreement with a point of view and/or the presentation of the comment (e.g., punctuation) may also shape how people perceive the civility of a comment.

It is also worth noting that although we see patterns in the types of speech that appear to be considered uncivil, the diversity in the reactions suggests that there was no consensus over what was considered uncivil. Patterns, yes. Consensus, no. Along with group means for the types of speech evaluated, Table 3.2 presents the standard deviations (SD) around those means. Those show that on average middle-aged participants were from 1.16 to 1.76 points away from the group mean and college participants were from 0.86 to 1.36 points away from the group mean. In other words, there were ranges of reactions to the statements.

Gender Differences in Perceived Incivility

If incivility perceptions shape political deliberation and engagement, for either good or ill, it is important to understand whether particular groups perceive discourse differently than do others. We focus here specifically on possible gender differences, because gender shapes human perceptions, intentions, and behaviors in subtle but significant ways. In politics, gender affects interest, knowledge, and participation. Women tend to express less political interest than do men (Bennett 1986; Kenski 2001), underperform their male counterparts on political knowledge tests (Delli Carpini and Keeter 1996, 2000; Kenski 2000; Kenski and Jamieson 2000), and participate less than do men in politics generally (Burns, Schlozman, and Verba 2001), with the exception of turning out at the polls during elections. Gender differences, moreover, are not confined to the United States (e.g., Coffé and Bolzendahl 2010). These modest but consistent gender differences affect the way political life looks. Consequently, understanding possible gender differences in perceptions of public discourse may provide insight into understanding gender gaps in political engagement. In this section, we examine how men and women interpret the civility of statements made by other members of the public.

Table 3.2 presents the mean incivility ratings for women and men. The last column on the right subtracts the male mean from the female mean. A positive gap rating means that women are more likely to perceive the type of speech as uncivil in comparison to men. This column shows that women were consistently more likely to perceive the statements as uncivil. The only exception to this trend is that middle-aged men evaluated the first control statement as more uncivil than did middle-aged women. In Kenski, Coe, and Rains (2017), we looked at gender as a predictor of incivility perceptions and found that being female was significantly associated with perceiving statements as uncivil controlling for other considerations, such as party identification, personality characteristics, and demographic variables. In other words, gender was important above and beyond these other factors.

Another way to examine incivility is to categorize all ratings above the midpoint as "uncivil" and below the midpoint as "civil," getting rid of the gradations or intensity of the evaluations. Using this dichotomous approach, we also see that gender is associated with incivility evaluations, as shown in Table 3.3. Across the 12 statements for the two samples, there were only four cases in which males were more likely than females to categorize a statement as uncivil. In two of these four cases, the gap was razor thin—the second control statement had a gap of −0.1% in the middle-aged sample, and the pejorative for speech "Quit crying over spilled milk" had a −0.4% margin in the college sample. In both samples, men were more likely to categorize the aspersion "Texting while driving is stupid" as uncivil than were women—with gaps of −5.3% for those in the middle-aged sample and −9.1% for those in the college sample. In that situation, neither group found the aspersion very uncivil, perhaps owing to agreement with the position. In all other statements, women categorically rated the statements as uncivil more so than did men.

In our college sample, we asked respondents, "How serious a problem is the lack of civil or respectful discourse in our political system?" Nearly two-thirds (65.7%) reported that it was a very serious or somewhat serious problem. Only 1.3% of subjects said that it was not a serious problem at all. We broke down these responses by gender and found that men and women tended to see the seriousness of the problem similarly, as shown in Table 3.4. Men were more likely to report that it was a "not too serious a problem" in comparison to women (16.5–9.9%), while women were more likely than men to say they didn't know (23.6–15.5%). This is consistent with research that has demonstrated that women in general are more likely than men to give "don't know" responses (Francis and Busch 1975; Mondak and Canache 2004; Rapoport 1981; Seltzer, Newman, and Leighton 1997; Shapiro and Mahajan 1986).

TABLE 3.3 Percentage of respondents rating statements as uncivil by gender

Statements	Type	40–65-year-olds sample			College-student sample		
		Female	Male	Gender gap (female–male)	Female	Male	Gender gap (female–male)
Just because something is not popular with the beer swilling Texas drawling NASCAR crowd here does not mean that the rest of the world agrees that it is worthless.	Name-calling	68.4%	60.1%	8.3%	67.5%	66.0%	1.50%
At least the morons in the state capital no longer have control of this process!	Name-calling	72.8%	60.3%	12.5%	90.6%	69.1%	21.50%
I hope the voters will kick that politician out on his pompous ass next election.	Vulgarity	65.3%	48.4%	16.9%	88.7%	75.3%	13.4%
That person said not one damn word in that article. All BS just like the politicians—the same crap.	Vulgarity	77.0%	65.9%	11.1%	87.3%	77.3%	10.0%
Americans have been screaming at the top of their lungs that this government is wrong, is corrupt, is lying, is deceiving the people, and is violating our constitution.	Lying accusation	29.9%	28.7%	1.2%	34.9%	24.7%	10.2%
We need to get everyone out of office and start fresh. Make it so that lawyers cannot run for office in the executive or legislative branches of government. They lie and should not be trusted.	Lying accusation	52.3%	41.3%	11.0%	65.6%	47.4%	18.2%
Quit crying over spilled milk.	Pejorative for speech	41.4%	26.5%	14.9%	42.9%	43.3%	−0.4%
I am sick and tired of people throwing tantrums.	Pejorative for speech	29.9%	27.4%	2.5%	38.2%	28.9%	9.3%
Our justice system is just as corrupt and lousy as any in the world.	Aspersion	49.4%	41.3%	8.1%	67.0%	48.5%	18.5%
Texting while driving is stupid.	Aspersion	20.1%	25.4%	−5.3%	14.6%	23.7%	−9.1%
95% of our students qualify for free or reduced lunches??? What in the world does that have to do with being able to pass a test. (sic) "Poor" is no excuse.	Control	58.0%	57.0%	1.0%	76.4%	71.1%	5.3%
The article was not correct with regard to the personnel required to fly and maintain the unmanned aerial vehicles. The article stated that three individuals were required to fly each UAV. The real number is two (Pilot and Sensor Operator).	Control	5.7%	5.8%	−0.1%	11.8%	8.2%	3.6%

Source: Authors' surveys.

TABLE 3.4 "How serious a problem is the lack of civil or respectful discourse in our political system?" by gender (college-student sample)

	Female	Male	Gender gap (female–male)
A very serious problem	19.8%	20.6%	−0.8%
A somewhat serious problem	45.3%	46.4%	−1.1%
Not too serious a problem	9.9%	16.5%	−6.6%
Not serious at all	1.4%	1.0%	0.4%
Don't know	23.6%	15.5%	8.1%

Source: Authors' college-student survey.

Substantively, women and men see the seriousness of the problem similarly, and yet as we showed in other analyses, when it comes to perceiving specific instances of incivility, women and men have different reactions. Depending on which group we use as a baseline, either women are more sensitive to incivilities than are men, or men are less sensitive than are women. The framing makes a difference in terms of how we collectively decide to pursue courses of action to mitigate uncivil speech.

Conclusions

In this chapter, we have noted that there is no consensus among scholars about what constitutes incivility. When it comes to the different dimensions, however, members of the public seem to agree that incivility in public discourse includes things perceived to be disrespectful, unnecessary, and rude. The public believes that incivility is a problem, but there is variation when specific speech acts are evaluated for their incivility. The patterns suggest that name-calling and vulgarity are the two types of speech that receive the highest incivility ratings. Patterns in the data also suggest that women are more likely to identify statements as uncivil than are men.

While much civility research has been pursued with concerns over public discourse and possible negative effects in mind (e.g., Anderson et al. 2014; Gervais 2015; Muddiman et al. 2017), some scholars have argued that the negative effects are overstated. Brooks and Geer (2007) contend that incivility does not hurt electoral engagement and that "the public will not melt in response to harsh exchanges—even those that are uncivil—and might even modestly profit from them in some cases" (12). It is not clear, however, whether the benefits of incivility are felt by all groups equally or received by some groups more than others. If incivility causes a sense of offense in some people but not others, it provides a possible explanation for why some people are comfortable engaging in politics while others avoid participating.

Exploring public perceptions of incivility, as we have done here, may also prove useful in weighing the normative implications of certain types of public speech. For example, as discussed earlier, accusations of lying were not perceived as particularly uncivil, falling just under the midpoint for the middle-aged sample and just over the midpoint for the college sample. Conceptually, an understanding of lying accusations as uncivil is grounded in congressional discourse (Jamieson and Hardy 2012). Normatively, however, it is unclear whether public discourse in general would benefit from lying accusations being viewed as uncivil—and thus, less likely to be offered. After all, facts are normatively desirable in public deliberation. If someone is not adhering to those facts, public discourse might be served by saying so. Our purpose here is not to declare that lying accusations are or are not uncivil, but instead to note comparing academic and public perspectives on this issue may aid a broader discussion about such issues.

Regarding our findings on gender, the literature is replete with studies showing that women are less politically engaged than are men. It may be the case that incivility plays a role in engaging men more than women. If one group (e.g., women) perceives political discourse as less civil than another group (e.g., men), group differences in interest, knowledge, and participation may result. If different people within a population do not agree on whether given statements break or are consistent with perceived social norms, it becomes difficult to address group differences in civic engagement. That leaves us with a call for future researchers to figure out whether the effects of incivility facilitate engagement among those already inclined to participate in the political system and among those less likely to see speech as uncivil and whether there is systematic political and deliberative avoidance by those who perceive incivility as pervasive in public discourse.

Note

1 Harman's single-factor tests were conducted on the four items for the 12 statements for each sample. This test involves entering the items into an exploratory factor analysis and examining "the unrotated factor solution to determine the number of factors that are necessary to account for the variance in the variables" (Podsakoff, MacKenzie, Lee, and Podsakoff 2003, 889). For each of the 12 statements examined independently, a single-factor solution emerged and accounted for a majority of the variance in the solution in both samples. One factor accounted for 76.99% to 83.97% of the variance in the sample of middle-aged adults. One factor accounted for 61.91% to 78.64% of the variance in the sample of college students. Notably, we took steps to mitigate against the possibility that the results could be the result of common method variance (see Podsakoff et al. 2003): the items were randomly rotated, two of them were reverse coded, and the descriptions on the ends of the scales were adjectives, making each side of the scale unique from the other items assessed.

Bibliography

Anderson, Ashley A., Dominique Brossard, Dietram A. Scheufele, Michael A. Xenos, and Peter Ladwig. 2014. "The 'Nasty Effect:' Online Incivility and Risk Perceptions of Emerging Technologies." *Journal of Computer-Mediated Communication* 19 (3): 373–387.
Bennett, Stephen Earl. 1986. *Apathy in America, 1960–1984: Causes and Consequences of Citizen Political Indifference.* Dobbs Ferry, NY: Transnational Publishers.
Borah, Porismita. 2014. "Does It Matter Where You Read the News Story? Interaction of Incivility and News Frames in the Political Blogosphere." *Communication Research* 41 (6): 809–827.
Brooks, Deborah Jordan, and John G. Geer. 2007. "Beyond Negativity: The Effects of Incivility on the Electorate." *American Journal of Political Science* 51 (1): 1–16.
Burns, Nancy, Kay Lehman Schlozman, and Sidney Verba. 2001. *The Private Roots of Public Action: Gender, Equality, and Political Participation.* Cambridge, MA: Harvard University Press.
Coe, Kevin, Kate Kenski, and Stephen A. Rains. 2014. "Online and Uncivil? Patterns and Determinants of Incivility in Newspaper Website Comments." *Journal of Communication* 64 (3): 658–679.
Coffé, Hilde, and Catherine Bolzendahl. 2010. "Same Game, Different Rules? Gender Differences in Political Participation." *Sex Roles* 62 (5–6): 318–333.
da Silva, Marisa Torres. 2013. "Online Forums, Audience Participation and Modes of Political Discussion: Readers' Comments on the Brazilian Presidential Election as a Case Study." *Communication and Society/Comunicación y Sociedad* 26 (4): 175–193.
Delli Carpini, Michael X., and Scott Keeter. 1996. *What Americans Know About Politics and Why It Matters.* New Haven, CT: Yale University Press.
Delli Carpini, Michael X., and Scott Keeter. 2000. "Gender and Political Knowledge." In Sue Tolleson-Rinehart and Jyl J. Josephson (Eds.), *Gender and American Politics: Women, Men, and the Political Process.* Armonk, NY: M. E. Sharpe, 21–52.
Francis, Joe D., and Lawrence Busch. 1975. "What We Now Know About "I Don't Knows."" *Public Opinion Quarterly* 39 (2): 207–218.
Gervais, Bryan T. 2015. "Incivility Online: Affective and Behavioral Reactions to Uncivil Political Posts in a Web-Based Experiment." *Journal of Information Technology and Politics* 12 (2): 167–185.
Jacobellis v. Ohio, 378 U.S. 184 (1964). (Stewart, J., concurring).
Jamieson, Kathleen Hall. 1997, March 1. *Civility in the House of Representatives.* APPC Report #10. The Annenberg Public Policy Center at the University of Pennsylvania. Retrieved from www.annenbergpublicpolicycenter.org/civility-in-the-house-of-representatives/.
Jamieson, Kathleen Hall. 2011, September 27. *Civility in Congress (1935–2011) as Reflected in the Taking Down Process.* APPC Report No. 2011–1. The Annenberg Public Policy Center at the University of Pennsylvania. Retrieved from www.annenbergpublicpoli cycenter.org/Downloads/Civility/Civility_9-27-2011_Final.pdf.
Jamieson, Kathleen Hall, and Bruce Hardy. 2012. "What Is Civil Engaged Argument and Why Does Aspiring to It Matter?" *PS: Political Science and Politics* 45 (2): 412–415.
Jamieson, Kathleen Hall, Allyson Volinsky, Ilana Weitz, and Kate Kenski. 2017. "The Political Uses and Abuses of Civility and Incivility." In Kate Kenski and Kathleen Hall Jamieson (Eds.), *The Oxford Handbook of Political Communication.* New York: Oxford University Press, 205–217.
Kenski, Kate. 2000. "Women and Political Knowledge During the 2000 Primaries." *Annals of the American Academy of Political and Social Science* 572: 26–28.

Kenski, Kate. 2001. "Explaining the Gender Gap in Political Knowledge: Tests of Eighteen Hypotheses." Paper presented at the National Communication Association convention in Atlanta, GA, November 1–4.

Kenski, Kate, Kevin Coe, and Stephen A. Rains. 2017, online first. "Perceptions of Uncivil Discourse Online: An Examination of Types and Predictors." *Communication Research.* doi: 10.1177/0093650217699933.

Kenski, Kate, Christine Filer, and Bethany A. Conway-Silva. 2018, online first. "Lying, Liars, and Lies: Incivility in 2016 Presidential Candidate and Campaign Tweets During the Invisible Primary." *American Behavioral Scientist.* doi: 10.1177/0002764217724840.

Kenski, Kate, and Kathleen Hall Jamieson. 2000. "The Gender Gap in Political Knowledge: Are Women Less Knowledgeable Than Men About Politics?" In Kathleen Hall Jamieson (Ed.), *Everything You Think You Know About Politics . . . and Why You're Wrong.* New York: Basic Books, 83–89, +238–241.

Massaro, Toni M., and Robin Stryker. 2012. "Freedom of Speech, Liberal Democracy and Emerging Evidence on Civility and Effective Democratic Engagement." *Arizona Law Review* 54: 375–441.

Mondak, Jeffery J., and Damarys Canache. 2004. "Knowledge Variables in Cross-National Social Inquiry." *Social Science Quarterly* 85 (3): 539–558.

Muddiman, Ashley. 2017. "Personal and Public Levels of Political Incivility." *International Journal of Communication* 11: 3182–3202.

Muddiman, Ashley, Jamie Pond-Cobb, and Jamie E. Matson. 2017, online first. "Negativity Bias or Backlash: Interaction With Civil and Uncivil Online Political News Content." *Communication Research.* doi: 10.1177/0093650216685625.

Muddiman, Ashley, and Natalia Jomini Stroud. 2017. "New Values, Cognitive Biases, and Partisan Incivility in Comment Sections." *Journal of Communication* 67 (4): 586–609.

Papacharissi, Zizi. 2004. "Democracy Online: Civility, Politeness, and the Democratic Potential of Online Political Discussion Groups." *New Media and Society* 6 (2): 259–283.

Pew Research Center. 2014, June 12. "Political Polarization in the American Public." Retrieved from www.people-press.org/2014/06/12/political-polarization-in-the-american-public/.

Podsakoff, Philip M., Scott B. MacKenzie, Jeong-Yeon Lee, and Nathan P. Podsakoff. 2003. "Common Method Biases in Behavioral Research: A Critical Review of the Literature and Recommended Remedies." *Journal of Applied Psychology* 88 (5): 879–903.

Rainie, Lee, Janna Anderson, and Jonathan Albright. 2017, March 29. "The Future of Free Speech, Trolls, Anonymity and Fake News Online." Retrieved from www.pewinternet.org/2017/03/29/the-future-of-free-speech-trolls-anonymity-and-fake-news-online/.

Rains, Stephen A., Kate Kenski, Kevin Coe, and Jake Harwood. 2017. "Incivility and Political Identity on the Internet: Intergroup Factors as Predictors of Incivility in Discussions of News Online." *Journal of Computer-Mediated Communication* 22 (4): 163–178.

Rapoport, Ronald B. 1981. "The Sex Gap in Political Persuading: Where the 'Structuring Principle' Works." *American Journal of Political Science* 25 (1): 32–48.

Santana, Arthur D. 2014. "Virtuous or Vitriolic: The Effect of Anonymity on Civility in Online Newspaper Reader Comment Boards." *Journalism Practice* 8 (1): 18–33.

Seltzer, Richard A., Jody Newman, and Melissa Vorhees Leighton. 1997. *Sex as a Political Variable.* Boulder, CO: Lynne Rienner Publishers.

Shapiro, Robert Y., and Harpreet Mahajan. 1986. "Gender Differences in Policy Preferences: A Summary of Trends From the 1960s to the 1980s." *Public Opinion Quarterly* 50 (1): 42–61.

Sobieraj, Sarah, and Jeffrey M. Berry. 2011. "From Incivility to Outrage: Political Discourse in Blogs, Talk Radio, and Cable News." *Political Communication* 28 (1): 19–41.

Strachan, J. Cherie, and Michael R. Wolf. 2012. "Political Civility." *PS: Political Science and Politics* 45 (3): 401–404.

Stryker, Robin, Bethany Anne Conway, and J. Tyler Danielson. 2016. "What Is Political Incivility?" *Communication Monographs* 83 (4): 535–556.

Sydnor, Emily. 2018. "Platforms for Incivility: Examining Perceptions Across Different Media Formats." *Political Communication* 35 (1): 97–116.

Weber Shandwick. 2016. "Nearly All Likely Voters Say Candidates' Civility Will Affect Their Vote; New Poll Finds 93% Say Behavior Will Matter." [Press release on January 28] Retrieved from www.webershandwick.com/news/article/nearly-all-likely-voters-say-candidates-civility-will-affect-their-vote.

4

SIGNALING INCIVILITY

The Role of Speaker, Substance, and Tone

Emily Sydnor[1]

In early 2016, the *New York Times* published an article entitled "The 199 People, Places and Things Donald Trump Has Insulted on Twitter: A Complete List" (Lee and Quealy 2016). By October 2017, the count had increased to 382. While entertaining to some, the article represents a continued focus by pundits, politicians, and citizens on incivility in political discourse. In 2013, 83% of survey respondents stated their belief that politics have become increasingly uncivil, and they point to politicians and the media as the ones to blame (Weber Shandwick, KRC Research, and Powell Tate 2013).

These pundits, politicians, and citizens wouldn't be wrong—research demonstrates that negativity and incivility have been increasing since the 1980s, and that this trend has an impact on a range of important political behaviors (Geer 2012; Shea and Sproveri 2012; Weber Shandwick et al. 2013). Americans exposed to incivility tend to exhibit greater close-mindedness, more polarized opinions, and lower political trust (Brooks and Geer 2007; Geer and Lau 2006; Mutz 2007; Mutz and Reeves 2005). As I will show in this chapter, incivility also influences our evaluations of others, particularly when we can identify their demographic characteristics. Given incivility's association with a range of negative political outcomes, scholars, politicians, and citizens alike need to consider strategies for minimizing its negative effects.

One of the biggest challenges in understanding these potentially harmful effects and in developing potential interventions to thwart them is clearly articulating what incivility means. What is incivility and what components of incivility produce the range of effects mentioned earlier? Understanding incivility requires a consideration of three elements—the message tone, the message substance, and the message sender. When people encounter online political messages, their assessment of the civility of that communication is determined by a combination of each of these three factors.

How It's Said: Style or Tone

Before reviewing the different ways that scholars have conceived of incivility, it is important to distinguish it from the broader concept of "negativity." To do this, we can draw on the literature on the effects of campaign advertising. Positive ads emphasize the positive attributes of the message sponsor; for example, Ronald Reagan's iconic positive ad, "Morning in America," told voters "under the leadership of President Reagan, our country is prouder, and stronger, and better" (Prouder, Stronger, Better 1984). Negative ads, in contrast, emphasize the negative attributes of the opponent. The infamous negative ad "Revolving Door," run by George H.W. Bush in 1988, attacked his opponent, Michael Dukakis, on a weekend furlough program run during his time as Massachusetts governor.

While positive messages are by definition civil, negative messages can be either civil or uncivil. As Brooks and Geer explain,

> Incivility [includes] claims that are inflammatory and superfluous. Some comments can, in fact, be quite critical of an opponent, and still not earn a classification as "uncivil." Incivility requires going an extra step; that is, adding inflammatory comments that add little in the way of substance to the discussion.
>
> *(2007, 5)*

In other words, a civil, negative message would be straightforward and opponent-focused: "Obama's restrictions on student expression on college campuses violate our First Amendment rights." An uncivil, negative message would include superfluous language, such as insults or name-calling: "*Self-centered, ignorant* Obama's restrictions on student expression on college campuses violate our First Amendment rights." Both statements are negative, but they vary in tone.

Many empirical tests of the effects of incivility focus on incivility as the style or tone of political discourse, rather than its content or substance. From this perspective, civility describes the manner in which political discussions are conducted, emphasizing adherence to cultural norms for polite, face-to-face conversation: "features of discussion that convey an unnecessarily disrespectful tone toward the discussion forum, its participants, or its topics" (Coe, Kenski, and Rains 2014, 3; Mutz 2015). Incivility, from this perspective, includes language that is consistently seen as outside social norms (racial slurs, obscenity) as well as sarcasm, finger-pointing, name-calling, and belittling (Berry and Sobeiraj 2014; Gervais 2015; Hwang, Kim, and Huh 2014; Mutz 2015; Thorson and Wells 2015; Coe et al. 2014). This conceptualization of civility in terms of a message's style or tone is consistent with how the average American thinks about civility. Respondents to a 2016 survey by Allegheny College emphasized interruption (51%), shouting (65%), belittling or insulting someone (74%), and personal attacks (71%) as against the rules for civility. In other words, people judge the civility of communication, in part, by the tone of a message.

What Is Said: Substance or Content

Others insist that civility goes beyond a polite tone of communication, and describes instead a message's substance and content. In this definition, civility isn't defined by compliance with widely shared norms about appropriate behavior, but by substantive content that demonstrates "deference to the social and democratic identity of an individual" (Papacharissi 2004, 267). In that same survey of people's perceptions of what constitutes incivility, over half of respondents reported that questioning someone's patriotism (52%), comments about someone's race or ethnicity (69%), and comments about someone's sexual orientation (65%) were against the rules for civility in politics ("Allegheny Survey" 2016). These responses align with three ways that a person might be labeled uncivil in his or her online commentary according to communication scholar Zizi Papacharissi (2004): making threats to democracy, assigning stereotypes, and threatening others' rights. In other words, incivility is determined by the content of the ideas within a message, and not just by the package carrying that message.

Who Is Saying It: Message Source

Finally, yet a third set of scholars argues that civility is about message source and issues relating to power. That is, identifying communication as civil or uncivil is inexorably tied to the nature and status of who is speaking, and to our perceptions of that individual. For example, consider Greensboro, North Carolina, in the early 1950s. As historian William Chafe explains, mid-twentieth-century Southern progressives prided themselves on their civility: "abhorrence of personal conflict, courtesy toward new ideas, and a generosity toward those less fortunate than oneself" (Chafe 1980, 7). In this environment, the emphasis on consensus and deference made it problematic for African Americans to assert their independence. It was only through "uncivil" acts—protests, sit-ins, direct challenges, and conflict—that they could move toward racial justice. Incivility, as such, continues to be a tool of marginalized groups to call attention to their concerns (Chafe 1980; Zerilli 2014).

Incivility is a function of an individual's place in the social and political hierarchy, but also of the individual characteristics and affiliations of both the speaker and the listener. In his June 16, 2015, announcement that he was running for president, Donald J. Trump referenced Mexican immigrants, noting, "They're bringing drugs . . . they're bringing crime. They're rapists. And some, I assume, are good people" (Engber and Bouie 2016; Lee and Quealy 2016; Milbank 2015).

Opponents were quick to criticize this claim. Hillary Clinton remarked that he had used "deeply offensive rhetoric" (Milbank 2015). Supporters, on the other hand, dismissed his rhetoric as "careless and undisciplined" (Engber and Bouie 2016). The difference between calling this language offensive and calling it careless was contingent on where the listener stood on the political spectrum.

Unsurprisingly, an individual's partisanship colors her perception of and reaction to uncivil language. When an individual's own party uses incivility, or when incivility is used in attacks against the individual's party, that individual is also more likely to use uncivil language. In contrast, people's responses to incivility toward out-groups are less emotionally charged (Gervais 2014, 2016). Incivility's ability to polarize the electorate also depends on its source. Incivility depolarizes partisans when it comes from their own party, but when it comes from a source associated with the other party (e.g., MSNBC for Republicans, Fox News for Democrats) it polarizes. As Druckman, Gubitz, Levendusky, and Lloyd (2017) explain, when Democrats hear incivility from MSNBC's Chris Hayes on the Dakota Access Pipeline, they express more partisan ambivalence than when they hear incivility from Tucker Carlson on Fox.

How, What, and Who?

In two different experiments conducted in July 2016 and July 2017, I explored how uncivil tone and message substance interact with perceptions of the speaker to influence people's perceptions of civility within a message. Participants were recruited through online survey platforms and randomly assigned to view one of several tweets (or exchanges on Instagram) that varied systematically in their presentation of the various elements discussed.

Study 1 involved three variations on the substance of a tweet about President Obama: rights-threatening, rights-affirming, and rights-neutral comments. In the rights-threatening condition, the tweet stated, "Obama restricts student expression on college campuses." The rights-affirming condition read, "Obama endorses student expression on college campuses at the expense of academic integrity." The rights-neutral tweet read, "Obama missed the funeral of another high-profile conservative." In order to manipulate differences in message tone, half of the messages in Study 1 included name-calling and character assassination, while the other half did not. For example, rather than simply saying, "Obama restricts student expression on college campuses," one set of treatments (the uncivil ones) said that "*self-centered, ignorant* Obama restricts student expression on college campuses."

Some literature on incivility as a function of speaker characteristics focuses on power differentials, specifically that members of marginalized or less powerful groups will be more likely to be labeled as uncivil (Zerilli 2014; Volpp 2014; Chafe 1980). Based on these assertions, in Study 1, tweets were attributed to a member of one of two groups, either the political elite or the group ostensibly being oppressed in the given political situation. The political elite was Congressman

Ken Buck (R-CO) (@RepKenBuck). The group member being threatened by the substantive content of the tweet (college students) was college student Ben Smith, a fictional character. We tried to highlight his status as a college student through his Twitter handle (@BulldogBen) and corresponding user photo (see Figure 4.1). Table 4.1 breaks down each experimental manipulation in Study 1 by category and type.

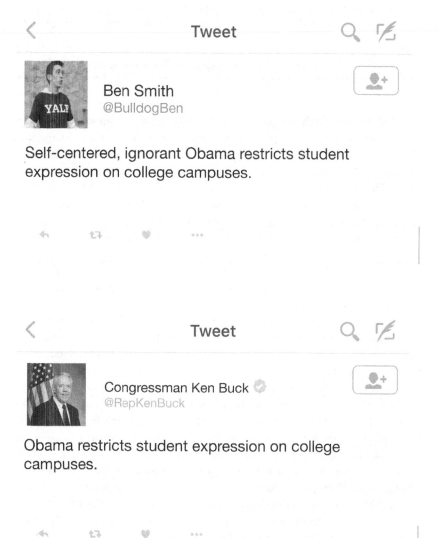

FIGURE 4.1 Study 1 treatments showing variation on speaker and tone.

TABLE 4.1 Experimental manipulations

	Type	Manipulation
Speaker	College student	College student @BulldogBen
	Congressperson	U.S. congressman @RepKenBuck
Substance	Democratic	Obama *endorses* student expression on college campuses *at the expense of academic integrity.*
	Anti-democratic	Obama *restricts* student expression on college campuses.
	Neutral	Obama *missed the funeral of another high-profile conservative.*
Tone	Polite	Obama. . .
	Impolite	*Self-centered, ignorant Obama. . .*

While the first study focuses on how all three message components (content, source, and speaker) work together, the second study focuses on the interplay between the speaker and tone, using a different set of issues and social groups. In Study 2, all participants were asked to watch a one-minute video from CNN about Richard Spencer's visit to Auburn University in April 2017. The video opens with shots of protestors at the university event, followed by clips of Spencer, a leader of the alt-right and a white supremacist, explaining his stance against racial diversity. Participants were told that the video was posted to CNN's Instagram account and that the comments that followed were excerpted from comments posted on Instagram. They were then randomly assigned to one of four comment conditions that varied in the level of civility and racial composition of the two speakers. The comments were either civil or uncivil and were attributed either to two white men or to one white man and one black man. Figure 4.2 shows two versions of the exchange—the civil exchange by the white men and the uncivil exchange by the diverse group—to give a sense of the variation across the treatments. The race of the speaker is clear from the small, circular picture next to each comment.

While the central argument of this chapter is that incivility is in the eye of the beholder (Herbst 2011), there are nonetheless criteria that reliably classify political communication as more or less uncivil. These criteria primarily focus on the tone of the message and include the use of obscenity, mockery, insulting language, character assassination, lying, pejoratives, and ideologically extremizing language, among others (Berry and Sobeiraj 2014; Gervais 2016). The comments used in Study 2 draw on these criteria and include name-calling ("you idiot"), insults ("a whiny pansy liberal"), extensive capitalization ("FREE SPEECH DOES NOT EQUAL HATE SPEECH"), and excessive punctuation use ("?!?!" and "!!!"). The civil condition still took a contentious, negative tone but without these specific indicators of incivility.

Civil x white treatment

 rossparker4 So colleges should just let anyone come speak even if it's someone like Spencer who stands for racism and white superiority? Things that I might add go against the historically diverse atmosphere of universities!

 jsmith Look, Spencer is a brave man representing a culture that continuously gets ignored in America! The left thinks that black people should be on top, that diversity means stripping white people of their rights. Absolutely not, Spencer is a hero and he should be allowed to spread his message any and everywhere!
50m   1 like   Reply

 rossparker4 No, you Alt-Right members don't understand how destructive this speech is! The students at Auburn University held a peaceful protest against white supremacy, white privilege, and in favor of diversity. They understand that someone like him shouldn't be allowed to say these things. Free speech does not mean hate speech.
43m   1 like   Reply

 jsmith @rossparker4 Oh look, a liberal...what a surprise. #freespeechisallspeech
37m   1 like   Reply

Uncivil x mixed treatment

 rossparker4 Wow, so colleges should just let anyone come speak even if it's just some asshole like Spencer who literally stands for racism and white superiority? Things that I might add go against the historically diverse atmosphere of universities?!?!

 jsmith Look, Spencer is a brave man representing a culture that continuously gets ignored in America!! You f#%&*@!% communists think that black people should be on top, that diversity means stripping white people of their God given rights. Absolutely not, Spencer is a hero and he must be allowed to spread his message any and everywhere!!!
50m   1 like   Reply

 rossparker4 No, you idiot Alt-Right members don't even understand how destructive this speech is! All the sensible students at Auburn University held a peaceful protest against white supremacy, white privilege, and in favor of diversity. They understand that a monster like him should never be allowed to spew this kind of hatred. FREE SPEECH DOES NOT MEAN HATE SPEECH.
43m   1 like   Reply

 jsmith @rossparker4 Oh look...a whiny liberal pansy what a surprise. #freespeechisallspeech
37m   1 like   Reply

FIGURE 4.2   Study 2 treatments.

In each study, after the participants had read their randomly assigned tweet or set of comments, they were asked about a variety of attitudes and perceptions, including their trust in politicians and the political system, the legitimacy of the arguments articulated in the posts, perceptions of the posts as undemocratic or uncivil, and their warmth toward the person making the comments. This approach lets us look first at the effects of each element of incivility separately, then at how elements—like the speaker and tone of communication—interact to affect our understanding of and reactions to incivility.

Like any experimental test, these studies have some inherent limitations. Because the treatments are designed to mirror social media posts, the results are not generalizable across all types of media. The experiments ask participants to evaluate a single communication incident at a single point in time, so we cannot evaluate the long-term effects of exposure to these sorts of messages. However, experiments like these are effective for isolating specific relationships, opening the door for several avenues of future research. By testing each conception of incivility in isolation and in interaction with one another, we get a sense of how theories of incivility play out in the average citizen's thought processes.

Does Message Content Matter?

Results indicate that on its own, substance seems to have little to no effect on identification of language as uncivil. Out of the two studies described earlier, only Study 1 manipulated content that has been tied theoretically with uncivil rhetoric: threats to individual rights. However, after holding the tone and speaker constant, there was no substantial or statistical difference in participants' perceptions of incivility. Figure 4.3[2] shows the difference in perceptions of incivility across the three different types of content. If anything, people found the rights–neutral treatment—the one that criticized Obama for missing a Republican funeral—more uncivil than either of the two tweets that focused on free speech, though these differences are not statistically significant.

Even though the message content did not affect participants' perceptions of message incivility, Figure 4.4 shows that message content *did* have a small impact on their *general* assessment of political civility. In comparison to those who saw the rights-restricting message, those who read the rights-neutral tweets reported that *they saw politics today as generally more civil* than those who read the rights-threatening tweet. These results weakly correspond with the results of survey data and scholarly research that tie the identification of incivility to stereotypes and threats to others' rights. The substance of communication can have small but significant effects on overall perceptions of politics as civil, even if it has only minor impact on assessment of the message itself.

Message Tone Definitely Matters

While changing the content of tweets did not have much effect on whether people saw the message as uncivil, changes to message *tone* produced a strong shift

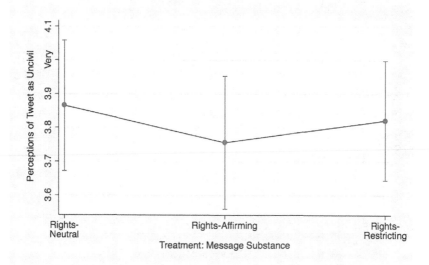

FIGURE 4.3 Message substance has little effect on perceptions of civility.

Source: Author's data.

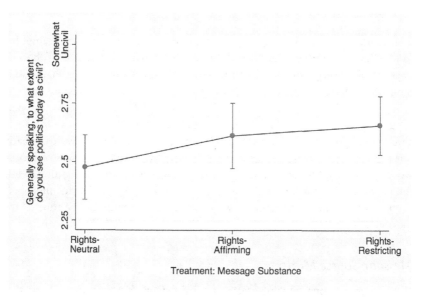

FIGURE 4.4 Substance impacts feelings that overall, politics is uncivil.

Note: Perceptions of incivility were measured on a 1 (extremely civil) to 4 (extremely uncivil) scale. Only the difference between the rights-restricting and rights-neutral treatments is statistically significant.

Source: Author's data.

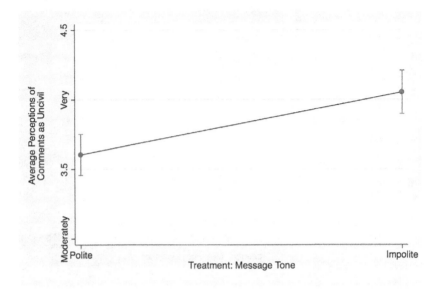

FIGURE 4.5 Study 1: Tone affects perception that tweets are uncivil.

Note: Perceptions of incivility were measured on a 1 (not at all) to 5 (extremely) scale.

Source: Author's first study data.

in assessments of incivility. In Study 1, participants rated tweets with an impolite tone as significantly less civil than the more polite tweets, regardless of the *substance* of the message or the person to whom it was attributed (see Figure 4.5). Similarly, in Study 2, the main factor shaping perceptions of incivility was the change in *tone* between the two treatments. As Figure 4.6 shows, the average perception of the treatments that used name-calling, capitalization, and so forth was almost a full point higher than the same treatments without those words. Clearly, our perceptions of incivility are driven primarily by our identification of certain words, phrases, and styles of writing that denote a rude or demeaning tone. While the public thinks that both style and substance matter in the abstract, their perceptions of incivility in specific messages are driven far more by the tone of the message than its content.

Message Source Matters

While message tone certainly seems to drive people's perceptions of message civility, characteristics of the speaker can shift these perceptions as well. Study 1 and Study 2 focused on two different characteristics of speakers—age and race— and point to two different sets of effects. In Study 1, tweets that were attributed to the college student were not seen as more or less uncivil than those that came

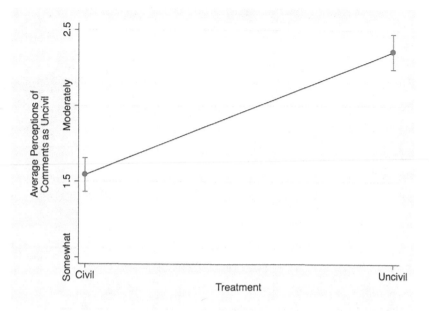

FIGURE 4.6   Study 2: Tone affects perception that comments are uncivil.

Note: Perceptions of incivility were measured on a 0–4 scale, with 0 indicating not at all uncivil. Verticle lines represent 95% confidence intervals from a bivariate regression of perceptions on treatment.

Source: Author's second study data.

from the congressman. However, in Study 2, when the exchange was presented between two white men, it was perceived as more uncivil than when it was between a black man and a white man, regardless of the use of name-calling, insults, and so forth. As Figure 4.7 shows, the difference is relatively small—certainly smaller than the effects we saw for tone—but nonetheless suggests that the race of the speakers mattered for perceptions of incivility in that situation.

Like with the substance of the message, the age and experience of the speaker in Study 1 did not affect perceptions of the message itself as civil or uncivil, but they did affect perceptions of politics more generally. This is shown in Figure 4.8. Unsurprisingly, people saw politics as more uncivil when the tweet came from the congress person than when it came from the college student.

How These Three Factors Interact

When one looks at tone, substance, and speaker individually, it's easy to declare that incivility is a product of a message's tone and leave it at that. However, it's in the interaction between these three elements where we can more clearly see the effects of the speaker and the message content on individual attitudes.

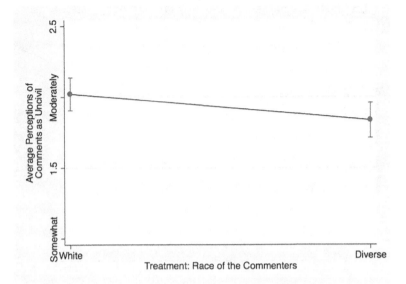

FIGURE 4.7 Study 2: White commenters are perceived as more uncivil.

Note: Perceptions of incivility were measured on a 0 to 4 scale, with 0 indicating not at all uncivil. Verticle lines represent 95% confidence intervals from a bivariate regression of perceptions on treatment.

Source: Author's second study data.

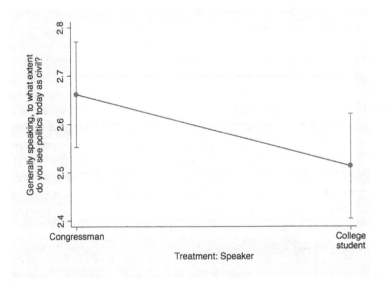

FIGURE 4.8 Feelings that politics is generally uncivil depend on who is talking.

Note: Perceptions of incivility were measured on a 1 (extremely civil) to 4 (extremely uncivil) scale.

Source: Author's first study data.

First, let's consider how perceptions of incivility shift with the interactions between the speaker, substance, and tone. Figure 4.9 shows perceptions of incivility for each treatment in Study 1. Higher bars demonstrate that, on average, people perceived the tweet as more uncivil. While the differences between treatments are not always statistically significant, there are clear patterns in which manipulation of each element changes perceptions of the tweet as uncivil. For example, impolite rhetoric from the congressman is seen as more civil as we move from rights-restricting rhetoric to rights-affirming to rights-neutral content. However, the same pattern is not present when the tweet is attributed to the student; here, rights-restricting rhetoric and rights-affirming rhetoric are seen as slightly more civil than rights-neutral commentary. Results from the same question in Study 2 demonstrate that tone has the strongest effect on perceived incivility, but that the race of the speaker also plays a role (Figure 4.10).

The combination of message speaker, substance, and tone affects not only individuals' identification of incivility in a message but also their broader political attitudes. Attitudes toward the speaker can be influenced by these factors, as can broad political attitudes, like trust in the government. The latter of these is particularly vital to the functioning of democracy, as citizens need to trust in their government in order for institutions to be considered credible, which aids in democratic health (Mutz 2015; Ferree, Gamson, Gerhards, and Rucht 2002). However, as the results from both studies show, the impact of political incivility on these attitudes depends on who is using it.

To investigate how incivility affects political trust, Study 1 asked individuals a series of questions about the extent to which they trusted both politicians and

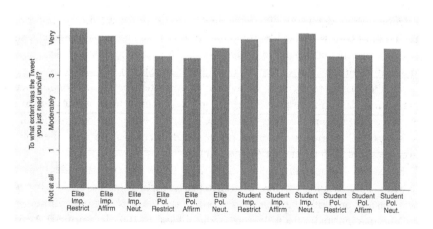

FIGURE 4.9 Perceived incivility of each treatment, Study 1.

Note: Treatments varied on the speaker (elite/student), tone (impolite/polite), and substance (rights-restricting, rights-affirming, and rights-neutral).

Source: Author's first study data.

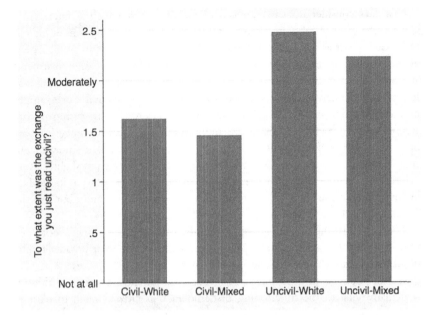

FIGURE 4.10 Perceived incivility of each treatment, Study 2.

Note: Treatments varied on the race of the speakers (white/mixed) and tone (impolite/polite).

Source: Author's second study data.

the political system as a whole. Previous studies have shown that uncivil discourse reduces citizens' trust in government (Mutz 2015; Mutz and Reeves 2007). Study 1 does not show significant differences in government trust as a function of tone. Yet, political trust is affected by the interaction of tone and speaker. Participants' trust in government was more affected by the tone of the political elite (congressperson) than by the tone of the college student. Specifically, when looking at tweets about rights restrictions, we see that an impolite tweet from a congressperson is more damaging to political trust—in the system or in politicians—than is the same tweet from a college student. Conversely, when the congressperson's tweet was polite, trust in government increased in comparison with the polite tweet from the college student (Figure 4.11).

Study 2 looked at feelings of warmth toward fellow citizens, rather than political elites. After reading the full online exchange, participants were asked to rate how warmly or coolly they felt toward one of the speakers (the one whose race was also manipulated) on a scale from 0 (the coldest) to 100 (the warmest). Again, assessments of the speaker varied as a function of both the message tone and characteristics of the speaker. As illustrated in Figure 4.12, on average, participants felt somewhat warmly toward the commenter when he used a polite tone and toward the African American speaker even when he used an impolite tone. Both speakers

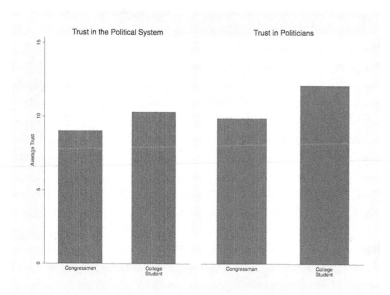

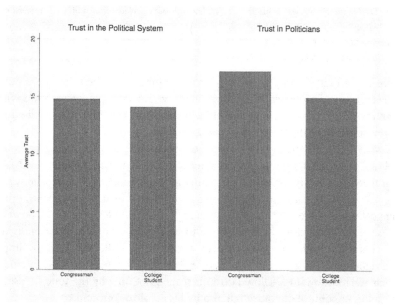

FIGURE 4.11 Joint effect of tone and speaker on trust.

Note: For impolite tweets: elite-peer differences are significant at $p < .03$ (system) and $p < .02$ (politicians). For polite tweets: the elite-peer difference in trust in politicians is significant at $p < .01$. Trust is measured on an additive scale, with higher numbers indicating greater trust. Treatments vary in who is speaking and their tone; the rights-restricting substance remains the same.

Source: Author's first study data.

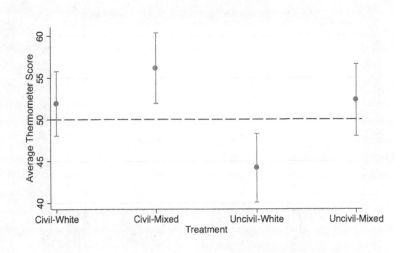

FIGURE 4.12 Joint effects of speaker and tone on feelings toward commenter.

Note: Dots represent averages, with 95% confidence intervals calculated from a bivariate regression of thermometer scores on the treatments.

Source: Author's second study data.

were viewed less warmly when they were impolite than when they were polite. However, participants had much more negative reactions to the impolite white man than they did to the impolite black man; in this condition alone did ratings of the commenter dip below the neutral 50 mark.

When we examine the interaction of the speaker, substance, and tone in a political message, it is clear that all three shape individuals' willingness to label that message as uncivil. A rights-restricting message from a politician who is calling his opponent names is identified as more uncivil than a rights-neutral message delivered politely by a college student. Beyond simple perceptions, however, we see that interactions between these three elements can also shape individuals' political attitudes. People's trust in government is affected more by impolite, rights-restricting tweets from a congressperson than from an average citizen. Their warmth toward a fellow citizen is shaped not only by the tone he uses in engaging in political discourse but also by his racial background.

Implications and Recommendations

From these results, we have learned that changing the tone of political communication matters. Adding just two words that cast character aspersions can change perceptions of how civil a message is. However, we cannot understand the effects of an impolite tone on political behavior without taking context into account. Impolite or uncivil rhetoric has a greater impact on individuals' trust in politicians when it is wielded by political elites than when it is used by a fellow citizen. When a white online commenter uses incivility to attack white supremacist Richard Spencer, people feel less warmly toward him than they do toward a black commenter using the same language. The speaker and substance of the message influence how we judge its incivility.

These findings are the result of two experiments that focus on incivility within the same medium: online social media. As such, they should not be taken to represent the ways that individuals perceive incivility in every context. The results are useful as a first step in trying to isolate the different components of incivility and to open doors for future research. To start, the results of these studies suggest that people perceive language differently when it comes from different speakers, but they do not offer a mechanism for *why* they see it differently. Consider the foregoing example—does the simple presence of a diverse set of speakers suggest an effort to speak across differences that is more civil? Is there a social desirability effect, where participants are less willing to admit they see incivility on the part of a black man as equally civil to that of a white man? Or is it that people see the black speaker as having more authority on the issue of speech that is demeaning to minority groups? Future research will have to consider these questions as they explore perceptions of incivility as they relate to democratic health.

Based on these findings, I have several recommendations for scholars and advocates for greater political civility. First, these efforts should be targeted at political elites over the general citizenry, as this top-down approach has the potential to mitigate some of the negative effects of incivility. Americans are not reacting to tweets by the average person the same way they react to tweets by their congressperson or president. Disregarding the effects of substance and tone, tweets from the congressman led participants to think that, in general, politics were more uncivil. This is especially important in the context of the current historical low in trust in government; a 2017 survey by Pew Research Center showed that only 20% of adults stated they trust the government to do what's right always or most of the time. As Mutz (2015, 90) points out, "Incivility in political discourse, rather than political conflict per se, may be the root of the problem of low regard for politics and politicians." The evidence from Study 1 supports that claim, with an important caveat. It's not simply incivility in political discourse but incivility in *elite* public discourse that has the most damaging effect on political trust. Conversely, elite messaging that does not contain an uncivil tone leads to greater political trust than the same language from a college student. We hold politicians to a higher standard in many parts of life; let's challenge them to rebuild trust by engaging in civil discourse.

Second, Study 2 participants' "punishment" of the white man for using an uncivil tone speaks to the broader debate about identity politics in America today. From pedagogical practices to Facebook memes, people are being encouraged to consider notions of systemic injustice and inequality. And along with this important and admirable focus, frequently, comes an additional refrain: a white male should not be the one conveying this message. If one identifies with groups that have historically been at the top of the social and political hierarchy, according to this line of argumentation, one cannot understand the experience of marginalization. Both men in the experiment were making an argument in favor of diversity and inclusion, and in so doing, employed some insults and online "shouting." We decry incivility because it breaks down the connections between citizens that are necessary for functioning democracy. Assuming one person has more of a right to uncivil speech than another by virtue of an ascribed trait leads to the same feelings of estrangement.

Finally, these findings offer insight for media companies that are trying to moderate online forums to encourage more productive conversation. Increasingly, academic research is being applied to media layout and web design in order to improve news organizations' ability to promote substantive discourse and help citizens expose themselves to and understand diverse views (see, e.g., the work being done by the University of Texas at Austin's Center for Media Engagement). Study 2 raises questions about the role of the avatar associated with certain social media or comment sections of media websites. On the one hand, the photo makes the commenter less anonymous. On the other hand, it has the potential to affect the way the commenter's message is viewed. Media organizations committed to minimizing incivility on their sites may want to consider alternatives to a user photo or whether they want to include them at all. Individuals who seek to use Facebook, Twitter, or Instagram as platforms for uncivil political messages may want to consider how their photo is affecting recipients' reactions to their message.

These studies left me with one final question: what do civil politics look like in modern political discourse? In the first study, the tweets that were designed to be the most civil read, "Obama endorses free speech on college campuses at the expense of academic integrity." While the statement is somewhat negative, emphasizing the trade-off between academic integrity and campus free speech, it reads more like a newspaper headline than an individual's opinion. Yet on average, participants who saw this tweet reported that it was somewhere between moderately and somewhat civil. Answering this question requires more thought about the role that social media, or media context more generally, might play in branding a political exchange as uncivil. Previous research suggests that we would see different results if these statements were made in a newspaper article or on the radio (Sydnor 2017) and certainly there is a widespread assumption that incivility is worse on the Internet. As Americans increasingly get their political news online, we must consider the ways in which the medium itself influences our experience of civility in political life.

Notes

1 The author would like to thank Southwestern University for its financial support of this project. Grace Atkins and Emily Tesmer provided invaluable assistance with the development of the treatments used for both studies.
2 Most of the figures in this chapter represent results from bivariate ordinary least squares (OLS) regressions of the treatments on relevant dependent variables. From these regressions, the figures are then created using Stata's margins plot function, which produces the predicted probability or marginal effects of each dependent variable, with a 95% confidence interval, for the specified levels of the independent variable. While I do not report the results of these regressions or analyses here, they are available at https://emily-sydnor.squarespace.com/s/SignalingIncivility_OnlineAppendix_12019-868g.pdf.

Bibliography

Allegheny Survey: 2016 Presidential Campaign Reveals Chilling Trend Lines for Civility in U.S. Politics "News and Events | Allegheny College–Meadville, PA," *Allegheny College News and Events*, October 17, 2016. Retrieved from http://sites.allegheny.edu/news/2016/10/17/allegheny-survey-2016-presidential-campaign-reveals-chilling-trend-lines-for-civility-in-u-s-politics/.

Berry, Jeffrey M., and Sarah Sobeiraj. 2014. *The Outrage Industry: Political Opinion Media and the New Incivility*. New York: Oxford University Press.

Brooks, Deborah Jordan, and John G. Geer. 2007. "Beyond Negativity: The Effects of Incivility on the Electorate." *American Journal of Political Science* 51 (1): 1–16.

Chafe, William H. 1980. *Civilities and Civil Rights: Greensboro, North Carolina, and the Black Struggle for Freedom*. New York: Oxford University Press.

Coe, Kevin, Kate Kenski, and Stephen A. Rains. 2014. "Online and Uncivil? Patterns and Determinants of Incivility in Newspaper Website Comments." *Journal of Communication* 64 (3): 658–679.

Druckman, James N., S. R. Gubitz, Matthew Levendusky, and Ashley Lloyd. 2017. "How Incivility on Partisan Media (De-)Polarizes the Electorate." Unpublished ms, Northwestern University. Retrieved from www.ipr.northwestern.edu/publications/docs/workingpapers/2017/wp-17-07.pdf.

Engber, Daniel, and Jamelle Bouie. 2016. "Donald Trump Is a Racist," *Slate*, November 11. Retrieved from www.slate.com/articles/news_and_politics/politics/2016/11/the_people_who_look_at_trump_and_don_t_see_a_racist.html.

Ferree, Myra Marx, William A. Gamson, Jürgen Gerhards, and Dieter Rucht. 2002. "Four Models of the Public Sphere in Modern Democracies." *Theory and Society* 31 (3): 289–324.

Geer, John G. 2012. "The News Media and the Rise of Negativity in Presidential Campaigns." *PS: Political Science and Politics* 45 (3): 422–427.

Geer, John G., and Richard R. Lau. 2006. "Filling in the Blanks: A New Method for Estimating Campaign Effects." *British Journal of Political Science* 36 (2): 269–290.

Gervais, Bryan T. 2014. "Following the News? Reception of Uncivil Partisan Media and the Use of Incivility in Political Expression." *Political Communication* 31 (4): 564–583.

Gervais, Bryan T. 2015. "Incivility Online: Affective and Behavioral Reactions to Uncivil Political Posts in a Web-Based Experiment." *Journal of Information Technology and Politics* 12 (1): 167–185.

Gervais, Bryan T. 2016. "More Than Mimicry? The Role of Anger in Uncivil Reactions to Elite Political Incivility." *International Journal of Public Opinion Research* 29 (3): 384–405.

Herbst, Susan. 2011. *Rude Democracy: Civility and Incivility in American Politics*. Philadelphia: Temple University Press.

Hwang, Hyunseo, Youngju Kim, and Catherine U. Huh. 2014. "Seeing Is Believing: Effects of Uncivil Online Debate on Political Polarization and Expectations of Deliberation," *Journal of Broadcasting & Electronic Media* 58 (4): 621–633.

Lee, Jasmine C., and Kevin Quealy. 2016. "The 239 People, Places and Things Donald Trump Has Insulted on Twitter: A Complete List." *New York Times*, January 28. Retrieved from www.nytimes.com/interactive/2016/01/28/upshot/donald-trump-twitter-insults.html.

Milbank, Dana Milbank. 2015. "Donald Trump Is a Bigot and a Racist," *The Washington Post*, December 1, 2015. Retrieved from www.washingtonpost.com/opinions/donald-trump-is-a-bigot-and-a-racist/2015/12/01/a2a47b96-9872-11e5-8917-653b65c809eb_story.html.

Mutz, Diana C. 2007. "Effects of 'In-Your-Face' Television Discourse on Perceptions of a Legitimate Opposition." *American Political Science Review* 101 (4): 621–645.

Mutz, Diana C. 2015. *In-Your-Face Politics: The Consequences of Uncivil Media*. Princeton, NJ: Princeton University Press.

Mutz, Diana C., and Byron Reeves. 2005. "The New Videomalaise: Effects of Televised Incivility on Political Trust." *American Political Science Review* 99 (1): 1–15.

Papacharissi, Zizi. 2004. "Democracy Online: Civility, Politeness, and the Democratic Potential of Online Political Discussion Groups." *New Media and Society* 6 (1): 259–283.

Pew Research Center. 2017. "Public Trust in Government Remains Near Historic Lows as Partisan Attitudes Shift." *Pew Research Center for the People and the Press*, May 3. Retrieved from www.people-press.org/2017/05/03/public-trust-in-government-remains-near-historic-lows-as-partisan-attitudes-shift/.

"'Prouder, Stronger, Better' Reagan, 1984." *Political Advertisement*. Retrieved July 24, 2018, from The Living Room Candidate, www.livingroomcandidate.org/commercials/1984/prouder-stronger-better.

Shea, Daniel M., and Alex Sproveri. 2012. "The Rise and Fall of Nasty Politics in America." *PS: Political Science and Politics* 45 (3): 416–421.

Sydnor, Emily. 2017. "Platforms for Incivility: Examining Perceptions Across Media." *Political Communication* 35 (1): 97–116.

Thorson, Kjerstin, and Chris Wells. 2015. "Curated Flows: A Framework for Mapping Media Exposure in the Digital Age." *Communication Theory* 26 (3): 309–328.

Volpp, Leti. 2014. "Civility and the Undocumented Alien." In Austin Sarat (Ed.), *Civility, Legality, and Justice in America*. New York: Cambridge University Press, 69–106.

Weber Shandwick, KRC Research, and Powell Tate. 2013. *Civility in America 2013*. Washington, DC: Weber Shandwick.

Zerilli, Linda M. G. 2014. "Against Civility: A Feminist Perspective." In Austin Sarat (Ed.), *Civility, Legality, and Justice in America*. New York: Cambridge University Press, 107–131.

PART II

Instances of Civility and Incivility in Contemporary American Political Discourse

5

"SHOWDOWNS," "DUELS," AND "NAIL-BITERS"

How Aggressive Strategic Game Frames in Campaign Coverage Fuel Public Perceptions of Incivility

Dannagal Goldthwaite Young, Lindsay H. Hoffman, and Danielle Roth

How the public perceives the level of civility in public life is dictated largely by our perceptions of the behavior of political elites. Importantly, though, these perceptions are mediated; they come to us through the news, social media, friends, and family, as well as other political programming. This means that subtle aspects of media production, selection, and framing might affect our perception of civility and how we respond to content more generally.

Extensive work by Diana Mutz (2015), for example, illustrates that political debate segments on cable news use close camera angles that emphasize negative emotions in a way that in turn affects how viewers learn from and respond to that content. A recent set of studies by Kate Kenski, Kevin Coe, and Stephen Rains (2017) is consistent with Mutz's finding about "in-your-face" politics on cable television. Kenski and her colleagues found that, compared to television news, talk radio, and online newspaper use, reading print newspapers was associated with people perceiving "name-calling" to be more civil. Perhaps reading about politics textually rather than having to witness people actually attacking each other on television makes that act seem less aggressive—and hence less uncivil.

The current project explores another aspect of contemporary news and how it affects audience perceptions of the civility of elites: strategic game frames. The media's tendency to cover elections (and politics in general) as a competition between two self-interested parties has been studied for decades (Cappella and Jamieson 1997; Patterson 1993). Scholars have demonstrated that in comparison to issue-based coverage, strategic game framing increases cynicism, reduces trust in government, increases negative emotional responses, and depresses political participation (see Cappella and Jamieson 1997; De Vreese 2004; De Vreese and Elenbaas 2008; Gross and Brewer 2007; Shehata 2013;Valentino, Beckmann, and Buhr 2001).We extend this line of research to explore how strategic game framing—which we call *aggressive* strategic game framing—can increase citizens' perceptions of incivility that exists among elites.

Strategy Frames in Political News

The concept of framing is not a new one for political scientists and communication scholars.According to Robert Entman, to frame is to "select some aspects of a perceived reality and make them more salient in a communicating text, in such a way as to promote a particular problem definition, causal interpretation, moral evaluation, and/or treatment recommendation for the item described" (Entman 1993, 52). Framing allows audiences to create mental models used to interpret incoming information and reconcile it with existing knowledge pertaining to a particular topic (Iyengar 1991; Rhee 1997; Scheufele and Tewksbury 2007). Political knowledge is organized in networks of information in memory, which can later be retrieved and activated. How campaign stories are framed can shape the content and structure of political information networks in our memories, hence affecting the kinds of judgments we form about politics (Cappella and Jamieson 1997).

Within the scope of election coverage, there are two opposing frames that scholars have identified in news content: issue and strategy frames. Issue framing focuses on policies and the substance of issues: what the issues or policies in question are, what possible solutions to those issues are, and what the consequences may be of those proposed problems and solutions (Patterson 1993). Strategic game frames, on the other hand, focus on a candidate's strategy for winning and on the horse-race aspect of a campaign, specifically who is ahead and behind, what actions candidates are taking to improve their standings, and candidates' own self-interests in motivating their competitive behaviors (Aalberg, Strömbäck, and DeVreese 2011; Graber and Dunaway 2014, 305; Jamieson 1992; Patterson 1993).

When strategic game frames focus on political winners and losers, and who is ahead or behind in the polls, we refer to this coverage as "horse-race coverage" (Aalberg et al. 2011).Within the broader category of strategic game frames, Aalberg et al. (2011) suggest we conceptualize strategy frames as those depicting political figures as disingenuous and strategic, usually operating out of self-interest rather than working in the interest of the public (Cappella and Jamieson 1997). These frames focus on specific events and are person-centered to emphasize the performance and personalities of political actors and the consequences of their actions in lieu of substantive conversations about political issues or policies (Aalberg et al. 2011; Iyengar 1991). It is important to note that while strategy and game framing have distinct elements, they most often appear together.

Strategic game framing is a staple of political news coverage, especially in the context of presidential elections. An analysis from 2007 found that 63% of campaign stories focused on tactical and political aspects, 17% on background of candidates, 15% on the candidate's actual ideas and policy proposals, and a mere 1% on the candidate's records or past public performance (Nisbet 2015). A 2004 election coverage report found that media (newspapers and television) used strategy tactics frequently, with 43% of the coverage in newspaper articles using strategy frames and 68% of the coverage on television (Druckman 2005). According to analyses of presidential primary election coverage from 2016, issue frames were almost completely absent from news content about the presidential primaries. A report by Harvard's Shorenstein Center found that 56% of primary coverage was dedicated to stories of the competitive game (who is ahead and behind) and another 33% to stories about the campaign process. This left only 11% of media content dedicated to substantive or policy-based concerns (Patterson 2016).

Strategic game framing is prominent in news coverage of campaigns largely because of the criteria used to prioritize content elements of news production. Strategic game frames are considered newsworthy because they focus on conflict and drama among political actors. By creating personalized stories of winners and losers, news directors may feel they are fueling audience interest in political campaigns (Bennett 2016; Lawrence 2000). Journalists may also embrace the game frame because it affords them objectivity—and avoids the appearance of taking sides politically (Lawrence 2000).

Strategic Game Framing Versus Aggressive Strategic Game Framing

Strategic game frames commonly use language and metaphors of games, sports, and competition, and, when especially aggressive, they incorporate language of wars and military battles (Jamieson 1992; Patterson 1993). Common strategy frames depict poll results in terms of "scoring in a ball game or leading/trailing in a horse-race" (Rhee 1997, 31). Even the very word "campaign" derives from military language. It is perhaps unsurprising then that language of war and combat is so salient in American journalistic descriptions of political activities. Aggressive verbs such as "attack," "blame," "hit," and "battle" dominate political campaign coverage (Rhee 1997).

Story headlines from a variety of sources during the 2016 election illustrate this aggressive form of strategic game framing. A *Huffington Post* headline from June 2016 stated that Clinton "*eviscerates* Trump in her best speech yet" (Lachman 2016). The blog Policy Mic discussed Clinton and Trump "*going to war*" over a variety of issues (*Presidential Debate* 2016). *Time Magazine* described why it's so hard for adversaries to *attack* Trump (Tsai 2016) and the *New York Post* recalled Trump thanking Bernie Sanders for the "anti-Hillary *ammunition*" (Fredericks and Campanile 2016). Other examples from CNN coverage of this year include candidates "hitting" swing states, "tackling" states, "fighting" for every last vote, and the Clinton team going on "attack" against Trump. References to the "battleground" states and "war rooms" are also popular terms used in election coverage. Such colorful examples illustrate the kinds of combative dialogue and rhetoric that are prevalent in discussions of politics in the news, particularly during election seasons. As this rhetoric becomes more and more the norm, journalists are likely uninclined to drift away from this framework.

Negative Effects of Strategy Frames

Years of research on strategy versus issue framing has highlighted the deleterious effects of constant exposure to such political coverage. At the heart of these critiques is the concern, summarized by Regina Lawrence, that when politics is presented as a game, "the actual substance of politics may be relegated to the sidelines" (Lawrence 2000, 94). Candidates are often portrayed as only trying to get ahead, doing or saying anything as a means to increase public support. Actions are generally not described as organic or authentic, but rather as deliberately planned efforts at courting a vote or getting back at an opponent. As Valentino et al. write, "the press interprets campaigns as games. Journalists view candidates as strategic players . . . devoid of sincere desire to identify and solve important societal problems" (Valentino et al. 2001, 348). The consequences for the public are potentially dire, ranging from shaping the mental frameworks that people use to make sense of politics (Rhee 1997) to increasing distrust of politicians and cynicism about political life (Cappella and Jamieson 1997; De Vreese 2004; De Vreese and Elenbaas 2008; Shehata 2013) to increasing voter anger and disgust (Gross and Brewer 2007) to reducing voter turnout, people's sense of civic duty, and how meaningful citizens perceive elections to be (Valentino et al. 2001).

The subtle cognitive mechanisms through which these news frames affect the public have consequences that extend beyond the processing of a particular news story. When news frames shape our mental frameworks associated with certain concepts or topics (e.g., politics), they also shape the kind of related information we will retain within that mental model, and the kinds of stories we tell ourselves about our political worlds (Cappella and Jamieson 1997). Once strategy frames are activated, biases will remain when recalling relevant information regarding related concepts in memory (Rhee 1997). As a result, even when topics are not presented through strategy frames, viewers will still activate those mental models—in which strategy and candidate self-interest dominate—making it more likely that new political scenarios will be interpreted through that same strategic, cynical lens (Cappella and Jamieson 1997).

Extending This Research to Perceptions of Civility

It is clear from the literature that strategic game framing affects people's mental models about politics and political candidates. Our goal is to understand how *aggressive* strategic game framing (coverage that relies heavily on language of battle and war) might shape people's mental frameworks about elections such that their perceptions of candidate civility will be affected. If election stories rely on aggressive strategic game frames with metaphors of violence and battle, the mental frameworks that would result from exposure to such content will likely emphasize aggression, ill-will, and conflict. Even if a given news story does not explicitly suggest discord between the candidates themselves, framing devices rooted in battle and war will likely trigger associations in our minds that cause us to perceive high rates of incivility between candidates.

A Note About Apples and Oranges in Strategic Game Framing Effects Research

The bulk of past research on the effects of strategic game frames compares this type of coverage to a fundamentally different kind of news content—issue- or policy-framed coverage. Since strategic game framing employs specific content elements that contrast in fundamental ways with the content elements of issue coverage, one of the potential drawbacks of this research is that it is actually examining the effects not just of two different frames of news coverage but of coverage of two totally different sets of content. In other words, the studies are often comparing apples (the experimental group exposed to strategic game-framed news) and oranges (the control group exposed to issue-framed news). To avoid this content-category confound, the current project explores various ways in which the strategy frame itself might be altered to mitigate the negative effects discussed earlier.

The Aggressive Strategic Game Frame and Some Alternatives

We studied people's reactions to—and perceptions of—three stories about the 2016 presidential campaign. The stories were consistent in content, but varied in the kind of frame employed. Interestingly enough, the story that served as an example of an "aggressive strategy frame" was taken verbatim from a CNN.com story dated May 24, 2016. The story emphasizes some of the war-like language often employed in strategic coverage of election campaigns. Words and phrases such as "battle," "nail-biter," "usurped," "duel," and "showdown" are part of the aggressive strategy frame and are all featured prominently here (battle language emphasized in boldface ahead):

Aggressive Strategy Frame
Will Trump Versus Clinton Be a Nailbiter?
May 24, 2016

Washington, D.C.—Democrats knew a general election battle between Hillary
Clinton and Donald Trump would be *rough*, but many never considered the
potential of a *nailbiter*.

During a primary in which Trump *usurped* the GOP establishment, *alienated* crucial sectors of the general electorate on issues like immigration and abortion
and *dinged* his own approval ratings, many Democrats salivated at talk of a
November *duel* with the billionaire.

Now, as Trump prepares for a general election *showdown* and a pair of new polls
show a statistical *dead heat*, veteran Democrats warn there is little room for
complacency.

"It will be close," said Mark Alderman, a veteran Democratic Party fundraiser
who worked on President Barack Obama's transition team.

The second news story in the study presented a "neutral" strategy frame constructed by simply removing the aggressive or war-like language and terminology
from the initial CNN.com story, toning down that language, while keeping the
rest of the content the same.

Neutral Strategy Frame
Trump and Clinton Look to November
May 24, 2016

Washington, D.C.—Democrats imagined that a campaign between Hillary Clinton and Donald Trump would be difficult, but many didn't consider how
close it would be.

During a primary in which Trump got the support of the GOP establishment,
in spite of his controversial statements on immigration and abortion, many
Democrats thought that Clinton's campaign against Trump would be easy.

Now, as Trump prepares for the general election and a pair of new polls shows the
candidates with equal public support, Democrats say that the party should
keep campaigning.

"It will be close," said Mark Alderman, a veteran Democratic Party fundraiser
who worked on President Barack Obama's transition team.

Finally, the third condition is what we refer to as a "citizen-centric frame."
The citizen-centric frame still includes aspects of the horse-race and language
in the original news story, but this time from the perspective of voters, not the
candidates. This frame was constructed by converting the language from political
jargon to more familiar terminology, such as "to say the least," "easy-peasy," "people like," and "Dems" to resonate more with how readers think and talk. But most
importantly, the citizen-centric frame shifted the subjects of some of the sentences
away from the politicians/candidates to the citizens themselves (citizen-centric
language emphasized in boldface ahead).

Citizen-Centric Frame
Voters Expressing Equal Affection for Hillary and Donald
May 24, 2016

Many voters imagined that a campaign between Hillary Clinton and Donald
　　Trump would be close, but many probably didn't think it would be this close.
In the spring, Trump earned the support of many Republican politicians and
　　voters—in spite of his comments on immigration and abortion that made
　　many people uncomfortable, to say the least. So, naturally, many *Democrats thought*
　　that Hillary's campaign against Trump would be *easy-peasy*.
Now, though, as Trump gets ready for November and a pair of new polls shows
　　that *people like* the two candidates about the same, *Dems* are urging their sup-
　　porters to keep campaigning.
"It will be close," said Mark Alderman, a veteran Democratic Party fundraiser
　　who worked on Obama's transition team.

We predicted that reading the aggressive strategic game frame would activate
concepts related to hostility and war in relation to candidates Clinton and Trump
in ways that would then inform readers' mental models related to the candidates
and the election. While the article itself is focused on how the two candidates have
equal support from voters, we anticipated that the aggressive strategic language
would increase readers' perceptions of the level of aggression and incivility in the
dynamics between the candidates. In other words, we imagined that the use of
aggressive strategic framing language would cause readers to misunderstand the
main point of the article (that the two candidates have equal support) in favor
of an inaccurate but hostile understanding (that the two candidates are throwing
insults back and forth). We also predicted that the aggressive strategy frame would
exacerbate these misperceptions compared to both the citizen-centric frame and
the more neutral strategic game frame.

To test these hypotheses, we embedded these three news stories in an online
survey that was administered September 28–October 27, 2016, through the Cooperative Congressional Election Study (CCES) to a nationally representative sample
of 999 people ages 18 and over in the United States. Respondents were randomly
assigned only one of the three news stories within their survey: the aggressive strategic game frame (seen by 347 participants), the neutral strategy frame (seen by 327
participants), or the citizen-centric frame (seen by 322 participants). Immediately
following the news story, all respondents were asked questions about the article,
including what they thought the article was about. They also answered questions
related to political interest, ideology, party, discussion, and news media use.

To understand to what extent aggressive strategic game framing may have
contributed to perceptions of candidate incivility, participants were asked, "How
much do you agree or disagree with each of the following statements? According

to the article you read earlier, Hillary Clinton and Donald Trump . . ." followed by three prompts: "are throwing insults back and forth"; "are receiving about equal public support in public opinion polls"; and "have notably different positions on many different political issues." These items were measured on a five-point Likert scale from strongly disagree (1) to strongly agree (5).

Figure 5.1 shows that, as expected, participants in the aggressive game frame condition were more likely to conclude from the article that candidates were "throwing insults back and forth" compared to participants in the neutral strategy frame. However, it is worth noting that the citizen-centric frame fared no better than the aggressive strategy frame in this regard. Recall that none of the stories dealt—even tangentially—with uncivil behavior between the candidates; none of the stories emphasized hostilities or the throwing of insults. Yet, the mere presence of aggressive battle-type language seems to have translated itself into "candidates being uncivil" in the minds of the readers.[1]

Perhaps the most troubling finding concerns the small number of people who accurately perceived the main point of the story itself: that the candidates had equal public support, or—framed in the language of game framing—that the candidates were running neck-and-neck in the polls. Given that this was the main premise of the news stories, it is striking that many people did not see that to be the driving point behind the story. Most notably, consider the finding that those who read the aggressive strategic game frame were significantly less likely to agree that this was a focus of the story compared to people who read the neutral or citizen-centric frame. The mere language of aggressive strategic game framing changed respondents' interpretation of the actual content of the news story.

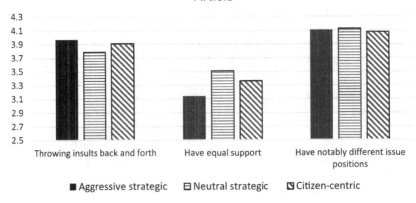

FIGURE 5.1 Framing effects on perceptions of candidates based on the article.

Source: Authors' survey.

Discussion

Most scholarly writings on democratic health place civility, among both citizens and elites, at their center. It is a democratic people's willingness and ability to engage in rational, honest, and polite discussion of ideas that allow democracy to thrive. Although we think of civility as something that stems from the actions of citizens or elites, it's also something that we experience and perceive in the world around us—a broad sense of how our society values thoughtful discourse. Although our perceptions are certainly shaped by the actions and words of citizens and elites, what we have explored in this chapter is how our perceptions of the level of rancor and discord in electoral politics are also informed by the practices of journalists and news producers. The dominance of the strategic game frame in American political coverage—and the aggressive strategic game frame, in particular—may be shaping our cognitive mental models about politics in a way that increases our perception of the level of hostility and incivility in elections.

The current project advances research in this area by comparing the impact of aggressive strategy-framing to a content-equivalent strategy-framed article that simply lacks the language of aggression and competition. This methodological choice is based on the assumption that given the pressures within the news industry to construct person-driven narratives that focus on aspects of competition, the strategic game frame is likely to continue to dominate news coverage. However, what we offer here is an alternative way to cover the race that may have less deleterious effects on audiences. Rather than just finding—once again—that strategic game framing is worse for citizens than issue framing, we propose that by working within the constraints of contemporary news norms, we can create less debilitating frames that still capture the aspects of competition that are central to contemporary campaign coverage.

Most interestingly, perhaps, is our finding that merely by framing politics in terms of war, battle, competition, and aggression, the most banal news story centering on who is ahead and behind in the polls can cause citizens to experience an election as hostile and rancorous. This raises a question: if the public perceives battle and war as inherently uncivil, could journalists' reliance on such language and metaphor be injecting incivility into our politics? This interpretation would imply that our findings are not evidence of news frames fueling public "misperceptions" of the level of political civility among elites, but rather that the battle itself constitutes uncivil behavior in the mind of the public.

Building on similar research by Diana Mutz and others, we contend that news organizations and the standard story formulas they use in covering politics are contributing in a negative way to citizens' perceptions of elections and how they experience their political world more broadly. As such, we urge journalists to reconsider the framing devices on which they rely in covering campaigns. Although many scholars urge an increased reliance on an issue-based frame in lieu of a strategy frame (which we also see as desirable), we acknowledge that strategic game frames lend themselves to news norms governed by personalized, narrative-driven stories. If strategic game frames are going to continue to be a staple of campaign coverage, journalists could employ small changes to minimize some of their deleterious effects on viewers. Simply by avoiding language of battle and aggression, opting instead for neutral strategic game language, or a more citizen-centric frame as illustrated here, journalists may find their audiences (a) better able to identify the main theme of their stories and (b) less likely to experience political campaigns as hostile and uncivil.

Note

1 One-way ANOVA with a post-hoc Bonferroni test was run to examine differences in emotional responses and article perceptions between the three experimental conditions. There were no significant differences in either positive or negative emotional responses as a function of experimental condition. Regarding perceptions of the news story, F tests reveal significant overall effects of condition on perceptions of the article portraying the candidates "throwing insults back and forth" ($F = 2.49$, $p < .08$) and "having equal public support" ($F = 8.84$, p $< .001$). Bonferroni tests indicated that when looking at perceptions of the news story portraying the candidates "throwing insults back and forth," the significant differences emerge between the aggressive strategy frame and the neutral strategy frame, with respondents in the aggressive condition more likely to say the candidates were throwing insults back and forth ($p < .09$). Keep in mind that the news story does not actually indicate anything about incivility between the candidates. Results also show that when respondents were asked about their perceptions of the article discussing the candidates having equal support, the aggressive strategy frame fostered significantly lower perceptions of "equal support" than either the neutral strategy frame ($p < .001$) or the citizen-centric frame ($p < .05$). In other words, the aggressive strategy frame produced significantly less understanding of the main premise of the article than the other two conditions. There were no significant differences between the neutral strategy and citizen-centric frames on any of the outcomes examined here.

Bibliography

Aalberg, Toril, Jesper Strömbäck, and Claes De Vreese. 2011. "The Framing of Politics as Strategy and Game: A Review of Concepts, Operationalizations and Key Findings." *Journalism* 13 (2): 162–178.

Bennett, W. Lance. 2016. *News: The Politics of Illusion*. 10th ed. Chicago: University of Chicago Press.

Cappella, Joseph N., and Kathleen Hall Jamieson. 1997. *Spiral of Cynicism: The Press and the Public Good*. Oxford University Press.

De Vreese, Claes. 2004. "The Effects of Strategic News on Political Cynicism, Issue Evaluations, and Policy Support: A Two-Wave Experiment." *Mass Communication and Society* 7 (2): 191–214.

DeVreese, Claes H., and Matthijs Elenbaas. 2008. "Media in the Game of Politics: Effects of Strategic Metacoverage on Political Cynicism." *International Journal of Press/Politics* 13 (3): 285–309.

Druckman, James N. 2005. "Media Matter: How Newspapers and Television News Cover Campaigns and Influence Voters." *Political Communication* 22 (4): 463–481.

Entman, Robert M. 1993. "Framing: Toward Clarification of a Fractured Paradigm." *Journal of Communication* 43 (4): 51–58.

Fredericks, Bob, and Carl Campanile. 2016, May 28. "Trump Thanks Bernie Sanders for the Anti-Hillary Ammunition." *New York Post*. Retrieved June 10, 2017 from http://nypost.com/2016/05/28/trump-thanks-bernie-sanders-for-the-anti-hillary-ammunition/.

Graber, Doris A., and Johanna Dunaway. 2014. *Mass Media and American Politics*. 9th ed. Washington, DC: CQ Press.

Gross, Kimberly, and Paul R. Brewer. 2007. "Sore Losers: News Frames, Policy Debates, and Emotions." *Harvard International Journal of Press/Politics* 12 (1): 122–133.

Iyengar, Shanto. 1991. *Is Anyone Responsible? How Television Frames Political Issues*. Chicago: University of Chicago Press.

Jamieson, Kathleen Hall. 1992. *Dirty Politics*. New York: Oxford University Press.

Kenski, Kate, Kevin Coe, and Stephen A. Rains. 2017. "Perceptions of Uncivil Discourse Online: An Examination of Types and Predictors." *Communication Research* 9365021769993. doi: 10.1177/0093650217699933.

Lachman, Samantha. 2016, June 2. "Hillary Clinton Eviscerates Donald Trump in Her Best Speech Yet." *Huffington Post*. Retrieved June 10, 2017, from www.huffingtonpost.com/entry/hillary-clinton-donald-trump_us_57508150e4b0eb20fa0d31f9.

Lawrence, Regina G. 2000. "Game-Framing the Issues: Tracking the Strategy Frame in Public Policy News." *Political Communication* 17 (2): 93–114.

MacDougall, Curtis. 1982. *Interpretative Reporting*. New York: Palgrave Macmillan.

Mutz, Diana C. 2015. *In-Your-Face Politics: The Consequences of Uncivil Media*. Princeton, NJ: Princeton University Press.

Nisbet, Matthew C. 2015. "Horse Race Coverage and the Political Spectacle." *Time Magazine*. Retrieved August 15, 2017, from http://bigthink.com/age-of-engagement/horse-race-coverage-the-political-spectacle.

Patterson, Thomas E. 1993. *Out of Order*. New York: Knopf.

Patterson, Thomas E. 2016. "News Coverage of the 2016 Presidential Primaries: Horse Race Reporting Has Consequences." Retrieved October 10, 2017, from https://shorensteincenter.org/news-coverage-2016-presidential-primaries/.

Pew Research Center. 2012. "Watching, Reading, and Listening to the News." Retrieved April 1, 2017, from www.people-press.org/2012/09/27/section-1-watching-reading-and-listening-to-the-news-3/.

Presidential Debate Liveblog: Clinton, Trump Go to War Over Sexist Remarks, Taxes and More. 2016, 9 October. Retrieved from https://mic.com/articles/156303/second-presidential-debate-liveblog-highlights-full-recap-of-clinton-vs-trump-showdown#.iajafnGTq.

Rhee, June Woong. 1997. "Strategy and Issue Frames in Election Campaign Coverage: A Social Cognitive Account of Framing Effects." *Journal of Communication* 47 (3): 26–48.

Scheufele, Dietram A., and David Tewksbury. 2007. "Framing, Agenda Setting, and Priming: The Evolution of Three Media Effects Models." *Journal of Communication* 57 (1): 9–20.

Shehata, Adam. 2013. "Game Frames, Issue Frames, and Mobilization: Disentangling the Effects of Frame Exposure and Motivated News Attention on Political Cynicism and Engagement." *International Journal of Public Opinion Research* 26 (2): 157–177.

Tsai, Diane. 2016, March 2. "Why It's So Hard to Attack Trump." *Time Magazine*. Retrieved June 10, 2017, from http://time.com/4245093/donald-trump-attacks-insults-criticism/.
Valentino, Nicholas A., Matthew N. Beckmann, and Thomas A. Buhr. 2001. "A Spiral of Cynicism for Some: The Contingent Effects of Campaign News Frames on Participation and Confidence in Government." *Political Communication* 18 (4): 347–367.

6

CRISES AND CIVILITY

Twitter Discourse After School Shootings

Deana A. Rohlinger and Cynthia Williams

Social media can play an important role before, during, and after a crisis. Officials, organizations, individuals, and journalists can simultaneously use platforms such as Twitter to share information that maximizes resources allocated to crisis response and minimizes loss of life (Houston et al. 2015). Social media, however, do more than share factual information among users following a given hashtag. Platforms such as Twitter allow individuals to collectively and collaboratively construct narratives, or shared understandings, about an event (Papacharissi and de Fatima Oliveira 2012). These narratives matter because they not only provide frameworks for discussing crises (Sadler 2017) but also create opportunities for interaction and deliberation among individuals holding diverse points of view (Polletta and Lee 2006).

The narratives that emerge on social media are not necessarily civil. There is ample evidence that Americans respond uncivilly to newspaper comments and YouTube videos (Coe, Kenski, and Rains 2014; Guo and Harlow 2014). For example, Arthur Santana (2015, 99) found that news stories regarding the anti-government positions and protests of the Tea Party movement, which involved peaceful demonstrations by U.S. citizens, generated more civil discourse in user comments than stories on undocumented immigrants from Mexico. In fact, over half of the comments about undocumented immigrants were uncivil, with some users advocating "shoot to kill" laws to deter "illegals" from coming "over the border." It is easy to imagine, then, that narratives constructed in the wake of crises are not always conducive to civil discourse.

Civility should not be confused with politeness (Papacharissi 2004). Civility may involve conflict as individuals holding diverse views come together and articulate their particularistic positions (Habermas 1989, 1996). These sometimes impolite disagreements are beneficial to deliberative processes writ large because they bring new ideas and "changes of will" at the periphery to the center of society (Habermas 1996, 85, 115), which maximizes the inclusion of different perspectives in public debate (Dahlberg 2005). Impolite disagreements are more likely in the digital era because real-life boundaries are broken down and relative anonymity allows more open—and sometimes more explicit and potentially offensive—exchanges (Papacharissi 2004; Suler 2004).

In this chapter we explore the relationship between crisis narratives on Twitter and civility. Specifically, we examine how four types of crisis narratives—personal stories, polemics, factual information, and misinformation—influence discourse civility. Drawing on an analysis of more than 10,000 tweets the week following two shootings that occurred on college campuses, we find that personal stories and factual information are associated with higher levels of civil discourse than polemics and misinformation. Additionally, we find that one or two individuals serve as "opinion entrepreneurs" (Blom et al. 2014; Dreier and Martin 2010) in the wake of crises and indelibly shape the course and civility of the broader, collective conversation.

Narratives and Civility in the Digital Age

Social media narratives are influenced by at least three related factors: news media coverage, the social media platform, and opinion entrepreneurs. First, news media coverage affects public attention and expression. The more news outlets cover an issue or event, the more salient it is with the broader public (McCombs and Shaw 1972). The more salient the issue is with the broader public, the more it is likely to be discussed on social media platforms like Twitter (King, Schneer, and White 2017). News media, however, do not simply signal what issues and events should matter to the citizenry. Coverage also provides frames for understanding how the public might interpret an issue or event. These frames are important to deliberative processes because, absent personal experience, they influence how citizens think—and talk—about social and political issues (Gamson 1992). The frames circulated via news media, especially those involving accidents and crises, may be sensationalistic and peppered with incorrect information (Grabe, Zhou, and Barnett 2001). This can be problematic because individuals are likely to accept information from news outlets on face value (Bessi et al. 2015; Del Vicario et al. 2016) and use it in their narrative construction. This may have implications for civility. News coverage that is sensationalistic or factually incorrect may cause individuals to construct crisis narratives that stoke political anxieties rather than discuss the substantive issues at hand (e.g., why a crisis occurred and whether there is a desired social response). These narratives can be problematic for civility if they generate insults, use ideologically extreme language, and mock individuals or groups of people—all of which shut down deliberative discourse (Berry and Sobieraj 2014; Sobieraj and Berry 2011).

Second, the social media platform used for the conversation influences narrative construction. Platforms like Facebook, for instance, can be used to create communication hierarchies that prioritize some individuals' ideas over others. This often is done in order to influence what narratives (and voices) dominate understandings of issues and events (Mercea 2013)—an effort made easier by the fact that users have to find and navigate to relevant Facebook pages in order to participate in the conversation. Twitter, in contrast, flattens communication hierarchies insofar as it makes it easy for individuals to participate in ongoing conversations on social and political issues. Unlike Facebook, Twitter users can simply search for a hashtag, read what others have to say, share posts of interest or posts with which they (dis)agree, and contribute their original thoughts (Burgess and Matamoros-Fernández 2016; Weller et al. 2014). While these conversations may be fragmented, "relatively stable narrative constellations"—or groups of tweets that are bound through the repetition of keywords, hashtags, "likes," and shares—naturally develop over time (Sadler 2017). Twitter discourse is susceptible to outside influences, like news media and the current political climate. Individuals can become immersed in Twitter narratives and see themselves as part of an "imagined community" in which others share their worldview (McLaughlin and Velez 2017).[1]

Imagined communities have potentially positive and negative implications for civility. On the one hand, imagined communities provide individuals who share a worldview a "free space" in which they may articulate their own values, interests, and visions of common good away from more dominant or opposing groups (Fraser 1989; Young 1997). This can ultimately aid civility and deliberative processes because these more insular discursive communities enable like-minded individuals to hash out their differences before engaging a broader public (Rohlinger 2007). On the other hand, imagined communities can become too insular and grow distant from the political mainstream. These communities may become uncivil insofar as those participating in them rely on insults, ideologically extreme language, and the mocking of individuals or groups of people to make their points—all of which undermine deliberative, democratic processes (Berry and Sobieraj 2014).

Finally, narratives often are shaped by one or two "opinion entrepreneurs," who shape the course of a broader, collective conversation (Blom et al. 2014; Dreier and Martin 2010) and the emerging narratives. Individuals can (un)intentionally become opinion entrepreneurs. For example, individuals can make and release "gotcha videos" that allegedly show a person or organization engaged in illegal behavior via social media. If these videos, such as the heavily edited one released by conservative activists that "shows" ACORN employees telling a pretend pimp and prostitute how to trick federal tax authorities, go viral, individuals can virtually dominate public discourse on an issue (Dreier and Martin 2010). The same is potentially true with crisis narratives. Individuals can share emotionally charged personal stories that are quickly shared and come to dominate crisis narratives

(Stieglitz and Dang-Xuan 2013). This dynamic can be problematic if the individuals driving discourse (un)intentionally engage in incivility (Blom et al. 2014).
Social scientists find that there is a "bandwagon effect" in online discourse, meaning that individuals take cues from and are more likely to share posts that are well
"liked" (Waddell 2017). For instance, if those driving online discourse use aggressive language, other users conform to the standard and use aggressive language in
subsequent posts—regardless of whether their posts are anonymous (Rösner and
Krämer 2016). It is easy to imagine one malicious opinion entrepreneur intentionally constructing untrue or intentionally polarizing narratives that skew crisis
narratives away from civility.

Campus Shootings: Data and Methods

In order to explore (in)civility in crisis narratives, this research analyzed more than
10,000 tweets that emerged in the week following two shootings that occurred on
college campuses. The first shooting occurred at Florida State University (FSU).
On November 20, 2014, at 12:25 a.m. Myron May, a 31-year-old FSU graduate, went in the university's library and opened fire with a .380 handgun. May
shot and injured three students before he was shot dead by police on an access
ramp leading into the library. While two of the students fully recovered, Farham
"Ronny" Ahmed, who was shot in the back by May, was paralyzed. In the days
following the shooting, it became clear that May was mentally ill. He believed that
"stalkers" were targeting him and that his behavior was being managed via mind
control and "invisible weapons" devised by the U.S. government (Bousquet and
Van Sickler 2014).

The second "shooting" occurred two years later at Ohio State University (OSU).
On November 28, 2016, at 9:52 a.m., Abdul Razak Ali Artan, an 18-year-old
Somali refugee, drove his Honda Civic into a crowd of people outside an OSU
building, deliberately striking pedestrians. Artan crashed the Civic, got out of the
car, and attacked students with a butcher knife. OSU police responded to the
attack, which injured 11 students, and Artan was fatally shot. Unlike the May case,
the motives for Artan's attack were not immediately clear (Smith and Perez-Pena
2016). However, as we discuss in more detail ahead, news outlets quickly cast
Artan's attack as an act of terrorism by a disaffected Muslim. Investigations by law
enforcement never uncovered any (in)direct links between Artan and terrorist
groups, such as ISIS. It is worth noting that since initial reports by OSU indicated
that there was an active shooter on campus, individuals tweeting about the event
used the #OSUShooting hashtag.[2]

Our analysis proceeded in the following steps. First, we deleted tweets from the
sample that were not directly related to the incident. We deleted tweets from the
sample, for instance, by companies that used the #FSUShooting and #OSUSh-
ooting hashtags to sell their products and services. Likewise, we excluded tweets
that discussed upcoming football games using the same hashtags. This process

left us with 6,138 tweets, including retweets. Retweets were kept in the sample because we were interested in what kinds of tweets were shared and played an important role in the construction of each crisis narrative (Sadler 2017). The tweets were coded using an open coding process. For example, if information was shared about the specifics of the incident, we would code this as an informational tweet and note whether the information was correct. We coded each tweet, including the hashtags, for up to three different ideas, although the vast majority of tweets included only one point. If multiple ideas were present in a tweet, they were coded in order in which they were presented. The first, or primary, code was used in the following analysis. Our coding process generated 43 unique codes. We collapsed these 43 codes into four broad categories of tweets: personal stories, information, misinformation, and polemics. We input these four general categories of content into Gephi, a network visualization tool, and then graphed the relationship between the Twitter users using ForceAtlas2, a force-directed layout where linked nodes (here, usernames associated with each tweet) are attracted to each other and pulled closer to the center of the network, and dissimilar nodes are pushed away from one another.

Finally, we coded whether each tweet was civil, uncivil, or unclear. We defined incivility as text that could shut down discussion or disrupt the flow of information because it contained insults, ideologically extreme language, and/or mocked individuals or groups of people (Berry and Sobieraj 2014). Civil tweets could have impolite language, discuss controversial topics, or contain incorrect information, as long as they contributed to, or did not shut down, the discussion (Papacharissi 2004). For example, an individual could argue that a school shooting proved that more guns were needed on college campuses. While the tweet is polemical, it potentially advances the conversation because it potentially represents a perspective that is not universally shared and is civil. In contrast, an uncivil tweet would make a similar argument about the need for more guns on college campuses, but note that the guns were necessary to kill a religious or ethnic minority or refugee. Unclear tweets were those that would otherwise be coded as civil, except that they contained incorrect information. This unclear category is important because we rarely know the intent of the individual and whether he or she is purposefully (re)tweeting misinformation. That said, there are cases where it was clear that an individual purposefully misrepresented an issue or event. As we discuss ahead, self-proclaimed comic Sam Hyde intentionally claimed credit for the OSUshooting, and his friends helped circulate this misinformation on Twitter. In these instances, tweets were coded as uncivil because they were clear incidents of misinformation designed to dominate the emerging crisis narrative and derail civil discourse.[3]

In the remainder of the chapter we explore the relationship between crisis narratives involving the #FSUShooting and #OSUShooting hashtags and civility. Specifically, we examine the relationship between personal stories, polemics, factual information, misinformation, and civility. We begin by visually showing the complete network of tweets associated with the two hashtags, highlighting whether the discourse included information, misinformation, a personal narrative, or polemics. Since we find that the networks are very different, we analyze each case in turn highlighting how opinion entrepreneurs affect discourse civility.

FSU and OSU: An Overview

Figures 6.1 and 6.2 show the network of individuals tweeting about the FSU and OSU shootings the first week after each incident. In the figures, each shade of gray represents a category of discourse: white represents informational tweets (e.g., news updates or information provided by the university), gray represents tweets that are factually incorrect, which we refer to as misinformation, dark

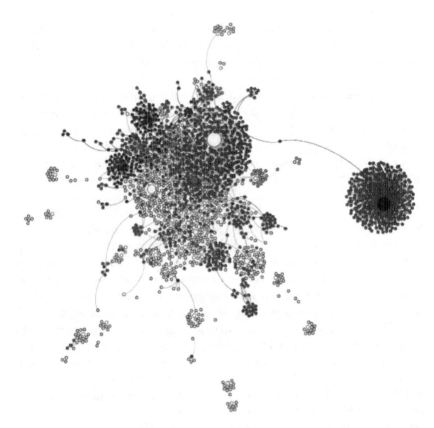

FIGURE 6.1 Overview of FSU discourse on Twitter.

White: information

Gray: misinformation

Dark gray: personal stories

Black: polemics

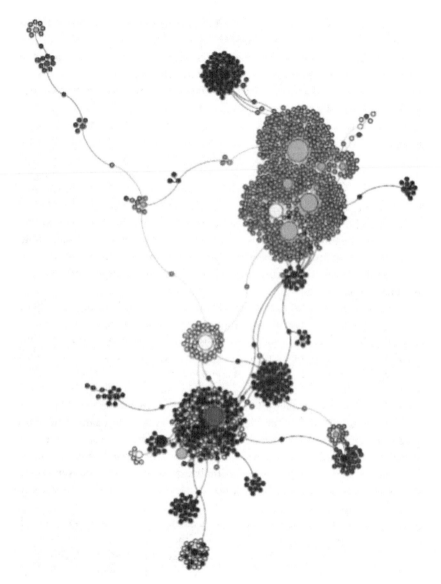

FIGURE 6.2 Overview of OSU discourse on Twitter.

White: information
Gray: misinformation
Dark gray: personal stories
Black: polemics

gray represents personal story tweets, and black represents polemical tweets (e.g., opposition to or support for gun rights). Gephi graphs are made up of nodes and edges. Each node represents an individual who is tweeting (or retweeting) about the incident, and the size of the node matters. The larger the node, the more important the individual is in a network. The edges are the lines that connect them, and represent their connections (e.g., retweeting).

There are clear differences between the FSU and OSU networks. First, the networks have very different shapes. The FSU network (Figure 6.1) is denser than the OSU network (Figure 6.2). In fact, the OSU network has several distinct clusters. Second, and related, the categories of discourse vary considerably by network. Notice that the FSU network is dominated by white (information), dark gray (personal stories), and black (polemics), which are interspersed. Even the smaller cluster is a mix of gray (misinformation) and black (polemics). This suggests that the discourse is relatively diverse. The OSU network clusters, however, often are dominated by a single discourse category—misinformation (gray) and polemics (black) with small pockets of white (information) and dark gray (personal stories).

These differences indicate that the individuals tweeting about the FSU shooting were connected to one another more directly and, consequently, potentially exposed to a broader range of discourse than those tweeting about the OSU incident. This diversity of ideas may bode well for civility insofar as individuals are potentially exposed to a variety of arguments about the FSU shooting, why it occurred, and how the incident was handled by the university and law enforcement. When we look at the OSU network it is clear that some individuals were enmeshed in imagined communities in which they were exposed to—and helped spread—polemics and misinformation. Again, polemic discourse is not necessarily uncivil. Polemics mixed with correct information, for example, can help create the conditions for robust discussion or simply expose individuals to diverse points of view. This is not necessarily true, however, when polemics are mixed with misinformation.

In the remainder of the chapter we look at these two networks more closely. First, we examine how they developed over the course of the week. Here, we want to get a better sense of what—or who—seems to drive the discourse and the shape of the network. Second, we take a closer look at whether the discourse is civil.

FSU Shooting: An Example of Civility Online

Table 6.1 gives insight into how the FSU network developed over the course of the week. The table indicates (1) the board discourse category in which a tweet fell (e.g., personal story) and (2) the more specific content of the tweet (e.g., a student comment about the event). Additionally, the table notes the frequency of the specific content within a particular time interval. Here, we analyze the

TABLE 6.1 Content of FSU tweets over one week

	General category	Specific content	Percentage
2 hours			
	Personal narrative	Thoughts/prayers about the event	24.8
	Personal narrative	Pictures/videos of/from the event	14.1
	Personal narrative	Student comment/content about the event	11.5
	Personal narrative	Personal comment/observation	10.3
	Information	Correct information about the event	6.0
			N = 1,324
1 day			
	Personal narrative	Thoughts/prayers about the event	19.3
	Personal narrative	Personal comment/observation	13.7
	Personal narrative	Student comment/content about the event	12.8
	Personal narrative	Pictures/videos of/from the event	10.3
	Information	Correct information about the event from media source	8.4
			N = 2,609
1 week			
	Personal narrative	Student comment/content about the event	18.6
	Personal narrative	Thoughts/prayers about the event	13.1
	Personal narrative	Personal comment/observation	12.2
	Information	Information/comment about victims from media source	8.4
	Information	Correct information about the event from media source	7.0
			N = 4,120

Source: Authors' data.

content of the tweets two hours, one day, and one week after the shooting.[4] We find that misinformation about the FSU shooting was quickly replaced by facts circulated by a reporter and personal narratives shared by students. The FSU crisis narrative, in fact, largely became a story of one student's survival. We also find that Twitter discourse about the FSU incident was largely civil, with users sharing "thoughts and prayers" with the FSU community and students circulating their personal stories.

The first hour after the FSU shooting, a lot of misinformation was spread via social media. In fact, almost half (42.9%) of the tweets contained incorrect information regarding the number of students injured and killed in the shooting (Table 6.1). However, by the second hour, misinformation was replaced by personal stories. Tweets sharing "thoughts and prayers," pictures or videos from inside the library, and personal comments or observations, some as simple as the tweet "#fsushooting really makes me sad," drive Twitter discourse. This rapid shift from misinformation to personal narratives in large part can be attributed to user @PerezLocal10, a Florida journalist who is represented by the large white node in Figure 6.1. He used his "official sources" to gather and share correct information about the shooting—and this information was retweeted frequently. As correct information spread, posts containing misinformation plummeted, and, by the end of the second hour, tweets spreading misinformation had all but disappeared. This suggests that opinion entrepreneurs, particularly ones with factually correct information, are very important to the course of a discussion. They not only ensure that important and potentially life-saving information gets to the public, including those affected by the event, but also can pivot discussions away from narratives that might generate incivility. We see here that once the facts have spread through a network, users turn their attention to other aspects of the incident.

In the case of the FSU shooting, users continued sharing their personal stories (54%) and information about the shooting and shooter (31%) for a week after the event. In particular, individuals retweeted and commented on a post shared by an FSU student who was shot in the back (this tweet is represented by the largest black node surrounded by the multitude of dark gray nodes in Figure 6.1). The bullet was stopped by several books he had just checked out from the library and loaded into his backpack. The student didn't realize until later that he had been shot, and, once home, he shared the pictures of the bullet-punctured library books on Facebook, claiming that his life had been saved by books on medieval thinker John Wyclif and by God. The student also tweeted his story, where it clearly struck an emotional chord and quickly spread with the #FSUShooting hashtag. His tweet was retweeted hundreds of times with notes like "Unbelievable. Thank God for helping this person."

The social media discourse around the FSU shooting also was remarkably civil (Table 6.2). Throughout the seven-day period civility never fell below 94%. Likewise, incivility was low overall (2.3%). Incivility was at its highest at the end of the first day (2.8%) and lowest two hours after the shooting (.3%). Uncivil tweets

TABLE 6.2 Civility in FSU tweets

	Discourse Quality	Percentage	N = 1,324
2 hours	Civil	94.0%	
	Uncivil	0.3%	
	Unclear	5.2%	
			N = 1,324
1 day	Civil	96.5%	
	Unclear	2.8%	
	Uncivil	0.7%	
			N = 2,609
1 week	Civil	96.0%	
	Uncivil	2.3%	
	Unclear	1.8%	
			N = 4,120

Source: Authors' data.

were often intentionally racist. For example, one tweet promoted stereotypes regarding race and education, noting, "All The Crackas & Foreignerz Scared For They Life. . . . All The Niggas Home Like â˜°ï¸ðŸ˜ðŸ’‰ðŸŽŠðŸ’‰ðŸŽŠ YES!!! I Never Go In The Library! #FSUshooting" (formatting in original). The reference to "foreignerz" alludes to Farham "Ronny" Ahmed, who was shot by May and paralyzed from the waist down. Another type of uncivil tweet was those that claimed the shooting was a hoax. For example, one individual tweeted, "Meet @BlairStokes the #FSUShooting #CRISISACTOR: #FalseFlag #NotOneMore #Hoax #Fake #2A #Treason #NWO #Agenda21." The tweet included an embedded link to a YouTube video, where an unidentified man argues that the shooting didn't happen and systematically tries to discredit videos and photos regarding the incident. These types of denials disrupt the flow of information and conversation about the incident and, consequently, were coded as uncivil.

In sum, we find that FSU crisis narratives were predominantly civil and focused on the personal stories of students—and one student in particular. This is largely a function of two factors. First, the early entry of a journalist circulating correct information about the shooting slowed the spread of misinformation. In this case, the journalist served as an opinion entrepreneur, who relayed information about the ongoing event. Since his tweets were devoid of incorrect or uncivil language, the narrative that ultimately emerged was a factual timeline of events. Second, the dramatic story (complete with photos) of an FSU student being saved by his library books was an emotional lightning rod that became a focal point for users' reactions and narratives (Polletta 2006; Stieglitz and Dang-Xuan 2013). Users connected their reactions to a "survival" narrative, which they shared broadly with the personal expressions of relief and thanks.

OSU Shooting: An Example of Incivility Online

Table 6.3 shows that discourse around the OSU "shooting" is dominated by misinformation. This is true in the hours, days, and week following the shooting. What changes over time is the nature of the misinformation. Two hours after the shooting, Twitter users shared accurate and inaccurate information about the event and assailant. Notice that misinformation was circulated at a much higher frequency than correct information. There are two reasons why misinformation ruled the Twitter conversation. First, journalist @DerekMyers reported incorrect information on Twitter and his tweet, which read, "BREAKING: My FF source says 4–5 people shot on campus. Shooter unknown whereabouts. #OSU-shooting," was shared hundreds of times. Of course, the "shooting" was really a "stabbing," meaning the only individual shot was the perpetrator within minutes after he initiated the attack. While it is impossible to say whether @DerekMyers knew the information was incorrect when he shared it, his status as a journalist

TABLE 6.3 Content of OSU tweets over one week

	General category	Specific content	Percentage
2 hours			
	Misinformation	Incorrect information about the assailant	35.4
	Personal Narrative	Thoughts/prayers about the event	10.8
	Misinformation	Incorrect information about the event	8.3
	Information	Correct information about the event	6.3
	Information	Information/comment on the assailant	6.1
	Polemics	Pro-gun comment advocating policy	6.1
			N = 576
1 day			
	Misinformation	Incorrect information about the assailant	29.3
	Personal Narrative	Thoughts/prayers about the event	8.5
	Polemics	Pro-gun comment advocating policy	6.4
	Polemics	Negative comment about Muslims/refugees	6.3
	Polemics	Pro-gun comment	5.1
			N = 1,803
1 week			
	Misinformation	Incorrect information about the assailant	28.0
	Polemics	Negative comment about Muslims/refugees	8.3
	Personal Narrative	Thoughts/prayers about the event	7.9
	Polemics	Pro-gun comment advocating policy	5.9
	Polemics	Pro-gun comment	5.7
			N = 2,018

Source: Authors' data.

who presumably had accurate information ensured that his tweet was circulated widely. Second, the spread of misinformation was exacerbated by the fact that so-called comedian Sam Hyde claimed credit for the shooting. Sam Hyde is the large dark gray node in Figure 6.2. A tweet proclaiming, "BREAKING NEWS! OSU shooter identified as Sam Hyde #OSUshooting," was retweeted hundreds of times. The tweet featured two photos of Sam Hyde—one of him smiling and taking a selfie and another one of him somber with a machine gun. Several versions of this tweet circulated, including tweets noting, "#OSUShooting hearing rumors that neo nazi leader, Sam Hyde is behind this atrocity, please stay safe" and "OSU shooter identified as Hillary supporter and Antifa activist Samuel Hydestein #osushooting." Hyde's references to ideological extremes (neo Nazis and the Antifa) is a clear effort to stoke political divisions and provoke an uncivil response. In short, both opinion entrepreneurs (un)intentionally circulated false information about the OSU incident, providing a foundation for crisis narratives based on untruths and cultural biases.

Narratives involving misinformation dominated tweets 24 hours and seven days later. Most of these tweets focused on the assailant and mistakenly argued that he was in the U.S. illegally, he was a terrorist, or he was affiliated with ISIS. In fact, it is worth noting that negative comments regarding Muslims and refugees increased in frequency over the course of the week. There are several possible explanations for these trends. First, mainstream media outlets immediately focused on Artan's possible terrorist connections. As discussed earlier, news media shape how citizens discuss political issues (King et al. 2017) and affect crisis narratives. In this case, journalists focused on a related incident; in Nice, Mohamed Lahouaiej-Bouhlel, a Tunisian resident of France, deliberately drove a cargo truck into a crowd, killing 86 people four months earlier. Journalists were quick to ask law enforcement whether the OSU incident was a terrorist attack and officers made this tentative link. Before long, Artan was branded a terrorist in news coverage. Second, days after the incident, ISIS claimed credit for the attack.[5] The FBI did not find any terrorist propaganda on Artan's computer or in his home, meaning the terrorist connection was tentative at best. Third, newly elected Donald Trump tweeted about the incident and his tweet received widespread media attention. Trump noted that ISIS was claiming credit for the attack and argued that Artan was "a Somali refugee who should not have been in our country" (Johnson and Wagner 2016). This anti-immigrant sentiment from a high-level politician likely caused a few misinformed individuals to gather new information (Graf and Aday 2008; Stroud 2010). Finally, Sam Hyde and his contemporaries continued to tweet and retweet incorrect information in which Hyde and later his "assistant" claimed credit for the shooting. In short, the nature of the controversy, which involved an immigrant, and the misinformation spread by "opinion entrepreneurs," which in this case included journalists, created a discursive environment in which narratives involving incorrect information could flourish and spread.

Not surprisingly, in the wake of Donald Trump's controversial presidential campaign, which included incendiary remarks concerning immigration and terrorism, the OSU incident generated a lot of polemical debate. In addition to attacks on Muslims and refugees, Twitter users argued that the OSU case was proof that guns were needed on campus and that politicians should pass legislation to this effect immediately (Table 6.3). The polemical nature of the online discussion around the event at OSU left ample room for incivility (as shown in Table 6.4), where we find that much of this discourse was uncivil. It is worth noting that only around 11% of the uncivil tweets in the OSU sample contain explicitly offensive language, and most of this discourse was directed at Artan—for example, the tweet "#OSUShooting— One suspect sent to hell," which included screenshots of Artan, deceased, on the ground and surrounded by two police officers. Another individual tweeted, "Do you see what happens when they let Refugees invade our Country #OSUStrong #OSUAttack #osushooting," using the word "invade" to suggest that refugees are unwelcome in the United States. The bulk of the (re)tweets were uncivil because they spread false information regarding Artan and the incident (Sam Hyde and later his assistant claiming credit for the "shooting"). The OSU case underscores how one or two opinion entrepreneurs can effectively dominate online discussions and cultivate narratives built on lies. While Hyde is clearly a troll who gets "lulz," or laughs, by intentionally spreading misinformation, this has implications for civility insofar as fake information hinders online conversation among individuals with diverse perspectives regarding the causes of and solution to school shootings. Rather than inviting (im)polite discussion, the OSU crisis narratives rehash stereotypes, express prejudices, and mock Artan's life and death.

TABLE 6.4 Civility in OSU tweets

	Discourse quality	*Percentage*
2 hours	Civil	47.1
	Uncivil	41.0
	Unclear	12.0
		N = 576
1 day	Civil	56.5
	Uncivil	34.1
	Unclear	8.5
		N = 1,803
1 week	Civil	58.3
	Uncivil	33.2
	Unclear	8.5
		N = 2,018

Source: Authors' data.

Discussion and Conclusion

We find that crisis narratives vary dramatically in terms of the kinds of topics discussed as well as the civility of the discourse, and both are largely consequences of the opinion entrepreneurs driving narrative construction and news media coverage of the incidents. The FSU crisis narratives predominantly focused on personal stories and community building, and were generally civil. In this case we see that opinion entrepreneurs played a critical role in the development of crisis narratives. A local journalist shared information about the FSU shooting quickly after the incident, which shifted the narratives away from misinformation. Personal stories—and one FSU student's dramatic story of survival in particular—quickly filled the gap and ultimately dominated FSU crisis narratives. While the FSU crisis narratives were predominantly civil, it is worth noting that the focus on personal stories and community building shifted the focus away from conversations about the causes of (and ways to prevent) school shootings. This may be problematic for deliberative processes. On the one hand, narratives that simply allow individuals to empathize with someone's personal story have value insofar as the story enables individuals to better understand another human being during a frightening moment—which, ultimately, benefits deliberative processes (Polletta and Lee 2006; Young 1997). On the other hand, an ongoing discussion regarding the causes of (and ways to prevent) school shootings would serve deliberative processes and democracy well.

In contrast, the OSU crisis narratives were shaped by both news coverage of Artan and opinion entrepreneurs. Individuals largely bought into and (re)circulated misinformation, created narratives based on false stories and prejudices, and, ultimately, about one-third of the tweets were uncivil (Table 6.4). The importance of news coverage and opinion entrepreneurs in shaping crisis narratives and facilitating civility is clear. While all of the tweets were in response to a violent incident on campus, the willingness of journalists to circulate incorrect information and Sam Hyde to exploit a network for his own amusement stoked incivility. To be clear, incivility was higher in OSU crisis narratives even before Hyde began tweeting. Recall that 11% of the uncivil tweets had nothing to do with Hyde's "comedy" but with Artan himself. If you consider the tweets about Artan alone, uncivil discourse in the OSU case is more than ten times that observed in the FSU case. Again, news coverage likely played an important role in this regard. Journalists were quick to frame Artan's actions as terrorism—a framework that both ISIS and Donald Trump embraced. Not only was the discourse uncivil but also the evidence suggests that individuals quickly formed imagined communities in which individuals discussed relatively few ideas (see Figure 6.2) and were exposed to relatively limited points of view.

More work needs to be done on the role of social media in crises and deliberative processes. Platforms such as Twitter are critical for sharing life-saving information during crises (Houston et al. 2015). However, these same platforms can be used to construct narratives about an event—and some of these narratives may be less than desirable. While the discourse surrounding Twitter narratives does not have to be polite, ideally these collective conversations would be civil and contribute to deliberative processes. While we find evidence that crisis narratives can be civil, more research is needed to determine whether there is a democratic benefit. For example, it would be worthwhile to analyze the imagined communities that emerge in the wake of the OSU incident. It is possible that the imagined communities create a free space in which individuals can articulate their values, interests, and visions of common good away from more dominant or opposing groups. If so, these communities may have benefits to democracy—regardless of whether they are civil. Likewise, it would be useful to analyze personal stories on Twitter to better assess whether (and how) these narratives help individuals empathize with others. Finally, it would be worthwhile to systematically analyze the relationship between news coverage and the construction of crisis narratives on Twitter to assess whether shifts in social media discourse mirror shifts in news coverage.

Notes

1 To be clear, it is beyond the scope of this chapter to comment on whether Twitter should play a more active role in fostering deliberative processes. The point here is that Twitter provides an open, public forum in which individuals can freely express themselves, and this has implications for crisis narratives and deliberative discourse more generally.
2 We collected 35 tweets associated with the #OSUStabbing hashtag. Given the small number of tweets we excluded them from this sample.
3 We did not verify the accounts of every individual participating in the discussion, nor did we check the veracity of every personal story shared via Twitter. Instead, we focused on those individuals driving the discussion and verified their accounts and identities.
4 Data were analyzed in hourly and daily increments. We present data where there were shifts in the Twitter discourse.
5 ISIS often claims credit for attacks on American soil.

Bibliography

Berry, Jeff, and Sarah Sobieraj. 2014. *The Outrage Industry*. New York: Oxford University Press.
Bessi, Alessandro, Fabiana Zollo, Michela Del Vicario, Antonio Scala, Guido Caldarelli, and Walter Quattrociocchi. 2015. "Trend of Narratives in the Age of Misinformation." *PLOS One*. 113 (3): 554–559. doi: doi.org/10.1371/journal.pone.0134641.
Blom, Robin, Serena Carpenter, Brian J. Bowe and Ryan Lange. 2014. "Frequent Contributors Within U.S. Newspaper Comment Forums." *American Behavioral Scientist* 58 (10): 1314–1328. doi: 10.1177/0002764214527094.
Bousquet, Steve, and Michael Van Sickler. 2014. "More Disturbing Details Emerge in FSU Shooting." *Miami Herald*, November 21.
Burgess, Jean, and Ariadna Matamoros-Fernández. 2016. "Mapping Sociocultural Controversies Across Digital Media Platforms: One Week of #Gamergate on Twitter, YouTube, and Tumblr." *Communication Research and Practice* 2 (1): 79–96. doi: 10.1080/22041451.2016.1155338.

Coe, Kevin, Kate Kenski, and Stephen A. Rains. 2014. "Online and Uncivil? Patterns and Determinants of Incivility in Newspaper Website Comments." *Journal of Communication* 64 (4): 658–679. doi: 10.1111/jcom.12104.

Dahlberg, Lincoln. 2005. "The Habermasian Public Sphere: Taking Difference Seriously?." *Theory and Society* 34 (1): 111–136.

Del Vicario, Michela, Alessandro Bessi, Fabiana Zollo, Fabio Petroni, Antonio Scala, Guido Caldarelli, H. Eugene Stanley, and Walter Quattrociocchi. 2016. "The Spreading of Misinformation Online." *Proceedings of the National Academy of Sciences* 113 (3): 554–559. doi: 10.1073/pnas.1517441113.

Dreier, Peter, and Christopher Martin. 2010. "How Acorn Was Framed: Political Controversy and Media Agenda Setting." *Perspectives on Politics* 8 (3): 761–792.

Fraser, Nancy. 1989. *Unruly Practices: Power, Discourse, and Gender in Contemporary Social Theory*. Minneapolis: University of Minnesota Press.

Gamson, William. 1992. *Talking Politics*. New York: Cambridge University Press.

Grabe, Maria Elizabeth, Shuhua Zhou, and Brooke Barnett. 2001. "Explicating Sensationalism in Television News: Content and the Bells and Whistles of Form." *Journal of Broadcasting & Electronic Media* 45 (4): 635–655. doi: 10.1207/s15506878jobem4504_6.

Graf, Joseph, and Sean Aday. 2008. "Selective Attention to Online Political Information." *Journal of Broadcasting & Electronic Media* 52 (1): 86–100. doi: 10.1080/08838150701820874.

Guo, Lei, and Summer Harlow. 2014. "User-Generated Racism: An Analysis of Stereotypes of African Americans, Latinos, and Asians in YouTube Videos." *Howard Journal of Communications* 25 (3): 281–302. doi: 10.1080/10646175.2014.925413.

Habermas, Jurgen. 1989. *The Structural Transformation of the Public Sphere*. Cambridge, MA: Massachusetts Institute of Technological Press.

Habermas, Jurgen. 1996. *Between Facts and Norms*. Translated by W. Rehg. Cambridge, MA: The MIT Press.

Houston, J. Brian, Joshua Hawthorne, Mildred F. Perreault, Eun Hae Park, Marlo Goldstein Hode, Michael R. Halliwell, Sarah E. Turner McGowen, Rachel Davis, Shivani Vaid, Jonathan A. McElderry, and Stanford A. Griffith. 2015. "Social Media and Disasters: A Functional Framework for Social Media Use in Disaster Planning, Response, and Research." *Disasters* 39 (1): 1–22. doi: 10.1111/disa.12092.

Johnson, Jenna, and John Wagner. 2016. "Trump says Ohio State Attacker Should not Have Been in the Country." *Washington Post*, November 30.

King, Gary, Benjamin Schneer, and Ariel White. 2017. "How the News Media Activate Public Expression and Influence National Agendas." *Science* 358 (6364): 776–780.

McCombs, Maxwell, and Donald Shaw. 1972. "The Agenda-Setting Function of Mass Media." *The Public Opinion Quarterly* 36 (2): 176–187.

McLaughlin, Bryan, and John A. Velez. 2017. "Imagined Politics: How Different Media Platforms Transport Citizens Into Political Narratives." *Social Science Computer Review* 0 (0): 0894439317746327. doi: 10.1177/0894439317746327.

Mercea, Dan. 2013. "Probing the Implications of Facebook Use for the Organizational Form of Social Movement Organizations." *Information, Communication & Society* 16 (8): 1306–1327. doi: 10.1080/1369118X.2013.770050.

Papacharissi, Zizi. 2004. "Democracy Online: Civility, Politeness, and the Democratic Potential of Online Political Discussion Groups." *New Media & Society* 6 (2): 259–283. doi: 10.1177/1461444804041444.

Papacharissi, Zizi, and Maria de Fatima Oliveira. 2012. "Affective News and Networked Publics: The Rhythms of News Storytelling on #Egypt." *Journal of Communication* 62 (2): 266–282. doi: 10.1111/j.1460-2466.2012.01630.x.

Polletta, Francesca. 2006. *It Was Like a Fever: Storytelling in Protest and Politics.* Chicago: University of Chicago Press.

Polletta, Francesca, and John Lee. 2006. "Is Telling Stories Good for Democracy? Rhetoric in Public Deliberation After 9/11." *American Sociological Review* 71 (5): 699–723.

Rohlinger, Deana. 2007. "American Media and Deliberative Democratic Processes." *Sociological Theory* 25 (2): 122–148.

Rösner, Leonie, and Nicole C. Krämer. 2016. "Verbal Venting in the Social Web: Effects of Anonymity and Group Norms on Aggressive Language Use in Online Comments." *Social Media + Society* 2 (3): 2056305116664220. doi: 10.1177/2056305116664220.

Sadler, Neil. 2017. "Narrative and Interpretation on Twitter: Reading Tweets by Telling Stories." *New Media & Society* 0 (0): 1461444817745018. doi: 10.1177/1461444817745018.

Santana, Arthur D. 2015. "Incivility Dominates Online Comments about Immigration." *Newspaper Research Journal* 36 (1): 92–107. doi: 10.1177/0739532915580317.

Smith, Mitch, and Richard Perez-Pena. 2016. "Ohio State Attacker may have been 'Inspired' by Al Qaeda, F.B.I. Says." *New York Times*, November 30, A15.

Sobieraj, Sarah, and Jeff Berry. 2011. "From Incivility to Outrage: Political Discourse in Blogs, Talk Radio, and Cable News." *Political Communication* 28 (1): 19–41.

Stieglitz, Stefan, and Linh Dang-Xuan. 2013. "Emotions and Information Diffusion in Social Media—Sentiment of Microblogs and Sharing Behavior." *Journal of Management Information Systems* 29 (4): 217–248. doi: 10.2753/MIS0742-1222290408.

Stroud, Natalie Jomini. 2010. "Polarization and Partisan Selective Exposure." *Journal of Communication* 60 (3): 556–576. doi: 10.1111/j.1460-2466.2010.01497.x.

Suler, John. 2004. "The Online Disinhibition Effect." *CyberPsychology & Behavior* 7 (3): 321–326. doi: 10.1089/1094931041291295.

Waddell, T. Franklin. 2017. "What Does the Crowd Think? How Online Comments and Popularity Metrics Affect News Credibility and Issue Importance." *New Media & Society* 0 (0): 1461444817742905. doi: 10.1177/1461444817742905.

Weller, Katrin, Axel Bruns, Jean Burgess, Merja Mahrt and Corneilus Puschmann, Eds. 2014. *Twitter and Society*, Vol. 89. Edited by S. Jones. New York: Peter Lang.

Young, Iris Marion. 1997. *Intersecting Voices: Dilemmas of Gender, Political Philosophy, and Policy.* Princeton, NJ: Princeton University Press.

7

CAN CIVILITY AND DELIBERATION DISRUPT THE DEEP ROOTS OF POLARIZATION?

Attitudes Toward Muslim Americans as Evidence of Hyperpolarized Partisan Worldviews

J. Cherie Strachan and Michael R. Wolf

The public's intense, divided reactions to the 2016 presidential election and Donald J. Trump's ensuing presidency have heightened both scholars' and pundits' interest in civility and deliberation as a remedy for partisan polarization. A resurgence of civil discourse is key to American democracy's viability. Democratic institutions simply cannot function without the threshold of civility required to sustain deliberation. Yet this chapter, which explores attitudes toward Muslim Americans to demonstrate the deep roots of partisan polarization, serves as a warning that cultivating more civil, deliberative public sphere will not be easy. Those prescribing civil discourse face a number of obstacles. Not least of these is the decades-long trend of party sorting that led to polarization, which coincided with the erosion of other large-scale civic organizations capable of mitigating the parties' current divisive influence on the electorate.

Despite these barriers, political civility deserves renewed attention because it serves the same function in public interactions as politeness does in interpersonal interactions—which is to minimize the effect of conflict on potential opponents' willingness or ability to interact with one another. Public political civility and private interpersonal politeness fulfill an important and similar function. They allow people who disagree with one another to sustain productive relationships (Brown and Levinson 1987; Strachan and Wolf 2012). Civil interactions, which are often purposefully undertaken to facilitate collaboration, are characterized by communication patterns that invite others to share and explain their preferences. Uncivil or rude interactions, on the other hand, are characterized by ad hominem attacks, name-calling, overt challenges, and interruptions. These are rhetorical moves that, often purposefully, diminish the likelihood of future collaboration.

Advocates of deliberation point out that when people continue to engage with one another despite their differences, they not only learn to how to listen but also may use new insights to develop shared solutions, sometimes referred to as the "third way" or "win-win" solutions, that could not be uncovered without deliberation. They also learn to set aside issues that will damage their ability to cooperate on less controversial items—which allows them to identify "shared-pain" or "shared sacrifice" solutions and to avoid gridlock. Those who rely on a civil tone to continue to engage despite disagreements increase their ability to explain not only their own positions but also that of their opponents. As a result, understanding and tolerance increase. In short, deliberative problem solving within diverse groups provides citizens with more nuanced understandings of collective problems, which enhance their abilities to exercise judgment (Guttman and Thompson 1996, 2004; Mutz 2006). This enables citizens and public officials to identify optimal solutions, or at the very least to find consensus whenever possible, even if they must "agree to disagree" on a smaller subset of intractable issues (Gutmann and Thompson 2004). From this perspective, the ongoing work of democratic governance requires mutual respect, which is undermined by public displays of incivility.

Unfortunately, evidence presented in this chapter suggests that intense partisan polarization among the U.S. electorate will impede the task of cultivating civil deliberation. It indicates that recent political events are the culmination of a decades-long process of partisan sorting, as the electoral strategies adopted by the two main political parties since the 1960s resulted in the recruitment of people with diametrically opposed worldviews into their coalitions. Promoting much-needed initiatives grounded in civility and deliberation is complicated not only by the erosion of the civic infrastructure required for widespread implementation of such initiatives, but also by the intense polarization of America's most active and engaged citizens—who are not particularly interested in seeking out opportunities for civil discourse across this partisan divide. Intense polarization, as indicated by strong partisans' polar reactions to current events highlighting attitudes toward Muslim Americans, already had deep roots by 2010. Discussion of how partisan Americans responded to the "9–11 Mosque" controversy and to National Public Radio's (NPR) decision to fire Juan Williams provides insight into the intensity of America's partisan polarization that advocates of civility and deliberation must find ways to address.

Why Focus on Muslim Americans?

Unlike most out-groups in the United States, Muslim Americans are ethnic-religious minorities but also practice distinct cultural traditions, a combination that heightens the perception that they threaten an "American" way of life. Media stories also often link their ethnic-religious status to recent terrorist acts and U.S. military engagements, which similarly heightens their perceived threat to

U.S. security. This ethnic, cultural, security "triple threat" makes Muslim Americans an especially likely target of scrutiny for those Americans who tend to be suspicious of any demographic minority or culturally deviant out-group perceived to pose a threat to the status quo. When offered the opportunity to explain their position on Muslim Americans, for example, some respondents in our 2010 national sample survey responded to an open-ended prompt with the following threat-based reactions:

> Because, you idiots, we are under attack from the Muslim religion, and anyone who can't figure that out has rocks in their head.
>
> Muslims are not Americans. They are here to destroy our country; they are here to destroy our religious beliefs; they are here to kill and maim; they are terrorists.
>
> Because Muslims shouldn't even be in America. They should be sent back to Afghanistan. They are all devils in a cult religion. We don't need the devils over here.
>
> They need to be dealt with. They need to be exterminated. Their beliefs, their organizations should not be tolerated, anywhere, not only in the United States, but in the world. They are terrorists. They are cowards. And they need to be exterminated.[1]

Such intense reactions would always be cause for concern, yet this reaction is exacerbated by the possibility that both elite and rank-and-file members of the two major U.S. political parties are polarized according to contested worldviews. So-called authoritarians, who have the strongest reactions to threats posed by such out-groups, may now be clustered in the Republican Party, while so-called non-authoritarians, who insistently prioritize protecting out-groups from any scrutiny that could be perceived as prejudice, may now be clustered in the Democratic Party. If so, the result is that those with a tendency to feel threatened by out-groups are far more apt to interact primarily with others who have even more intense fears. Meanwhile, Democrats are more apt to interact with intense ideologues who insist on suppressing discussion of such concerns altogether. The resulting dynamic—heightened fears on the right and suppression of conversations about those concerns on the left—does not bode well for the ability to promote civility and deliberation across partisan lines.

We use data from a unique two-wave cross-sectional national study of the 2010 midterm election to assess this possibility. The questionnaire was administered just as visceral public debate over a proposed Islamic-American cultural center, to be built close to the World Trade Center site, unfolded. Some pundits believed this project was an affront to victims of 9/11, because those who attacked the Twin Towers were Islamic and the new cultural center was located too close to "ground zero." Others supported religious leaders' right to develop land that they already owned as a cultural and religious center. Many such pundits were also worried by the tone of the criticism aimed at Muslim Americans during this debate, expressing concern that an increasingly hostile political environment threatened Muslim Americans' civil rights (Barnard 2010).

Cable news and talk radio "talking heads" argued over whether it was appropriate for political commentators to express strong, negative opinions about Muslim Americans. Meanwhile, one of their own, Juan Williams, was fired from NPR after claiming, as a guest on Fox News, that he was afraid to fly with fellow passengers dressed in Muslim "garb" (Farhi 2011; Williams 2010). This commentary further inflamed the cultural divide, and the rhetoric the controversy inspired provides insight into the foundational causes of contemporary party polarization, giving us the opportunity to probe whether partisan identity overlaps with differing worldviews that also drive Americans' opinions about treatment of Muslim Americans.

A substantial number of our respondents replied that it was not okay for pundits to say such negative things—which suggests that they preferred protecting a marginalized minority group from criticism more than they valued a pundit's free speech rights. Yet respondents who indicated that it was appropriate for pundits to say negative things about Muslim Americans rarely grounded their concerns in protection of free speech. When given an opportunity to provide an open-ended explanation for their position, the most frequent justifications were grounded in concerns that Muslim citizens represent not simply a threat to Americans' traditional values and way of life but also a threat to their physical safety. Respondents' reliance on their own words to describe Muslim Americans in this manner, despite the fact that commentary on Williams's firing focused almost exclusively on his free speech rights and political correctness, supports those who claim that contemporary political fault lines are rooted in diametrically opposed worldviews (Hetherington and Weiler 2009).

What Do We Know About Authoritarianism, Tolerance, and Democracy?

Citizens of liberal democracies must always decide how much freedom to permit to those perceived to threaten their existence (Sullivan, Piereson, and Marcus 1982). Scholars have labeled citizens inclined toward restrictions on "others" believed to pose such a threat as authoritarians because they have a heightened threat perception that makes them fear instability and prefer order. Early survey research documented that a substantial portion of the American electorate, similar to that of most other established democracies, was authoritarian, with widespread intolerance of minority groups and willingness to suppress their civil rights—especially when members of minority groups were not only disliked but also feared (Key 1949; Stouffer 1955; Prothro and Grigg 1960; McClosky 1964). This finding was met with some dismay, especially when overall levels of intolerance (albeit directed at new groups as targets) remained static across the decades

(Sullivan, Piereson, and Marcus 1979, 1982). Yet the geographic and institutional diffusion of U.S. political power meant that those with the most authoritarian sentiments were rarely clustered together in ways that allowed them to wield power over national policy (Sullivan et al. 1982, 17–21). Rather, those most willing to suppress minority rights were more likely to come into contact not only with moderates who could soothe their fears but also with those most strident about protecting minorities. The polarization of partisans by distinct worldviews, along with geographic sorting as people purposefully moved to neighborhoods and regions to live among like-minded neighbors, means that substantive interactions across these very different worldviews are now less likely to occur than in the past (Hetherington and Weiler 2009; Bishop 2008).

How Has Party Polarization Isolated People With Separate Worldviews?

Over the past six decades, the political parties have become more ideologically pure following the realignment of southern, conservative Democrats into the Republican Party (Black and Black 2002) and northeastern, liberal Republicans into the Democratic Party (Reiter and Stonecash 2011). Political scientists agree that parties are more deeply divided than at any point in modern American history (Hetherington 2002; Layman, Carsey, and Horowitz 2006; Abramowitz 2010). Hetherington and Weiler (2009) concur, adding the explanation that this polarization is grounded not simply in familiar conservative and liberal ideologies but also in diametrically opposed worldviews. They argue that Americans with authoritarian worldviews were gradually recruited into the Republican Party since the1960s, while those with non-authoritarian worldviews shifted over to the Democrats. This shift occurred because some issues (most recently gay rights, the Iraq War, terrorism, and immigration) triggered a heightened perception of threat (either to traditional cultural practices or to physical safety) among authoritarians, who were attracted to the Republican Party's appeals to tradition and security. Non-authoritarians, repelled by Republican policy positions, shifted their loyalty to the Democratic Party. The result of this rolling realignment around distinct worldviews has resulted in partisans not only with dramatically different policy preferences but also with vastly different approaches to deliberation and governance. Navigating these differences can make civil discourse difficult.

Authoritarians are motivated by an overwhelming need to maintain order and security. Sustained anxiety over threats to stability, combined with the perception of stark choices rather than nuanced options, encourages swift decision making based on gut instincts, established social norms, and esteemed authority figures (Adorno, Frenkel-Brunswick, Levinson, and Sanford 1950; Altemeyer 1996; Stenner 2005). Authoritarians seek to minimize threats—not only to physical security but also to stability in the social order (which makes them suspicious of and potentially hostile toward racial/ethnic minorities and "deviant" groups)

(Altemeyer 1996; Barker and Tinnick 2006; Huddy, Feldman, Taber, and Lahav 2005).

Non-authoritarians, characterized by commitment to fairness and deep aversion to ethnocentrism, not only reject these issue preferences but also are repulsed by them. Non-authoritarians seek to protect the very minorities and "deviant" out-groups that authoritarians often see as a threat. They also prioritize personal autonomy—which means security threats almost never justify sacrificing anyone's civil rights. Further, non-authoritarians value accuracy and prefer informed, deliberative decision making, thus finding authoritarians' steady deference to the established social order disturbing. Yet this commitment to deliberation does not mean that non-authoritarians are unwilling to censure expression of certain types of concerns. Given non-authoritarians' protection of minority rights, they are apt to suppress sharing concerns that a particular demographic group poses a threat—which may well be the type of concern that authoritarians believe needs to be discussed the most (Hetherington and Weiler 2009).

Given these tendencies, it is important to keep in mind that calls for civility, from the left or from the right, should not be used to suppress dissent. Rather, civility should be seen as an essential tool for peacefully resolving disagreements. Otherwise,

> when arguments are curtailed too early, the public sphere can produce an illusion of agreement that disguises differences by class and income, race and gender, excluding the unorthodox and eliding ideological fractures in ways that are convenient for those in authority.
>
> *(Edwards 2014, 77)*

On the other hand, strongly communicated disagreement—which is not only an acceptable but also an inevitable characterization of political discourse—must be juxtaposed with intransigence based on efforts to undermine others' abilities to participate in decision making or rejection of an open-ended process. Efforts to exclude others, for example, are likely to be characterized by name-calling and ad hominem attacks rather than reason-giving and explanation. Alternatives to inclusive deliberation as a way to make decisions are most likely to be undertaken when people rigidly embrace specific outcomes (recommended by their own value preferences) over those discovered through an open-ended process. "Rude" contributions that leverage unheard voices or perspectives in deliberative processes should be tolerated even if they are annoying; rude politics intended to undermine inclusive decision making should not. Playing by these rules for healthy deliberation is particularly difficult when issues divide intense partisans according to distinct authoritarian and non-authoritarian worldviews.

The treatment of Muslim Americans meets the criteria of an issue apt to divide partisans at the most extreme ends of these respective worldviews. Muslim Americans are an ethnic, cultural, and potential security "triple threat" minority out-group, which should encourage authoritarians (who are increasingly apt to be part of Republicans' voting bloc) to view them with suspicion, while simultaneously encouraging non-authoritarians (who are increasingly apt to be part of Democrats' voting bloc) to protect them from discrimination.

What Do We Already Know About Attitudes Toward Muslim Americans?

Muslim Americans have always faced prejudice in the United States. As a religious minority with distinct cultural practices, affect toward them is influenced by a person's attitudes both toward racial/religious out-groups (e.g., Jews or African Americans) and toward cultural out-groups (e.g., undocumented immigrants or gays) instead of just one or the other (Kalkan, Layman, and Uslaner 2009, 848).

Generally low levels of information about Muslims and Islam also mean that opinions have the potential to be shaped by current events, media coverage, and opinion leaders (Nisbet, Ostman, and Shanahan 2009). For example, the perception of a physical security threat from Muslim Americans resulted in episodic violent backlash against the Muslim community immediately after 9/11 (Peek 2011). Yet the broader American public was more informed about, as well as more tolerant of, Muslims in the aftermath of 9/11 (Panagopoulos 2006; Nisbet et al. 2009), perhaps reflecting President George W. Bush's use of the bully pulpit to make overt calls for religious tolerance, which contributed to positive media coverage of Muslim Americans at this time (Nacos and Torres-Reyna 2007).

Scholars, however, disagree on the long-term effects of 9/11 on American public opinion. Some argue that negativity is grounded in fear of physical threat, noting that 9/11 resulted in a "Bin Laden effect" encouraging Americans to view all Muslims, including U.S. citizens, as "The Enemy" (Cesari 2004). Wike and Grim (2010) use 2006 PEW global attitudes data to assess opinion in five Western democracies and find that perceived security threats best predict negativity toward Muslims. Cultural and religious differences exacerbate safety concerns, but are not the primary source of such attitudes. Americans also often fail to differentiate between Muslim Americans and Muslims overall, specifically labeling them as violence-prone and untrustworthy (Sides and Gross 2013). A substantial portion of Americans claim to fear Muslims and Muslim Americans, with 39% believing Muslim Americans are not loyal to the U.S., 34% claiming they are sympathetic to al-Qaeda, and 44% indicating they have extreme religious beliefs (Nisbet et al. 2009, 170). Without a reprieve from ongoing world events that highlight terrorism and military engagements, such scholars find "little hope that many Americans will be able to think of Muslims as anything but enemies" (Sides and Gross 2013, 597).

Others disagree, contending that views of Muslim Americans hinge on their out-group status. They point to evidence that Americans' information levels and affect reverted back to pre-9/11 patterns, when negative attitudes were not grounded in fears of another terrorist attack (Kalkan et al. 2009; Panagopoulos 2006). From this perspective, 9/11 primarily solidified the "non-white otherness" of Arab and Muslim Americans (Jamal and Naber 2008, 318), triggering a "lingering resentment" of Muslim Americans along with "growing anxiety" about Islam's compatibility with Western values (Panagopoulos 2006, 608).

Perhaps these discrepancies result from focusing on two different types of Americans. Negative attitudes characterize a plurality, rather than a majority, of the American electorate. Not everyone wants to revoke Muslim Americans' civil rights. Nisbet et al.'s (2009) exhaustive study finds that a desire to curtail Muslim American civil liberties hinges on political and religious beliefs, as well as media information sources. Use of television over print news—and in particular exposure to Christian news outlets, conservative opinion leaders, and right-wing media—leads to a heightened perception of the threat Muslims pose, which is used to justify limiting their civil rights (Kalkan, Layman, and Uslaner 2009; Nisbet et al. 2009). These scholars conclude that the American public is polarized in its attitudes toward Islam, just as Hetherington and Weiler's (2009) account of party polarization grounded in distinct worldviews would predict.

Our observations, gathered during the 2010 general election, provide an additional opportunity to assess whether views toward Muslim Americans support the claim that average Americans—and not just politicians and political elites—are polarized by distinct worldviews, as well as to consider the implications of such polarization on civility and deliberation.

What Happened in 2010?

Our study tests partisans' responses to current events in 2010, to determine if their attitudes toward political commentary during the debates about the "9–11 Mosque" and Juan Williams were grounded in partisan polarization. In particular, it explores whether Republicans are more apt to react to Muslim Americans as a deviant, threatening out-group. In turn, are Democrats more apt to prioritize protection of minority civil rights over free speech that appears critical of these groups?

Data come from two waves of a nationwide survey of registered voters, which primarily asked questions about political civility. These were automated surveys fielded by SurveyUSA, with the first wave implemented as the general election heated up during September 14–17, and the second wave running from October 28 through November 1, the eve of the general election.[2]

In the time frame immediately preceding implementation, two current events having to do with Muslim Americans, terrorism, and 9–11 were prominent topics on cable news and talk radio. First, the proposed establishment of an Islamic cultural center near ground zero sparked controversy during September 2010, as did the intense criticism leveled by some political commentators at those sponsoring the project. This time frame is especially important, given the media's ability to shape opinions about Muslim Americans (Kalkan et al. 2009, 858). Incorporating a question about these incidents allowed us to assess attitudes toward Muslim Americans by asking respondents to answer whether they thought it was appropriate or not "for political commentators to use language that could be seen as being negative toward Muslim Americans."

To further understand *why* respondents might view negative comments about Muslim Americans as appropriate, the second wave (in late October and early November, 2010) added a voice capture allowing respondents to explain why they deemed such criticisms appropriate. This open-ended question helped us to determine whether justifications were grounded in defense of free speech, concern that Muslim Americans' religious and cultural traditions threaten an "American" way of life, fear that Muslims are a threat to physical security, or an entirely different rationale.

Second, just days before our final wave, Juan Williams, a guest on the cable news program *The O'Reilly Factor*, admitted that fellow airline travelers dressed in "Muslim garb" made him nervous. His NPR editors stated that admitting such sentiments disqualified Williams as an objective political analyst, and they fired him. Critics argued that NPR caved to political pressure and undermined the American principle of free expression. These very public debates provide a natural experiment to determine whether media priming would result in an overwhelming number of respondents citing the First Amendment to justify their support of public criticisms of Muslim Americans. Hence, serendipity, combined with this open-ended question, also helped us to gauge whether media priming or entrenched worldviews had a bigger influence on respondents' answers.

Other potential explanations for people's responses to this question included how strongly they identified with a particular party, whether they embraced a liberal or a conservative political ideology, and whether they were willing to adopt the label of a Tea Party Republican. Party identification and political ideology typically drive many political attitudes, while the latter became particularly influential in the 2010 midterm election. Our questionnaire also included an important measure of respondents' worldviews: one's preference for politicians who stand firm on principle versus a preference for politicians who compromise to get things done (Barker and Carman 2012). We would expect that compromise would appeal to non-authoritarians, given their preference for deliberative problem solving, while a willingness to stand firm in support of principles would correlate with authoritarians' concern for defending the status quo. We also included questions that measured respondents' political attentiveness, age, gender, and religiosity.

We begin the data analysis here by examining individual-level attitudes about pundits' negative commentary. We provide descriptive statistics, as well measurements of how this attitude is affected by respondents' demographic traits and preferences for an uncompromising politician. Finally, the results of a content analysis of respondents' justifications provided in the voice captures are described. As these voice captures could not be linked back to the individual-level data, there is no way to determine whether each particular comment was made by a Democrat or Republican. Nevertheless, the two sections separately provide individual-level explanations of whether attitudes toward Muslim Americans reflect worldview-based polarization in contemporary American politics, while also providing unfiltered reasons about why Americans hold such views. The unique contributions of this project are that it does not entirely rely on secondary measures of attitude toward Muslim Americans, and that it was conducted at a time when intense real-world conditions provided a rich information flow on these issues.

What We Learned About Party Polarization in 2010

Negativity Toward Muslim Americans and Partisan Worldviews

As Table 7.1 demonstrates, a majority of Americans did not think it was appropriate for political commentators to say negative things about Muslim Americans. Views on appropriateness did not shift significantly between the two waves; the vividness of the so-called 9/11 Mosque issue fading from its September high point and the late addition of the Juan Williams's controversy apparently did little to alter these views.

What appears to drive opinions on the issue the most is an interrelated set of political variables that revolve around partisanship. First, a plurality of Republicans endorsed political commentators' negativity. Only a tiny number of Democrats shared this position, and this percentage, in fact, dropped by half between the two waves. Whether this decline among Democrats was due to the Williams's controversy we cannot tell. Second, a majority of Tea Party identifiers and males indicated that negative statements were appropriate. These patterns are not surprising, given the 78% of Tea Partiers who identified themselves as Republicans and the gender gap between the major parties. Third, an additional political attitude, the respondent's preference for politicians who stand firm, was also influential. Republicans are more likely to hold this view than are Democrats, and this sentiment reflects a deep-rooted, gut-level political division between the parties (Barker and Carman 2012; Wolf, Strachan, and Shea 2012).

Two additional patterns are also noteworthy. Willingness to criticize Muslim Americans did not reflect older respondents' suspicions about a new, unfamiliar minority, as younger cohorts were most inclined to believe that negative comments were appropriate. In addition, neither religious affiliation nor religiosity was related to reactions to Muslim Americans.[3]

Taken as a whole, these patterns indicate that this stark division of attitudes appears to be driven by political and partisan orientations. If opinions on this issue

TABLE 7.1 Socio-demographic characteristics and whether it is appropriate to say negative things about Muslim Americans

	September				October–November			
	Appropriate	Not sure	Not appropriate	N	Appropriate	Not sure	Not appropriate	N
All respondents	32.8 %	11.4 %	55.8 %	1,242	28.1 %	14.8 %	57.1 %	1,253
Party identification								
Republican	47.3 %	15.6 %	37.2 %	556	44.1 %	20.6 %	35.3 %	559
Pure independent	35.3 %	13.2 %	51.6 %	220	36.1 %	16.2 %	47.7 %	192
Democrat	14.4 %	5.6 %	80.1 %	466	7.1 %	7.9 %	85.0 %	501
Tea Party identification								
Tea Party identifier	55.4 %	14.9 %	29.7 %	470	55.3 %	17.0 %	27.8 %	462
Non–Tea Party identifier	18.0 %	6.6 %	75.4 %	628	10.6 %	11.0 %	78.5 %	683
Age cohorts								
18–34	37.1 %	9.0 %	54.0 %	361	30.3 %	14.1 %	55.6 %	359
35–49	36.8 %	9.1 %	54.1 %	344	32.5 %	15.9 %	51.7 %	329
50–64	30.4 %	13.3 %	56.4 %	316	25.5 %	15.8 %	58.7 %	339
65 +	23.0 %	16.2 %	60.8 %	222	22.1 %	12.9 %	65.0 %	226
Church attendance/religiosity								
Regular	33.6 %	12.0 %	54.4 %	584	29.4 %	17.5 %	53.1 %	599
Occasionally	30.4 %	11.9 %	57.7 %	307	26.3 %	13.7 %	60.0 %	324
Almost never	34.2 %	9.6 %	56.2 %	308	27.5 %	11.1 %	61.5 %	329
Gender								
Male	41.4 %	9.0 %	49.6 %	593	34.7 %	13.2 %	52.5 %	611
Female	24.9 %	13.6 %	61.5 %	649	21.8 %	16.4 %	61.8 %	642
Compromise								
Compromise to get things done	20.9 %	7.8 %	71.3 %	541	16.0 %	9.7 %	74.3 %	579
Not sure	29.2 %	23.4 %	47.3 %	59	23.8 %	30.5 %	45.8 %	61
Stand firm on principle	43.1 %	13.3 %	43.6 %	642	40.0 %	18.1 %	42.0 %	613

Note: Data are weighted. The number of respondents within each category excludes non-respondents and will not sum to the number of overall respondents.

Source: Authors' surveys.

reflect partisan polarization, however, then the divide should be greatest among attentive, strong party identifiers.

Figure 7.1 provides evidence that distinct views on the appropriateness of such criticism are especially acute among the most politically attentive partisans. Democrats almost always view such negativity as inappropriate, especially when these Democrats follow politics very closely. Republicans who follow politics somewhat or not very closely also tend to view negativity toward Muslim Americans as inappropriate, although far less frequently than either Democrats or Independents. The most significant finding reported here is that the majority of Republicans who follow politics very closely think such comments are appropriate. Divergent positions are greatest among the most politically attentive, as one would expect if this were an issue connected to party polarization.

As with political attentiveness, Table 7.2 shows stark differences between strong Republicans' and strong Democrats' views about whether negative commentary is appropriate. Polarization around the issue seems to be linked to worldviews as well, because strong Republicans who prefer firm stances on principle were far more likely to say such statements were appropriate. This is the modal group of all voters in both waves, so the effect here is particularly remarkable. Taken together, Figure 7.1 and Table 7.2 show that opinions on this issue split the most dramatically between the most polarized partisans.[4]

At this point, our analysis supports the claim that the non-authoritarian inclination to protect minority rights and to promote egalitarianism appear to underpins Democrats' preferences. Strong, attentive Democrats were far more likely to respond "no" to our filter question—suggesting that they were more committed to suppressing critical commentary about a marginalized minority group than to protecting free speech. While this response lacked an open voice capture, it is likely that at least some of these respondents were motivated by the same ideological commitments motivating far-left efforts to stifle free speech on college campuses—including recent high-visibility incidents at Evergreen College, Middlebury College, and the University of California at Berkeley.

Why It Is Appropriate to Say Negative Things About Muslim Americans

It would be a mistake, however, to assume that those who endorsed negative commentary about Muslim Americans were motivated by a commitment to free speech. Americans hold the First Amendment in high regard, making this response socially desirable. Respondents should also have been primed to provide this explanation by media framing of Juan Williams's firing. Yet these respondents were much more apt to explain their fears than they were to celebrate free speech.

Content analysis of our voice captures indicated that respondents typically provided at least one of four reasons to support their position. These answers ranged from support for the First Amendment (given least frequently) to three

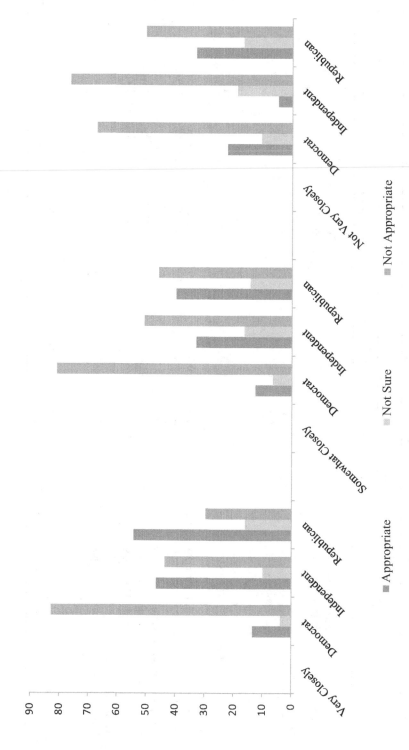

FIGURE 7.1 Appropriateness of negativity of Muslim Americans by how closely people follow politics.

Source: Authors' surveys.

TABLE 7.2 Views on appropriateness of political commentators saying negative things about Muslim Americans by party identification strength and views of whether people want politicians to compromise to get things done or stand firm on principle

	September				October–November			
	Appropriate	Not sure	Not appropriate	N	Appropriate	Not sure	Not appropriate	N
Strong Democrat								
→compromise > stand firm on principle	13.1 %	2.6 %	84.4 %	127	6.5 %	7.5 %	86.0 %	190
→stand firm on principle > compromise	9.4 %	3.6 %	87.1 %	76	5.1 %	8.7 %	86.2 %	76
Weak Democrat								
→compromise > stand firm on principle	14.7 %	9.6 %	75.7 %	97	6.1 %	5.3 %	88.6 %	86
→stand firm on principle > compromise	30.0 %	3.5 %	66.5 %	53	14.2 %	8.6 %	77.2 %	34
Independent leans Democratic								
→compromise > stand firm on principle	5.1 %	4.5 %	90.5 %	71	6.8 %	6.0 %	87.2 %	74
→stand firm on principle > compromise	29.2 %	10.5 %	60.3 %	20	8.2 %	17.2 %	74.6 %	20
Independent								
→compromise > stand firm on principle	22.8 %	6.8 %	70.5 %	97	22.2 %	16.2 %	61.6 %	85
→stand firm on principle > compromise	47.1 %	16.6 %	36.4 %	106	51.2 %	11.5 %	37.3 %	96
Independent leans Republican								
→compromise > stand firm on principle	44.4 %	13.7 %	41.8 %	49	47.1 %	10.9 %	42.0 %	40
→stand firm on principle > compromise	52.3 %	18.7 %	29.1 %	95	41.6 %	27.2 %	31.2 %	104
Weak Republican								
→compromise > stand firm on principle	31.1 %	15.2 %	53.7 %	59	28.4 %	18.5 %	53.1 %	51
→stand firm on principle > compromise	41.1 %	19.8 %	39.1 %	78	42.6 %	20.9 %	36.5 %	77
Strong Republican								
→compromise > stand firm on principle	40.4 %	9.7 %	49.9 %	41	34.0 %	10.3 %	55.8 %	52
→stand firm on principle > compromise	54.3 %	13.2 %	32.5 %	214	52.9 %	20.5 %	26.6 %	207

Note: Data are weighted.

Source: Authors' surveys.

additional reasons grounded in dislike of Muslim Americans as "others" and in the authoritarian perception that these "others" represent a threat. The categories included: rejecting political correctness in order to make accurate (but negative) claims about Muslim Americans, making explicit references to 9/11 and/or the War in Iraq to imply that Americans are at war with all Muslims (including Muslim Americans), and claiming that the existence of Muslims (and/or Islam) is an overt threat to Americans or the American way of life.

Some respondents provided more than one reason to bolster their position. While those who offered free speech as a justification often gave concise one-reason answers, those with explanations grounded in threat perceptions were apt to talk longer and to provide additional reasons for their position. These four categories were not mutually exclusive; one verbose respondent gave all four primary reasons to justify his position. Others provided only one, but many offered a combination of reasons.[5]

As reported in Table 7.3, 66 people, or 22% of these respondents, provided the First Amendment as at least one of the reasons why political commentators' criticism of Muslim Americans was appropriate. This justification was offered by the fewest number of respondents, despite the fact that free speech concerns had been primed by the elite-level discussion of the Juan Williams firing. Most who offered free speech concerns as an answer did so succinctly, simply stating the First Amendment or free speech before hanging up. Others offered brief explanations, such as "Our country was founded on freedom of speech," "We live in America, so anyone can say whatever they want," or "The First Amendment has a slippery slope." Only 44 people, or 14% of the respondents, relied solely on free speech justifications for their position. These are the only respondents who failed to include some aspect of an authoritarian worldview in their answers.

Coverage of the Williams controversy may have primed respondents to claim that political correctness played too much of a role in his dismissal, as 139 people, or 46% of the respondents, included this justification in their answers. Political correctness was carefully coded to ensure respondents were not simply rephrasing First Amendment concerns. While the cross-over between these categories could have been large, the anti–political correctness responses actually were overwhelmingly used to endorse negative stereotypes about Muslims. Examples of comments in this category include abrupt comments, such as "Because it's a fact and I'm sick and tired of political correctness," or "Because the truth hurts." Others provided in-depth explanations:

> It's not about using language that is inappropriate. It is a matter of telling the truth. And if all roads and all clues lead to a certain area that has caused havoc and world-wide terrorism, then let's talk about the truth. Let's not worry about political correctness.
>
> I think there are a lot of negative things that could be said about what is going on in the Muslim community. I feel like a lot of people. I don't trust

TABLE 7.3 Content analysis of reasons given for saying it is appropriate for political commentators to say negative things about Muslim Americans

Primary content categories				Secondary content categories				
First Amendment	Anti–political correctness	9/11 USA at war	Muslims are threat	Destroy Muslims	Juan Williams	Sharia law	Obama	Christian
23% (66)	46% (139)	24% (74)	39% (118)	2% (6)	5% (16)	4% (12)	2% (7)	10% (29)

Note: N = 304. Categories are not mutually exclusive so will not sum to total N.

Codes:

1st Amend.: Respondent explicitly refers to the First Amendment or the right of free speech, or uses a phrase that is clearly grounded in the First Amendment (e.g., we have a free country, so they can say what they want).

Anti-PC: Respondent explicitly refers to political correctness as a problem, or the respondent implies that the fear of offending people (social desirability) is not a good reason for suppressing speech. Note that many of these responses are based on an underlying stereotype or discriminatory component. Respondents very often asserted that negative things about Muslim Americans were the truth. Rather than explaining their position based on threat and so forth, respondents focus on political correctness (e.g., pundits say mean things about other groups of people, so why do we only get upset when it's about Muslims? Or: because it's the truth, and we shouldn't be afraid to say so).

9/11/war: Respondent explicitly references 9/11, or indicates that we are "at war" with Muslims. These responses are often based on an underlying prejudice about Muslims as a threat, but the respondent has not explicitly described his or her beliefs about Muslims (e.g., well, they blew up our buildings, and we are at war with them).

Threat: Respondent describes stereotypes about inherent beliefs, values, or characteristics of Muslims in order to explain why Muslims are a threat to Americans, or to characterize them as "other," an "out-group," and/or a threat (e.g., their religion advocates violence, or also very frequently: even the moderates won't stand up against the radicals and side with America).

Destroy: Respondent explicitly calls for the extermination or the destruction of Muslims, either within the United States or worldwide. Euphemisms for extermination count here as well (destroy, obliterate, crush).

Juan W.: Mentions Juan Williams's incident.

Sharia: Mentions threat of sharia law.

Obama: Mentions Obama directly; either Obama administration is too soft, or he is Muslim.

them. And I think people are entirely too politically correct today. People ought to speak up, while they still can.

I believe it is appropriate because we are so politically correct that we blind ourselves to the truth. As long as we are afraid to speak the truth and what is in our hearts, then we are doomed to fall, and we will be a Muslim nation, just like the rest of the world.

Political correctness has gotten far too out of hand. . . . Fort Hood and other incidents would have been avoided if we were willing to stereotype.

Some respondents grappled with concerns that Muslim Americans should not be held accountable for the actions of all Muslims worldwide, explaining that not all Muslims are bad. Yet most were quick to blur these categories as a way to justify negative commentary. After admitting that there might be some good Muslims, one respondent quickly cautioned that there certainly were not very many of them. Another differentiated between good Muslims and crazy Muslims, but concluded that there were far more "crazies" than one might suspect. Another common approach was to accuse moderate Muslims of silence and inactivity in the face of radical Islamists, behavior that was then interpreted at best as cowardice and at worst as tacit endorsement of violence.

Furthermore, all of the comments coded as concerns over political correctness convey frustration with perceived overprotection of Muslim Americans. This frustration reflects the tension between authoritarians' desire to be adequately warned—and to warn others—of the threat posed by a perceived dangerous minority group and non-authoritarians' simultaneous need to protect the same group from racial and ethnic stereotyping. Some respondents were more explicit, expressing resentment that accusations of prejudice suppressed adequate scrutiny of Muslims. They indicated the news media were "extremely soft" on Muslim Americans, a group described as having achieved a "privileged status" that placed them beyond legitimate criticism. As the following comments indicate, many respondents believe that Muslim Americans (and other minorities) receive unfair, "kid-glove" treatment:

Most people have opinions and express them. They just don't get in trouble for it unless it has to do with the Muslims.

Because it's all right to use language to be negative to all other Americans, so why isn't it okay to be negative to Muslim Americans like it is everyone else?

Well, the media is negative about a lot of religions, so why should the Muslims be an exception?

While the threat Muslim Americans pose is implied in most of the responses that focused on political correctness, many respondents were also much more explicit about such concerns. The most simplistic of these justifications referenced 9/11 to claim that America had been attacked by and/or was at war with Muslims. Some respondents simply shouted "9/11" or "nine-one-one" into the phone. Others provided slightly longer explanations, such as the following:

> Because they killed 3,000 people on 9/11.
> Our president is a Muslim, and we shouldn't have Muslims because they blew up the World Trade Center. That is my response.
> Simply because they attacked us on September 11th, and everybody seems to want to forget that. That's why!
> Because Muslim Americans are the ones who started the war in the first place!

As the last comment indicates, respondents were typically incapable or unwilling to differentiate between Muslim Americans and Muslims in general. Even when they recognized that the question referenced Muslim *Americans* as the focus of commentators' criticism, they blurred all Muslims, regardless of nationality, into a single category.

This pattern also occurred in the last coding category, when 118 respondents, or 39%, used the opportunity to fully explain the threat posed by Muslim Americans. A handful (21%) of these descriptions were generic and could not be classified as a threat either to American culture or to American security, such as the respondent who claimed Muslims posed a threat because they were "born and bred with that heritage," making it impossible to decipher her precise meaning. Even fewer respondents (16%) focused exclusively on the need to protect American values, such as the woman who claimed to dislike Muslims, along with other immigrant groups, because, "they want to change our Constitution and our way of life." Additional value-based explanations focused on preserving Christianity as America's predominant religious tradition (because "Allah is a false god"), or protecting a government founded on Judeo-Christian values. It is interesting to note, however, that only 29, or 10%, of all the open-ended responses contained a specific reference to Christianity, which bolsters the claim that negative affect toward Muslim Americans is not primarily triggered by religiosity.

Meanwhile, close to half (45%) of the respondents who explicitly described Muslims as threatening focused on security concerns, such as the respondent who said, "The Muslim Nation is trying to kill Americans. . . . They've got it out for Americans." The remaining responses in this category (19%) described a threat to both values and security. But when respondents articulated both types of threats, concerns that Arabic cultural traditions and Islamic religious traditions are inherently violent were used to bolster concerns about the threat to physical security. Not surprisingly, these respondents sound much more militant than those with only "clash of culture" concerns:

> I think it is necessary, because I don't believe that any Muslim is peaceful. Their Koran says to kill anyone who doesn't agree with you. I think that

is their religion. And I don't care if they say they are peaceful or peace-loving . . . they are not! The Muslim religion is trying to take over America, and I think it has to be stopped. If that's what it takes, then that is what we have to do.

Because they . . . want to take over the world, and they are a sick organization of blind, ignorant followers of maniacs.

We have to communicate to the American people, the Muslims are here for one reason and one reason only, and that is the destruction of our country and the compromising of our principles via the establishment of sharia law. And they will kill us. They are not a religion. They are a cult with a political agenda and their own soldiers, and their own laws, and their own army.

One weakness of this research is that specific open-ended voice captures cannot be linked to individual respondents. It is certainly likely that some Republicans who answered these questions were among those who celebrated free speech. Some among the small handful of Democrats who responded may also have grounded their answers in perceptions of threat. In the aggregate, however, strong, attentive Tea Party Republicans who also reject political compromise were far more likely to endorse negative commentary about Muslim Americans. In the aggregate, they were also those most apt to justify their endorsement of criticism by describing Muslim Americans as a threat to America's physical security.

What Are the Consequences of Polarization for Civil Discourse?

Our findings raise troubling concerns that go far beyond merely reinforcing the now long-standing finding that a substantial number of Americans have (and likely always have had) authoritarian tendencies (Key 1949; Stouffer 1955; Prothro and Grigg 1960; McClosky 1964). In the past, these sentiments were checked when those most apt to be afraid still interacted with those capable of addressing their fears. A classic example is the interaction between then-presidential candidate Senator John McCain and a potential supporter at a 2008 town hall meeting. When an audience member fearfully described Barack Obama as a radical Muslim, McCain not only corrected her but also went on to describe Obama as a "good man" with whom he (McCain) just happened to disagree. Our findings suggest these types of interactions are less and less likely to occur. Of course, not all Republicans are authoritarians. Yet so-called authoritarians, who have the strongest reactions to perceived threats to cultural tradition and physical security, are now clustered in the Republican Party. Similarly, not all Democrats are non-authoritarians, but so-called non-authoritarians, who insistently prioritize protecting out-groups from any scrutiny that could be perceived as prejudice, are now clustered in the Democratic Party.

Hence one of the most troubling consequences of entrenched polarization is the inability to engage in conversations that soothe rather than exacerbate risk-averse authoritarians' fears. Our content analysis indicates that authoritarians' opposition to political correctness is grounded in underlying fear for their physical safety and/or fear of the consequences of social change—and these underlying fears encourage them to embrace policies that undermine democratic values. This phenomenon in American politics is not new. Seminal political science research underscores the irony of democracy—which is that political elites have historically been not only more committed to democratic values but also more committed to applying these abstract values to concrete, real-world situations (Key 1949; Stouffer 1955; Prothro and Grigg 1960; McClosky 1964; see also Schubert, Dye, and Ziegler 2016). Even before political science research confirmed the importance of political leadership in appropriately channeling the electorate's angst and suppressing undemocratic tendencies, the founding fathers understood these tasks as integral to their own civic responsibilities. Thomas Jefferson's preferred response to citizen uprisings (specifically Shay's Rebellion), for example, was not to avoid future unrest by diminishing citizens' ability to participate, nor was it to play on their fears and passions in order to gain political advantage. Rather he argued that since the people "cannot be all, and always well informed" and would be "discontented in proportion to the facts they misconceive," leaders should educate and lead the public. Specifically leaders should "set them right as to the facts, pardon, and pacify them" (Jefferson 1787).

Partisan polarization makes it increasingly unlikely that political leaders will be capable of following Jefferson's advice. Rather, the far left exacerbates fears by suppressing such dialogue all together. The left's emphasis on protecting minority groups from scrutiny limits interaction not only between the left and the right but also within the left. Some feminists, for example, have recently argued that discussion of the potential for inherently different interests between transgendered and cisgendered women is not occurring—in public discourse or critical academic work—despite the widespread acceptance that cross-cutting demographic traits (or intersectional identities) mean that women have very different lived experiences that often lead them to embrace different issue priorities. Yet social desirability suppresses these conversations, as those making comments either directly claiming or implying fundamental differences between transgendered and cisgendered women are often labeled transphobic and called TERFs (trans-exclusionary radical feminist) (Flaherty 2018). As noted earlier, name-calling is a rhetorical move intended to discredit opponents and shut down conversations altogether.

While those on the far left suppress difficult conversations to protect marginalized groups, however, those on the far right purposefully play on fear of others to gain political advantage. In anticipation of the 2018 midterm elections, President Trump resurrected the racist and xenophobic appeals that he used to "rev up" Republican base voters in his 2016 presidential campaign by, for example, linking prominent Democrats to a violent Hispanic street gang and reigniting conflict with kneeling athletes in the NFL. Republican consultants and candidates, worried that their emphasis on tax cuts and economic policy had done little to mobilize their base—especially when midterm fortunes often turn on voter intensity—welcomed Trump's "cultural cudgels," with some primary candidates mimicking his approach (Brownstein 2018; Drucker 2018; Sargent 2018a, 2018b). These tactics are purposefully intended to play on the anxiety of older, blue-collar, evangelical, and rural white voters who have described diverse, young millennials as "a hostile force trying to take their country away from them" (Anderson 2018).

Such polarization means that fewer strong partisans on either side will view the centrist politicians most apt to make appeals to democratic values (e.g., free speech, religious tolerance or civil rights) as respected authority figures capable of shaping their political attitudes and beliefs. Barring a substantial change in the political environment—an influx of new voters in the electorate, different rules for nominating and electing candidates, a fundamental shift in campaign practices, a resurgence of large-scale civic initiatives that bolster bridging social capital—partisan polarization will continue to suppress opportunities for civil discourse and deliberation.

In short, this research underscores that the partisan polarization in the electorate is not a superficial reaction to the 2016 election or the Trump administration. Donald J. Trump's successful candidacy, along with his high level of support from the Republican base throughout his volatile first year in office, is the culmination of partisan polarization, not its root cause. It took over a half a century of campaign rhetoric and partisan appeals to sort the electorate into its current, polarized configuration. The resulting dynamic—heightened fears on the right and suppression of conversations about those very concerns on the left—makes the task of cultivating bipartisan civil discourse difficult. Several features of the current political landscape further exacerbate this task. First, about one-third of the electorate describe themselves as strong partisans, which means they are more apt to seek reinforcement from the like-minded than they are to embrace bipartisan deliberation. Second, the two major political parties will likely continue to frame political issues in a way that reinforces worldview polarization among rank-and-file voters because mobilizing these voters is the way they win elections. Barring a historic critical election, where the voting blocs that support the two major parties are disrupted and realigned in new ways, the current party system, and the politicians who seek office within it, will reinforce existing political fault lines well into the future. Finally, the effect of a polarized party system is exacerbated because the two major political parties are some of the last remaining federated voluntary associations capable of facilitating mass mobilization around a common identity and issue agenda. The erosion of civic infrastructure means that few large-scale federated voluntary associations capable of fostering bridging social capital and cross-cutting alliances are available to serve as a counterweight to the parties' polarizing influence.

Many scholars and political observers (the authors of this chapter included) believe that the most viable solution to the dysfunctional polarization gripping the country is for people and politicians to embrace civility and deliberation *especially* when we disagree with one another. The findings presented in this chapter make it clear, however, that addressing this problem by encouraging civil deliberation is a long-term goal. There is, unfortunately, no "quick fix" for the partisan polarization gripping the nation. Increasing the American electorate's desire and capacity for civil deliberation will require not only persistence and innovation. It will require also a commitment to rebuilding a robust, inclusive, deliberative civil society capable of undermining the polarizing effects of our current party system.

Notes

1 Not only were these responses collected via a voice capture but also the surveys used to collect the data were automated. The fact that respondents never interacted with a human interviewer likely minimized the effect of social desirability on the way they responded to this prompt. These features of the survey likely increased the number of overtly rude and politically incorrect responses.
2 The margin of error typically was +/−2.5 or less for each question. Furthermore, the generic House ballot results for our sample and SurveyUSA's other samples were very accurate relative to other generic House ballot results.
3 This finding is supported by the open-ended voice captures as well, as only 29 respondents made any reference to Christianity.
4 We also conducted a multivariate analysis that allowed us to assess the combined effects of these characteristics on the way respondents answered our filter question. The predicted probabilities included in this analysis revealed that the strongest, conservative, Tea Party Republicans who wanted politicians to stand firm were 71% more likely to say "yes" than the strongest liberal Democrats who preferred politicians who compromise.
5 The agreement across both co-authors' coding decisions for each of these binary, nominal categories ranged from a low of 89.7% to a high of 98.3%. In addition, as reported in Appendix 3, calculating the three most common measures of inter-coder reliability resulted in one category with substantial scores (in the .07 range) and three categories with nearly perfect scores (in the .90 range) (Krippendorff 2004, 244–250; Landis and Koch 1977; Neuendorf 2002, 153–158).

Bibliography

Abramowitz, Alan. 2010. *The Disappearing Center: Engaged Citizens, Polarization, and American Democracy*. New Haven, CT: Yale University Press.
Adorno, Theodor W., Else Frenkel-Brunswick, Daniel J. Levinson, and Nevitt Sanford. 1950. *The Authoritarian Personality*. New York: Harper.
Altemeyer, Robert. 1996. *The Authoritarian Specter*. Cambridge, MA: Harvard University Press.
Anderson, Kristin Soltis. 2018. "Conservatives Have a Millennial Problem." *The Weekly Standard*, May 11. Retrieved from www.weeklystandard.com/kristen-soltis-anderson/how-conservatives-can-find-a-way-to-appeal-to-millennials.
Barker, David, and Christopher Carman. 2012. *Political Representation in Red and Blue America: How Cultural Differences Shape Democratic Expectations and Outcomes*. New York: Oxford University Press.

Barker, David, and James D. Tinnick. 2006. "Competing Visions of Parental Roles and Ideological Constraint." *American Political Science Review* 100 (2): 249–263.

Barnard, Anne. 2010. "For Mosque Sponsors, Early Missteps Fueled Storm." *New York Times*. August 10. Retrieved from www.nytimes.com/2010/08/11/nyregion/11mosque.html.

Bishop, Bill. 2008. *The Big Sort: Why the Clustering of Like-Minded America Is Tearing Us Apart.* New York: Houghton Mifflin Harcourt.

Black, Earl, and Merle Black. 2002. *The Rise of the Southern Republicans.* Cambridge, MA: Harvard University Press.

Brown, Penelope, and Stephen C. Levinson. 1987. *Politeness: Some Universals in Language Usage.* New York: Cambridge University Press.

Brownstein, Ron. 2018. "The Republican Party's Generational Bet." *The Atlantic*, May 17. Retrieved from www.theatlantic.com/politics/archive/2018/05/the-gop-is-betting-its-majority-on-older-white-voters/560537/.

Cesari, Jocelyn. 2004. *When Islam and Democracy Meet: Muslims in Europe and the United States.* New York: Palgrave Macmillan.

Drucker, David M. 2018. "Republicans Think They've Found the Answer to Midterm Victory." *Washington Examiner*, June 6. Retrieved from www.washingtonexaminer.com/news/campaigns/republicans-winning-midterms-strategy-trump.

Edwards, Michael. 2014. *Civil Society.* 3rd ed. Malden, MA: Polity Press.

Farhi, Paul. 2011. "Editor Who Fired Juan Williams Resigns After NPR Interview." *The Washington Post*, January 6. Retrieved from www.washingtonpost.com/wp-dyn/content/article/2011/01/06/AR2011010603649.html.

Flaherty, Colleen. 2018. "By Any Other Name." *Inside Higher Education*, June 6. Retrieved from www.insidehighered.com/news/2018/06/06/philosophy-really-ignoring-important-questions-about-transgender identity?utm_source=Inside%20Higher%20Ed&utm_campaign=2aaa561d00-DNU_COPY_01&utm_medium=email&utm_term=0_1fcbc04421–2aaa561d00-199951349&mc_cid=2aaa561d00&mc_eid=246c34c3c8.

Guttman, Amy, and Dennis Thompson. 1996. *Democracy and Disagreement.* Cambridge, MA: Harvard University Press.

Guttman, Amy, and Dennis Thompson. 2004. *Why Deliberative Democracy?* Princeton, NJ: Princeton University Press.

Hetherington, Mark J. 2002. "Resurgent Mass Partisanship: The Role of Elite Polarization." *American Political Science Review* 95 (3): 619–631.

Hetherington, Mark J., and Jonathan D. Weiler. 2009. *Authoritarianism and Polarization in American Politics.* New York: Cambridge University Press.

Huddy, Leonie, Stanley Feldman, Charles Taber, and Gallya Lahav. 2005. "Threat, Anxiety, and Support of Anti-Terrorism Policies." *American Journal of Political Science* 49 (3): 611–625.

Jamal, Amaney, and Nadine Naber. 2008. *Race and Arab Americans Before and After 9/11.* Syracuse, NY: Syracuse University Press.

Jefferson, Thomas. 1787. "Extract from Thomas Jefferson to William Stephens Smith Thomas Jefferson Encyclopedia." Thomas Jefferson Monticello Museum. Retrieved June 8, 2018, from http://tjrs.monticello.org/letter/100.

Kalkan, Karem Ozan, George. C. Layman, and Eric. M. Uslaner. 2009. "Band of Others? Attitudes Toward Muslims in Contemporary American Society." *Journal of Politics* 71 (3): 847–862.

Key, V. O. 1949. *Southern Politics in State and Nation.* Knoxville: The University of Tennessee Press.

Kalkan, Kerem Ozan, Geoffrey C. Layman, and Eric M. Uslaner. 2009. "'Bands of Others?' Attitudes Toward Muslims in Contemporary American Society." *Journal of Politics* 71 (3): 1–16.

Krippendorff, Klaus. 2004. *Content Analysis: An Introduction to Its Methodology.* 2nd ed. Thousand Oaks, CA: Sage Publications.

Landis, Joanne, and Gary H. Koch. 1977. "An Application of Hierarchical Kappa-Type Statistics in the Assessment of Majority Agreement Among Multiple Observers." *Biometrics* 33 (2): 363–374.

Layman, Geoffrey C., Thomas M. Carsey, and J. M. Horowitz. 2006. "Party Polarization in American Politics: Characteristics, Causes, and Consequences." *Annual Review of Political Science* 9: 83–100.

McClosky, Herbert. 1964. "Consensus and Ideology in American Politics." *American Political Science Review* 58 (3): 361–382.

Mueller, John. 1988. "Trends in Political Tolerance." *Public Opinion Quarterly* 52 (1): 1–25.

Mutz, Diana. 2006. *Hearing the Other Side Deliberative Versus Participatory Democracy.* New York: Cambridge University Press.

Nacos, Brigitte L., and Oscar Torres-Reyna. 2007. *Fueling our Fears: Stereotyping, Media Coverage and Public Opinion of Muslim Americans.* Lanham, MD: Rowman and Littlefield.

Neuendorf, Kimberley A. 2002. *The Content Analysis Guidebook.* Thousand Oaks, CA: Sage Publications.

Nisbet, Erik C., Ronald Ostman, and James Shanahan. 2009. "Public Opinion toward Muslim Americans: Civil Liberties and the Role of Religiosity, Ideology, and Media Use." In Abdulkader H. Sinno (Ed.), *Muslims in Western Politics.* Bloomington: Indiana University Press, 161–199.

Panagopoulos, Costas. 2006. "Arab and Muslim Americans and Islam in the Aftermath of 9/11." *Public Opinion Quarterly* 70 (4): 608–624.

Peek, Lori. 2011. *Behind the Backlash: Muslim Americans After 9/11.* Philadelphia: Temple University Press.

Prothro, James W., and Craig M. Grigg. 1960. "Fundamental Principles of Democracy: Bases of Agreement and Disagreement." *Journal of Politics* 22 (2): 276–294.

Reiter, Howard, and Jeffrey Stonecash. 2011. *Counter Realignment: Political Change in the Northeastern United States.* New York: Cambridge University Press.

Sargent, Greg. 2018a. "GOP Candidates Are Now Mimicking Trump's Authoritarianism, That's Ominous." *The Washington Post*, April 23. Retrieved from www.washingtonpost.com/blogs/plum-line/wp/2018/04/23/multiple-gop-candidates-are-now-mimicking-trumps-authoritarianism/?utm_term=.3218ed78eff7.

Sargent, Greg. 2018b. "Get Ready for a Brutal Election About Trump's Racism and Authoritarianism." *The Washington Post*, June 6. Retrieved from www.washington-post.com/blogs/plum-line/wp/2018/06/06/get-ready-for-a-brutal-election-about-trumps-racism-and-authoritarianism/?noredirect=on&utm_term=.dd7d98e40290.

Schafer, Chelsea E., and Greg M. Shaw. 2009. "Tolerance in the United States." *Public Opinion Quarterly* 73 (2): 404–431.

Schubert, Louis, Thomas Dye, and Harmon Ziegler. 2016. *The Irony of Democracy, An Introduction to American Politics.* 17th ed. Boston, MA: Cengage.

Sides, John, and Kimberley Gross. 2013. "Stereotypes of Muslims and Support for the War on Terror." *Journal of Politics* 75 (3): 583–598.

Stenner, Karen. 2005. *The Authoritarian Dynamic.* Cambridge, MA: Cambridge University Press.

Stouffer, Samuel A. 1955. *Communism, Conformity, and Civil Liberties*. Garden City, NJ: Doubleday.

Strachan, J. Cherie, and Michael R. Wolf. 2012. "Calls for Civility: An Invitation to Deliberate or a Means of Political Control? In Morris P. Fiorina and Daniel M. Shea (Eds.), *Can We Talk? The Rise of Rude, Nasty and Stubborn Politics*. New York: Pearson Longman, 41–52.

Sullivan, John, James Piereson, and Gregory Marcus. 1982. *Political Tolerance and American Democracy*. Chicago: University of Chicago Press.

Sullivan, John, James Piereson, and Gregory Marcus. 1979. "An Alternative Conceptualization of Political Tolerance: Illusory Increases, 1950s–1970s." *American Political Science Review* 73 (4): 781–794.

Wike, Richard, and Brian J. Grim. 2010. "Western Views Toward Muslims: Evidence From a 2006 Cross-National Survey." *International Journal of Public Opinion Research* 22 (1): 4–25.

Williams, Juan. 2010. "I Was Fired for Telling the Truth." *Fox News*, October 21. Retrieved from www.foxnews.com/opinion/2010/10/21/juan-williams-npr-fired-truth-muslim-garb-airplane-oreilly-ellen-weiss-bush/.

Wolf, Michael R., J. Cherie Strachan, and Daniel M. Shea. 2012. "Forget the Good of the Game: Political Incivility and Lack of Compromise as a Second Layer of Party Polarization." *American Behavioral Scientist* 56 (12): 1677–1695.

APPENDIX 7.1

Survey Questions

1. How closely do you follow politics? Very closely? Somewhat closely? Not very closely? Or not at all?
10. Which do you think is more important in a politician: the ability to compromise to get things done, or a willingness to stand firm in support of principles?
11. Is it appropriate? Or not appropriate? For political commentators to use language that could be seen as being negative toward Muslim Americans?
12. Please speak up and tell me why you feel that way. At the beep, you may talk for as long as you'd like. . . . Why do you think it is appropriate for commentators to use language that could be seen as being negative to Muslim Americans? [beep; record voice]

[Demographic questions follow, unchanged from first wave]

Just a few questions for statistical purposes:

If you are a man, press 1.

A woman, 2.

Please enter your age. [Terminate <18]

Generally speaking, do you think of yourself as a Republican? Democrat? Independent? Or a member of some other party?

[Those who are other or not sure skip to demographic Q4. Democrats continue with A below, Republicans skip to B, Independents to C.]

    A Do you think of yourself as a strong Democrat? Or do you lean Democratic?
    B Do you think of yourself as a strong Republican? Or do you lean Republican?
    C Do you lean Democratic? Lean Republican? Or do you not lean?

If you are a: conservative, press 1; moderate, 2; liberal, 3; not sure, 4.

Do you, yourself, identify with the Tea Party movement?

Who did you vote for in the 2008 election for president?

If you attend religious services. . .

    Regularly, press 1.
    Occasionally, 2.
    Almost never, 3.

APPENDIX 7.2

Inter-coder Reliability Statistics

	Percent agreement	Scott's pi	Cohen's kappa	Krippendorff's alpha (nominal)	N Agreements	N Disagreements	N Cases	N Decisions
First Amendment	98.3	0.946	0.946	0.946	57	1	58	116
Anti–political correctness	89.7	0.73	0.734	0.733	52	6	58	116
9/11 USA at war	96.6	0.922	0.922	0.922	56	2	58	116
Muslims are a threat	98.3	0.966	0.966	0.966	57	1	58	116

8

DISENTANGLING UNCIVIL AND INTOLERANT DISCOURSE IN ONLINE POLITICAL TALK

Patrícia Rossini

Uncivil discourse has been a topic of scholarly concern in the past decades due to the perceived rise of political polarization and partisan media (Herbst 2010; Mutz 2016), and the pervasiveness of incivility in computer-mediated communication (Anderson, Brossard, Scheufele, Xenos, and Ladwig 2014; Coe, Kenski, and Rains 2014; Papacharissi 2004). The potential benefits of online political discussion are often questioned, or dismissed, due to the elevated presence of uncivil discourse (Rowe 2015; Santana 2014). However, as discussed in other chapters in this book (see Muddiman; Sydnor), incivility is a challenging concept to define. As a result, what scholars consider to be uncivil varies in definition and operationalization (Jamieson et al. 2017; Muddiman 2017).

Most of these studies, however, have focused on the US or the UK context, and little is known about civility in online discussions in non-English speaking democracies. This chapter fills that gap by analyzing uncivil discourse in Brazil, the fifth largest population in the world (Un.org 2017). By looking at a developing country with a high rate of Internet use,[1] this chapter contributes to a broader understanding of how citizens in non-U.S. contexts engage in uncivil and intolerant behavior when discussing political news online.

In this chapter, I advocate for a nuanced understanding of incivility in online political talk, and argue that uncivil discourse, in itself, does not necessarily prevent online discussions from producing beneficial outcomes. I argue that uncivil discourse, in which people express their perspectives with foul language and anti-normative intensity, should be understood as a rhetorical act. Second, I argue that the true threat to democracy is *intolerant* discourse, in which groups of people or individuals are attacked in ways that threaten democratic pluralism.

Distinguishing incivility and intolerance provides scholars with a better theoretical framework to evaluate not only the presence of uncivil discourse in online environments but also the extent to which online discussions represent an actual threat to democratic pluralism and equality. Moreover, understanding incivility as a rhetorical act that is both sensitive to context and shaped by individuals' understanding of prevailing norms allows us to avoid the trap in which uncivil discourse is all deemed bad and offensive (Herbst 2010). To discuss the merits of such a nuanced approach to uncivil discourse, this chapter opens with an overview of how incivility is conceptualized and operationalized in both online and offline contexts. I then present a conceptual approach that disentangles uncivil and intolerant discourse, and explain how it can be used to better understand incivility in online political discussion with a study testing the validity of this theoretical model. This chapter makes an important theoretical contribution by advancing an understanding of incivility as a rhetorical act, hence differentiating behaviors that are inherently harmful and offensive from those that are not.

Uncivil Discourse and Online Political Talk

The Internet offers citizens many opportunities to engage in informal political talk, a practice that is central to democratic citizenship (Barber 2003; Mansbridge 1999; Stromer-Galley and Wichowski 2011). It is through political talk that citizens learn about matters of public concern, form and clarify their opinions, and learn about others' views. Everyday political talk may increase political knowledge, foster shared values, and enable participants to learn and understand matters of public concern. Some scholars argue that politically meaningful talk should be characterized by deliberative criteria, such as a rational and respective exchange of arguments that are driven by the common good instead of personal gains (Mansbridge 1999). Other researchers have shown that several of these benefits have been measured using self-report, suggesting that informal discussions have positive outcomes for participants even when they are not measured as a function of deliberative criteria (Eveland and Hively 2009; Valenzuela, Kim, and Gil de Zúñiga 2012).

The discussion around the democratic potential of the Internet is as old as the commercial Internet itself. Structural affordances of the Internet—such as the ability to communicate with others beyond geographic boundaries, find people with similar interests, and be exposed to a variety of perspectives—were all predicted to facilitate political participation (Coleman and Blumler 2009; Stromer-Galley and Wichowski 2011). However, the hope that the Internet would revolutionize citizenship and renew political engagement by fostering political discussion was rapidly replaced by cynicism. Scholars quickly found that the characteristics of political discussion online did not live up to the standards of a public sphere governed by Habermasian principles, such as rational and respectful argumentation in which participants engage with a broad range of ideas (Coleman and Moss 2012). Although some have questioned whether online political talk can live up to the high standards of deliberation (Chadwick 2009; Freelon 2010), most agree that the potential benefits of political discussion online are undermined by the presence of uncivil discourse (Hmielowski, Hutchens, and Cicchirillo 2014; O'Sullivan and Flanagin 2003). Several studies have flagged the elevated presence of profanity, rude language, and disrespect, as well as trolling and flaming as indicators that these environments were toxic for democracy (Reagle Jr. 2015; Santana 2014). In the context of computer-mediated communication, behaviors such as name-calling, ad hominem attacks, profanity, stereotyping, and interpersonal disrespect are consistently flagged as uncivil (Coe et al. 2014; Papacharissi 2004; Sobieraj and Berry 2011). The list may also include graphic representations of shouting (e.g., writing in all caps) (Chen and Lu 2017). Even though there is overlap in how researchers have flagged expressions of incivility, it is relevant to note that differences in how scholars operationalize this wide range of expressions pose a challenge for comparing research results (Stryker, Conway, and Danielson 2016).

Incivility is a challenging concept to define (Jamieson et al. 2017). Authors have operationalized the concept in many ways (see Muddiman, this volume, and Sydnor, this volume). To some extent, it can be argued that the perception of incivility lies "in the eye of the beholder" and is sensitive to contextual factors and the flexible nature of social interactions—an expression perceived as uncivil in the workplace, for example, may be perfectly acceptable among friends (Herbst 2010). In short, there are two main approaches to incivility. One perspective is deeply rooted in deliberative theory, and approaches incivility as the lack of respect or unwillingness to acknowledge and engage with opposing views (Mutz and Reeves 2005). Another tradition is rooted in politeness theory, and considers rude or vulgar remarks, personal attacks, and disrespectful language as uncivil (Jamieson et al. 2017). Muddiman (2017) differentiates these two traditions under the concepts of personal-level and public-level civility. Personal-level civility is violated by behaviors such as rudeness, emotional speech, and name-calling. Public-level incivility includes behaviors such as refusing to engage with others or to recognize the legitimacy of opposing views, spreading misinformation, and prioritizing personal gains over the common good. Distinguishing different types of incivility is relevant to understand its effects. For instance, citizens appear to rank personal-level incivility as more uncivil than public-level incivility, suggesting that heated arguments around political issues are seen as less problematic than attacks on someone's character (Muddiman 2017). Stryker et al.'s (2016) study also suggests that citizens are sensitive to personal attacks, but consider some level of incivility acceptable in political discussions. The authors have also found that more "extreme" forms of incivility, such as racial, sexist, ethnic, or religious slurs, as well as threats—which, in my view, are expressions of intolerance—are consistently deemed as extremely uncivil, thus providing further evidence that these types of harmful expressions need to be disentangled from more acceptable and less dangerous forms of incivility.

Considerations of "Intolerance" Rather Than "Incivility"

These models emphasize a need to understand different forms of uncivil expression and their potential consequences. They demonstrate that context affects how citizens interpret political incivility and shed light on the fact that incivility may be expressed in many different ways—not all of which are necessarily offensive or problematic.

In fact, some level of rudeness may be deemed acceptable in heated political discussions when participants hold diverging views. The idea that incivility is, in itself, a threat to democratic norms ignores the nuances of uncivil discourse. For instance, some behaviors that are considered uncivil are not necessarily used to offend others or to disrupt the conversation. One might use profanity to express an opinion in a heated discussion and emphasize a point, or to get attention (Herbst 2010; Mutz 2016).

I align with the perspective that civility is a communicative practice and can be understood as a rhetorical act (Benson 2011; Herbst 2010), or "a tool in the strategic and behavioral arsenals of politics" (Herbst 2010, 6). In that sense, Papacharissi's (2004) perspective that incivility is a threat to democratic norms might be too strong. Civility is best understood as a set of shared norms of interaction that are flexible and contextual (Herbst 2010). The concept of incivility should not conflate rude or impolite discourse with that which threatens democratic pluralism—such as attacks on groups of people or on core values of a democratic society.

I argue that the concept of *political intolerance* is better suited than the concept of *incivility* to identify practices and behaviors that are inherently threatening to democracy (Gibson 1992; Hurwitz and Mondak 2002). Intolerant behaviors are less dependent on context than incivility, as they necessarily offend or undermine particular groups based on personal, social, sexual, ethnic, religious, or cultural characteristics. Political intolerance signals a lack of moral respect—a basic condition for individuals to be recognized as free and equal in a plural democracy (Habermas 1998; Honneth 1996). Although it can be argued that the level of perceived "intolerance" of a given behavior depends on a country's political system, culture, and rules, intolerant behaviors are more clearly distinguishable than the wide array of behaviors considered to be uncivil because they are rooted in democratic values and norms that are shared in the country. In fact, prior studies have identified behaviors such as racial slurs, threats to harm others, and encouragement of harm as "extreme" expressions of incivility and found that individuals are more likely to classify them as "very uncivil" (Stryker et al. 2016)—indicating that behaviors that convey intolerance are consistently perceived as violations of interactive norms.

Incivility as a Rhetorical Tool

Incivility, then, should be interpreted as a rhetorical asset that people may use to express opinions and justify positions (Herbst 2010). As such, incivility is not necessarily incompatible with democratically relevant political talk. Thinking of incivility as a rhetorical act and not as a set of pre-defined rules means accepting the complex and flexible nature of interaction norms that might occur across contexts. Hence, "uncivil" online political discussion might still be capable of contributing to opinion formation and learning about others' positions. Moreover, relying on predetermined standards of political civility may silence particular forms of expression or limit the types of discourse that are accepted in the public sphere. This critique is often directed at theoretical models that rely too much on procedural discourse and expectations of argumentative rationality, such as deliberation (Benson 2011; Fraser 1990). Incivility may also be associated with positive outcomes, such as improving attention, learning, and recall of opposing arguments in political discussions (Mutz 2016).

In examining incivility and intolerance online, it is important to go beyond the simple presence of certain words or expressions that might characterize them. To fully understand how expressions of incivility or intolerance are used in the context of online political talk—and the extent to which they are used to attack other participants in a discussion—it is crucial to identify the target of these expressions (Papacharissi 2004; Rowe 2015). While online discussions might be uncivil, one cannot infer that participants are actively offending one another simply because they use uncivil rhetoric.

This approach helps advance our understanding of political discussions online by acknowledging that incivility may be used as a rhetorical asset to mark positions and explain arguments in heated conversations, as well as to bring attention to one's perspective, particularly in heterogeneous conversations. Although the nature of online discourse may facilitate the use of uncivil rhetoric—due to reduced social and contextual cues, as well as weak or non-existent social ties (Hmielowski et al. 2014; Papacharissi 2004; Rowe 2015; Santana 2014)—I argue that these expressions are not necessarily incompatible with democratically relevant political talk online, nor they should prevent these discussions from having similar positive outcomes often attributed to face-to-face political conversation, such as increasing political knowledge, providing context and meaning to public affairs, and fostering social ties. Conversely, intolerant discourse signals moral disrespect and profound disregard toward individuals or groups, and as such—by definition—cannot be compatible with normative values of democratic pluralism, freedom of expression, and equality (Gibson 1992; Hurwitz and Mondak 2002). Expressions of political intolerance are therefore potentially damaging to democracy and should raise concerns as to the factors that may facilitate it in digital environments.

Moreover, discussion partners in online environments are often unknown, therefore provoking "the disinhibition effect" (Suler 2004) and facilitating antinormative behavior (Hmielowski et al. 2014; Rowe 2015). In this context, incivility is a rhetorical asset that individuals use to ensure their political claims stand out, and the diversity of viewpoints in online political discussions might encourage participants to rely on uncivil discourse. In fact, online discussions tend to be more uncivil precisely when participants disagree (Stromer-Galley, Bryant, and Bimber 2015), and those who discuss politics online more frequently are more likely to adopt uncivil rhetoric (Hmielowski et al. 2014). The same pattern should not be true for political intolerance, as intolerant behaviors tend to become salient in homogeneous environments (Crawford 2014; Wojcieszak 2011).

To demonstrate the validity of this theoretical model, I analyze political discussions around a variety of political topics in two distinct online environments— social networking sites and news websites. By doing so, I provide further evidence of how platform affordances may shape political discussion online. By disentangling incivility and intolerance in online political talk, I hypothesize that intolerant discourse is less frequent than incivility in public and informal venues of interpersonal interaction online.

Prior research suggests, for instance, that Facebook users are less likely to be uncivil than commenters on news websites (Rowe 2015). Because platforms shape the ways participants engage in political talk, this study also investigates whether there are significant differences in types and volume of intolerant and uncivil discourse in news websites and Facebook news pages.

Finally, both uncivil and intolerant discourse may be directed toward other people or groups, which may or may not be a part of the conversation. Thus, it is relevant to consider the targets of uncivil and intolerant expressions to understand the extent to which online spaces facilitate or constrain interpersonal offense.

Understanding "Uncivil" and "Intolerant" Comments in Context

To understand the prevalence of uncivil and intolerant political discussion, I analyzed online comments from news sources based in a Brazilian context. The study examined online comments in response to political stories posted on Facebook, as well as online comments posted in response to those same stories at their original online news site. This data was collected from Portal UOL's Facebook page— the most accessed online news outlet in Brazil, with over 6.7 million followers on Facebook. Portal UOL was selected as the source for Facebook comments because it is the country's largest online portal and hosts several media outlets. I used the constructed week sampling technique to ensure that the variability of news on weekdays is properly represented in the sample (Riffe, Lacy, and Fico 2005). Two constructed weeks were built to represent six months of online news coverage (Luke, Caburnay, and Cohen 2011).

To conduct my comparative analysis, I first identified all posts from Portal UOL on Facebook as either political or non-political news, adopting a broad conception of politics that also includes topics of public concern such as education, security and violence, social programs, minorities, activism, and social movements. I then followed the links in all political posts in order to collect comments located at the source, which was an official news outlet—mostly UOL and *Folha de São Paulo*, Brazil's most important newspaper, or political blogs.[2] This approach ensures that discussants on both platforms are engaging with the same stories. I analyzed comments on a total of 157 news topics and created a random stratified sample[3] from a universe of 55,053 comments on Facebook and on news sites, respecting the proportion between comments on Facebook (70%) and sources (30%), and number of comments per thread. The content analysis was therefore conducted on 12,337 comments. To analyze threaded discussions, I randomly sampled consecutive messages in each platform.

Separating "Uncivil" From "Intolerant" Comments

This study employs systematic content analysis (Neuendorf 2002) as its main methodology.[4] The coding scheme developed is broadly inspired by, and expands upon, prior research (Coe et al. 2014; Stromer-Galley 2007). The unit of analysis is a comment. The main coding categories are disagreement, opinion expression, incivility, and intolerance. The subcategories under "uncivil messages" include (a) dismissive or pejorative language toward public policies or political institutions; (b) profanity or vulgarity; (c) personal attacks focused on demeaning characteristics or personality; (d) attacks focused on arguments; and (e) pejorative language toward the way a person communicates. Intolerant messages have a harmful intent toward people or groups, attack personal liberties, and deny others equal rights and participation in the "free market" of ideas (Gibson 1992, 2007; Sullivan and Transue 1999). In practical terms, intolerant behaviors were coded in the following subcategories: xenophobia, racism, hate speech, violence, homophobia, religious intolerance, and attacks toward gender, sexual preferences, or economic status. Intolerant and uncivil messages are also coded by target—such as other users, political actors, people or groups featured on news stories, the media, and political minorities. This category identifies whether uncivil and intolerant discourse is targeted at other discussants—which in turn would undermine interpersonal respect and potentially affect the discussion—or at third parties who are not a part of the conversation—such as politicians, political parties, and minorities. Uncivil and intolerant messages can also be unfocused, when there is no clear target.

The results of this analysis support the hypothesis that expressions of political intolerance (which I argue are the real threat to democracy) are occurring less frequently online than are uncivil expressions (which I argue are less of a threat to democracy). As demonstrated in Table 8.1, the presence of incivility is substantial in both platforms: 40.9% of the comments on news websites and 36.5% of the comments on a news page on Facebook are flagged as uncivil. As predicted, intolerant discourse is observed substantially less often than incivility.

The main type of incivility observed on both platforms is attacking other people or groups, which includes *ad hominem* attacks, pejorative language, lying, and defamation. The second most frequent type of incivility is pejorative language

TABLE 8.1 Incivility x platform

	Facebook comments	News comments
Civil	5407 (63.5%)	2261 (59.1%)
Vulgarity or profanity	119 (1.4%)	6 (0.2%)
Attacks towards people or groups	2491 (29.3%)	981 (25.6%)
Pejorative/dismissive language towards institutions or policy	345 (4.1%)	421 (11%)
Attacks towards arguments	130 (1.5%)	152 (4%)
Pejorative for communication	19 (0.2%)	5 (0.1%)
Total	8511	3826

Note: $X^2(5) = 336.3893, p < 0.001$

Source: Author's data.

TABLE 8.2 Intolerance x platform

	Facebook comments	News comments
Absent	7702 (90.5%)	3664 (95.8%)
Intolerance towards political views/values	55 (0.6%)	50 (1.3%)
Racism	17 (0.2%)	7 (0.2%)
Social discrimination	9 (0.1%)	31 (0.8%)
Gender discrimination	24 (0.3%)	8 (0.2%)
Sexual discrimination	251 (2.9%)	6 (0.2%)
Religious intolerance	15 (0.2%)	7 (0.2%)
Offensive stereotyping	45 (0.5%)	26 (0.7%)
Incitement to violence/harm	393 (4.6%)	27 (0.7%)
Total	8511	3826

Note: $X^2(8) = 280.9623, p < 0.001$.

Source: Author's data.

toward political institutions, government, and policy. Both the volume of intolerant discourse and the types of intolerance are sensitive to different platforms (Table 8.2). Specifically, intolerance is more likely to be expressed in Facebook comments as compared to news websites, a result that could be partially explained due to the active presence of moderators in news websites and the lack of dedicated tools to moderate comments on Facebook pages.[5] Notably, the types of intolerance were also different across platforms. On Facebook, most comments coded as intolerant featured incitation to violence/harm, followed by sexual discrimination, intolerance toward political ideas, and offensive stereotyping. Conversely, the main expression of intolerance in news comments is toward political views and values, followed by social discrimination, offensive stereotyping, and incitation to violence or harm.

I additionally analyzed the targets of uncivil and intolerant discourse to understand whether people are intentionally offending other discussants or targeting particular groups. The main targets of uncivil discourse are politicians, political parties, and institutions on both platforms. However, while the second main target of incivility on Facebook is people or groups mentioned in the stories, the second main target of uncivil comments on news websites is other users.

Intolerant comments on the Facebook page were mostly targeted at minorities—such as LGBTQ and women, as well as socially disadvantaged individuals—and the second main target was the topic and actors mentioned in the news (Table 8.3). Politicians, parties, and institutions are the third main target of intolerant discourse on Facebook. The topics and actors mentioned in the news stories are the main focus of intolerant discourse, while the political sphere comes in second place and minorities are the third preferred target. It is also relevant to note that while intolerant discourse is seldom targeted at other users on Facebook, that is not the case for news websites, where 11.5% of all intolerant comments were interpersonal. These results suggest that those in less identified digital platforms might feel less constrained to adopt an offensive discourse toward other participants in the discussion than those who engage in political talk in social networking sites, where social ties could arguably exert some pressure for participants to refrain from interpersonal offense.

TABLE 8.3 Targets of incivility and intolerance per platform (%)

	Incivility		Intolerance	
	Facebook comments	*News comments*	*Facebook comments*	*News comments*
Unfocused	0.6%	0.4%	0.6%	3.7%
Other users	12%	16.4%	0.5%	11.1%
News topic and actors	25.6%	7.5%	39.6%	31.5%
Politicians, parties, institutions	48.5%	62.4%	10.5%	23.5%
Minorities	4.2%	1.3%	40.7%	16%
Journalist/news media	5.4%	7%	0.2%	0.6%
"Brazilians"	2%	1.9%	0.4%	7.4%
Others	1.7%	3.1%	0.3%	1.3%
Total	100%	100%	100%	100%

Note: Incivility: $X^2(7) = 270.3431, p < 0.001$; intolerance: $X^2(7) = 106.1873, p < 0.001$.

Source: Author's data.

Does It matter If It's Uncivil?

Digital platforms—such as social networking sites, discussion groups, communities, and news websites—provide citizens with a wide array of opportunities to engage in political discussion. Nonetheless, online political talk is often questioned as a democratically healthy activity due to elevated levels of incivility. In this chapter, I advance the argument that these venues for political discussion should not be dismissed just because participants often resort to uncivil discourse to express opinions and views. Considering political talk as a vital activity for democratic citizenship, I question the perspective that the volume of uncivil discourse in online interactions is inherently problematic or that it impedes the ability of such conversations to produce democratically desirable outcomes, a view that has been broadly endorsed (Hmielowski et al. 2014; Rowe 2015; Santana 2014) and is heavily informed by theories of deliberation and expectations that online political talk should live up to standards of deliberative discourse (Freelon 2010; Mendonça 2015; Stroud, Scacco, Muddiman, and Curry 2014). I argue that this approach disregards some key features of interpersonal communication in the digital age, in particular the fact that interaction norms are flexible and highly affected not only by context but also by the nature of relationships.

Prior studies have adopted various approaches to incivility that do not rigorously disentangle behaviors that denote lack of interpersonal respect or adherence to interaction norms from those that are inherently harmful or threatening to core democratic values—which are necessarily undermining the intrinsic value of political talk. Although some authors have suggested the need to accept impolite and rude behaviors as inherent to online political talk (Papacharissi 2004), conceptualizing incivility as democratically threatening behaviors seems disconnected from most approaches of civil discourse that are grounded in interpersonal norms and politeness theories (Jamieson et al. 2017). In this chapter, I have advocated for a conceptual distinction between intolerant behaviors and uncivil ones, which assumes the latter constitutes a rhetorical act that people may use strategically to advance their political opinions, which might be acceptable in online environments. This perspective builds upon the idea that online conversation may be compatible with uncivil expressions insofar as participants are less constrained by social sanctions that are present in face-to-face interactions and may interpret some types of incivility as tolerated or acceptable.

The results presented in this chapter suggest that different online platforms may shape how participants engage in uncivil and intolerant discourse. For instance, uncivil discourse is more frequently observed on news websites, whereas intolerance is more likely to be expressed on Facebook. These results might be interpreted in different ways. First, Facebook pages are less controlled than news websites, as page administrators have limited capabilities to moderate comments on a large scale. Thus, intolerant comments are not systematically moderated. Secondly, if people perceive that their opinions will be broadly shared by others, they might be more willing to make intolerant public comments. That is, Facebook users could potentially be more likely to express intolerance if they believe that their imagined audience will share their views—which is consistent with studies that indicate that intolerance is associated with the perception of a homogeneous public opinion environment (Askay 2014; Crawford 2014; Wojcieszak 2010). Prior research has demonstrated that Internet users are affected by their perception of a favorable opinion environment and are less inclined to express their views if they believe others will not share them (Askay 2014; Gearhart and Zhang 2014; Liu and Fahmy 2011).

This study also demonstrated that incivility is not necessarily used to offend other participants in online discussions. Rather, uncivil discourse is more frequently targeted at politicians and political actors—which suggests that those who engage in political talk online might be "critical" or monitorial citizens who like to express their opinions about public affairs (Norris 2000; Zaller 2003). Considering that Brazilian citizens have been witnessing repeated corruption scandals and took to the streets in large demonstrations against the political sphere in 2013, 2014, and 2015, it is not surprising that those who discuss politics online are vocal about their dissatisfaction and mistrust by targeting uncivil attacks at political actors.

Notably, platform affordances have a significant impact in the extent to which citizens engage in interpersonal incivility—that is, when they purposefully offend others with uncivil discourse—which happens more frequently in the comments section of news websites. However, interpersonal incivility constitutes a fraction of the uncivil expressions in online environments, a finding that should serve to calm those who believe that the uncivil nature of online political talk is necessarily harmful for democracy. The fact that citizens are likely to target politicians, political actors, and others is consistent with findings on perceptions of incivility suggesting that personal attacks are seen as more uncivil and inappropriate than incivility targeted at politicians or political positions (Kenski, Coe, and Rains 2017; Muddiman 2017; Stryker et al. 2016), which supports the argument that perceived interaction norms are flexible and contextual.

The finding that incivility occurs more frequently in comments on news websites, despite the fact that these spaces are often moderated (Huang 2016), suggests that some expressions of incivility are not generally perceived as undesirable or incompatible—as they are not flagged by participants nor excluded by moderators. By contrast, intolerant discourse was less likely to take place on news websites, suggesting that expressions of racism, hate speech, violence, and the like may be consistently deemed as inappropriate by moderators. Users, being aware of that active moderation, may be more likely to refrain from these types of comments on news sites. These findings are corroborated by studies investigating perceptions of incivility (Stryker et al. 2016) that show that racial slurs and threatening or harmful discourse are considered extremely uncivil by most people.

This study demonstrates that the types of uncivil discourse to which people are exposed online do not represent threats to democratic values or indicate a hostile environment for political debates. Although incivility might come with the territory when people engage with political news online, most discussions do not cross the boundaries of intolerant discourse and therefore should not be treated as inherently problematic for democracy. The potential benefits of informal political talk online should not be readily dismissed just because its users often behave in uncivil ways. As most research on the benefits of political talk is based on self-reported measures (Huckfeldt and Mendez 2008; Moy and Gastil 2006; Xenos and Moy 2007), it stands to reason that the quality of political discussions is less relevant than its frequency to produce positive outcomes.

This chapter has made three contributions. First, I offered a theoretical model that helps one understand the rhetoric uses of uncivil discourse in online political talk. By showing that incivility and intolerance can be meaningfully distinguished and analyzed, this study advances theory and helps identify the extent to which citizens engage in anti-democratic behaviors when discussing politics online. Second, the results suggest that incivility might be accepted—and even normalized—in political discussions online, being more frequently used to talk about political affairs than to offend other participants. These results are consistent with prior research suggesting that those who discuss politics online more frequently are also more likely to be uncivil, suggesting that these behaviors might be perceived as acceptable or appropriate (Hmielowski et al. 2014). The main focus of uncivil discourse across both platforms was politicians, parties, and institutions, thus revealing dissatisfaction with the political sphere. This finding supports the argument that incivility is a rhetorical act commonly used to expose individual opinions about the world. Finally, the platform through which political discussion takes place significantly shapes the ways individuals express themselves. Participants are more likely to attack others when they participate in more anonymous environments, such as news websites, than when they are discussing politics on Facebook. In contrast, uncivil and intolerant comments on Facebook are more frequently directed at those who are not a part of the conversation—politicians, people, and groups who are subjects of news stories—and seldom directed at other participants. This finding suggests that platform affordances that are specific to social networking sites—such as the "public displays of connections" and the use of personal profiles (Boyd 2012, 29–31; Ellison and Boyd 2013)—may influence users to refrain from confrontation.

This chapter provides a theoretical model that differentiates behaviors that are inherently threatening to democracy from those that are not. This is not to say that incivility is a positive aspect of online conversations. Rather, as this chapter has shown, one needs to scrutinize the different types of incivility and examine the targets of these expressions to determine the extent to which online platforms may contribute to offensive communicative styles. Future research needs to shift

Coe, Kevin, Kate Kenski, and Stephen A. Rains. 2014. "Online and Uncivil? Patterns and Determinants of Incivility in Newspaper Website Comments." *Journal of Communication* 64 (4): 658–679.

Coleman, Stephen, and Jay G. Blumler. 2009. *The Internet and Democratic Citizenship: Theory, Practice and Policy*. 1st ed. New York: Cambridge University Press.

Coleman, Stephen, and Giles Moss. 2012. "Under Construction: The Field of Online Deliberation Research." *Journal of Information Technology & Politics* 9 (1): 1–15.

Crawford, Jarret T. 2014. "Ideological Symmetries and Asymmetries in Political Intolerance and Prejudice Toward Political Activist Groups." *Journal of Experimental Social Psychology* 55 (2): 284–298.

Ellison, Nicole B., and Danah Boyd. 2013. "Sociality Through Social Network Sites." In W. H. Dutton (Ed.), *The Oxford Handbook of Internet Studies*, 1st ed. Oxford University Press, 151–172.

Eveland, William P., and Myiah H. Hively. 2009. "Political Discussion Frequency, Network Size, and "Heterogeneity" of Discussion as Predictors of Political Knowledge and Participation." *Journal of Communication* 59 (2): 205–224.

Fraser, Nancy. 1990. "Rethinking the Public Sphere: A Contribution to the Critique of Actually Existing Democracy." *Social Text* 25/26: 56–80.

Freelon, Deen G. 2010. "Analyzing Online Political Discussion Using Three Models of Democratic Communication." *New Media & Society* 12 (7): 1172–1190.

Gearhart, Sherice, and Weiwu Zhang. 2014. "Gay Bullying and Online Opinion Expression: Testing Spiral of Silence in the Social Media Environment." *Social Science Computer Review* 32 (1): 18–36.

Gervais, Bryan T. 2014. "Incivility Online: Affective and Behavioral Reactions to Uncivil Political Posts in a Web-Based Experiment." *Journal of Information Technology & Politics* 12 (2): 1–19.

Gibson, James L. 1992. "The Political Consequences of Intolerance: Cultural Conformity and Political Freedom." *American Political Science Review* 86 (2): 338–356.

Gibson, James L. 2007. "Political Intolerance in the Context of Democratic Theory." In Russell J. Dalton and Hans-Dieter Klingemann (Eds.), *Oxford Handbook of Political Behavior*. New York: Oxford University Press, 323–341.

Habermas, Jurgen. 1998. *Between Facts and Norms: Contributions to a Discourse Theory of Law and Democracy*. Cambridge, MA: The MIT Press.

Herbst, Susan. 2010. *Rude Democracy: Civility and Incivility in American Politics*. Philadelphia: Temple University Press.

Hmielowski, Jay D., Matthew J. Hutchens, and Vincent J. Cicchirillo. 2014. "Living in an Age of Online Incivility: Examining the Conditional Indirect Effects of Online Discussion on Political Flaming." *Information, Communication & Society* 17 (10): 1196–1211.

Honneth, Axel. 1996. *The Struggle for Recognition: The Moral Grammar of Social Conflicts*. Cambridge, MA: The MIT Press.

Huang, Chia Lun. 2016. *Do Comments Matter? Global Online Commenting Study 2016*. Frankfurt, Germany: The World Association of Newspapers and News Publishers (WAN-IFRA). Retrieved from www.wan-ifra.org/reports/2016/10/06/the-2016-global-report-on-online-commenting.

Huckfeldt, Robert, and Jeanette Morehouse Mendez. 2008. "Moths, Flames, and Political Engagement: Managing Disagreement Within Communication Networks." *The Journal of Politics* 70 (1): 83–96.

Stromer-Galley, Jennifer. 2007. "Measuring Deliberation's Content: A Coding Scheme." *Journal of Public Deliberation* 3 (1): 12.

Stromer-Galley, Jennifer, Lauren Bryant, and Bruce Bimber. 2015. "Context and Medium Matter: Expressing Disagreements Online and Face-to-Face in Political Deliberations." *Journal of Public Deliberation* 11 (1): 1.

Stromer-Galley, Jennifer, and Amber Wichowski. 2011. "Political Discussion Online." *Handbook of Internet Studies* 11: 168.

Stroud, Natalia Jomini, Joshua M. Scacco, Ashley Muddiman, and Alexander L. Curry. 2014. "Changing Deliberative Norms on News Organizations' Facebook Sites." *Journal of Computer-Mediated Communication* 20 (2): 188–203.

Stryker, Robin, Bethany A. Conway, and J. Tyler Danielson. 2016. "What Is Political Incivility?" *Communication Monographs* 83 (4): 535–556.

Suler, John. 2004. "The Online Disinhibition Effect." *CyberPsychology & Behavior* 7 (3): 321–326.

Sullivan, John L., and John E. Transue. 1999. "The Psychological Underpinnings of Democracy: A Selective Review of Research on Political Tolerance, Interpersonal Trust, and Social Capital." *Annual Review of Psychology* 50 (1): 625–650.

Valenzuela, Sebastian, Yonghwan Kim, and Homero Gil de Zúñiga. 2012. "Social Networks That Matter: Exploring the Role of Political Discussion for Online Political Participation." *International Journal of Public Opinion Research* 24 (2): 163–184.

Wojcieszak, Magdalena. 2010. "'Don't Talk to Me': Effects of Ideologically Homogeneous Online Groups and Politically Dissimilar Offline Ties on Extremism." *New Media & Society* 12 (4): 637–655.

Wojcieszak, Magdalena. 2011. "Pulling Toward or Pulling Away: Deliberation, Disagreement, and Opinion Extremity in Political Participation." *Social Science Quarterly* 92 (1): 207–225.

Xenos, Michael, and Patricia Moy. 2007. "Direct and Differential Effects of the Internet on Political and Civic Engagement." *Journal of Communication* 57 (4): 704–718.

Zaller, John. 2003. "A New Standard of News Quality: Burglar Alarms for the Monitorial Citizen." *Political Communication* 20 (2): 109–130.

PART III
Learning From the Past

9

SEEKING A MUTUALITY OF TOLERANCE

A Practical Defense of Civility in a Time of Political Warfare

John Gastil

Americans believe they live in an age of incivility. In the spring of 2016, 78% of those surveyed rated the 2016 Republican primary as "rude," with 41% rating the Democratic primary that way. Nearly 60% admit to behaving in an uncivil manner toward their fellow citizens, with three in four Americans seeing a decline in manners across society generally (AP-NORC 2016). A 2017 survey found that 79% rated the presidential election as uncivil, and a large majority believed civility had declined to "crisis" levels (Weber Shandwick, Powell Tate, and KRC Research 2017).[1]

The key terms themselves—civility and incivility—have been part of American discourse for centuries, and their use has been on the rise since the Reagan era.[2] The chapters in this volume attest to the range of meanings those terms carry, but here I refer to civility as engaging with political adversaries in a manner that is honest and respectful. It does not require politeness, but it avoids animus or contempt (see Benson 2011; Herbst 2010). The past decade has witnessed a rise in the number of foundations and institutes calling for civility in politics—from the National Institute for Civil Discourse to Beyond Civility and dozens of local, state, and university-based centers.

The campaign and election of Donald Trump, however, brought the so-called civility crisis to a head. His 2016 presidential campaign wagered that he could behave disrespectfully toward his opponents—and many other public targets—to galvanize an alienated base. Each taunt, nickname, and insult he hurled toward detractors served a purpose, while marking a new low in presidential debate rhetoric (Olson 2017). As the elected president, Trump has governed as "insulter-in-chief" (Thomas 2017). From the White House, Trump has used taunts and invective as a weapon against not only Democrats but also Republicans in Congress, his own staff, the media, foreign leaders, or anyone he views as opposing his agenda. To quote a former Republican president, he has degraded public discourse with "casual cruelty" (Wilkie 2017).

Worse still, former White House chief strategist Steve Bannon promised that Trump's victory was only a beginning and declared a coming "season of war" against perceived enemies within his own party. "This is not my war," he said in the fall of 2017 to an audience of Christian conservatives at the Values Voter Summit. "This is our war, and y'all didn't start it. The establishment started it. But I will tell you one thing—you all are going to finish it" (Taylor 2017).

Only in metaphor do politics and war conflate. Even famous military strategist Carl von Clausewitz (2008, 605) observed that "war is simply a continuation of political intercourse, with the addition of other means." American discord has not yet sparked a second civil war, but a survey of experts who study such wars averaged their estimates to say the odds of such a conflict are one in three (Wright 2017). By way of comparison, on the eve of the 2016 general election, the meta-polling site FiveThirtyEight and Trump's own campaign strategists estimated his odds of victory at the same percentage (Silver 2016). A 2018 poll had an ominous parallel: roughly one in three Republicans and Democrats alike fears that "the United States will experience a second civil war sometime in the next five years" (Rasmussen 2018).

The deadly clash that ensued at a white nationalist rally in Charlottesville, Virginia, in August 2017 suggested to some that a guerrilla war was already underway (Heim 2017). The car that drove into a crowd and killed a counter-demonstrator enacted a right-wing fantasy to "run down" protestors, as expressed in the gruesome meme "All Lives Splatter" (Grabar 2017).

Events in Charlottesville created an opening for anti-fascists, self-described as "antifa," to assert their political relevance. Contrasted against the pacifist civil disobedience of most organized counter-demonstrators, antifa partisans prepare themselves to use force, if necessary, to stop white supremacists hoping to march or speak in public. Unlike passive resisters, they often mask their identities to avoid identification and incarceration (Beinart 2017). Bennett (2011) reminds us that to quell dissent, officials often label protest—however peaceful—as "incivil," but those who choose to enact political violence make no pretense of civility.

Civility's Sullied Reputation

The Charlottesville example represents an extreme case, but those who participate in everyday political discussions online can incur psychic wounds from invective, insults, and trolling that occur as often *within* ideological camps as between them (King 2016; also see Lim, Cortina, and Magley 2008). Whether at a protest or interacting online, pleas for civility can seem out of place, naïve, or even unwelcome.

I experienced this first-hand when I came to the reluctant defense of a colleague on Facebook. He'd agreed with the content of a sexual assault prevention petition but declined to sign it because of the posting's uncivil tone toward college administrators at his alma mater. Within minutes, insults rained down. After a commenter dubbed my friend "truly the worst of people," I intervened by pointing out that ad hominem attacks only proved my friend's point about the need for more civility. "I wasn't inclined to agree with [my friend] (and often disagree with him)," I explained, "but after reading this thread? Dude's got a point." Later that evening, the commenter thanked us both for "such an illustrative display of rape-enabling mentalities."

In choosing to share the preceding example, I felt as much trepidation as when I hit the "Post" button during the preceding exchange. Calls for civility can ring hollow, particularly when made by a person (e.g., myself) who writes from a position of demographic and professional privilege. Would readers look past the awkward timing of my friend's Facebook post (in the middle of the petition campaign) and see that he was trying to prevent an unforced rhetorical error? Would my own intervention sound preachy, rather than being a plea for solidarity among those with common goals? One commenter in the Facebook thread engaged these points, but louder voices insisted that our discussion of tone and strategy revealed nothing more than our personal defects, political complicity, or worse.

Stepping back from this particular anecdote, many people who took a strong position on social media during the Democratic primary probably felt such barbs when the fight between "Hillary's army" and the "Bernie bros" became increasingly acrimonious (but see Marcetic 2016). It was cold comfort to learn that the Russian government had used trolls and bots to exploit these many other political divides to help elect their preferred presidential candidate in the 2016 election (McCarthy 2017).

Though the nature and degree of incivility differ between the left and right, owing to the more diverse social coalitions underlying the Democratic Party, calls for civility often meet resistance from both sides in the conflict (Grossman and Hopkins 2016). Activists on the left and right question civility as a viable strategy in the midst of all-out political warfare. If civility means showing respect for the opposition's views and the people who express them, it amounts to unilateral disarmament in the midst of an arms race that involves ever-more sophisticated propaganda apparatuses, particularly on the political right. Civility has to make an affirmative case for its use, but partisans are skeptical for at least three reasons.

First, civility achieves nothing in and of itself. A hostile audience rejects it as subterfuge or condescension if they can even recognize its use. Those few members of Congress who sought to hold genuine town halls have witnessed this challenge first-hand, and few campaign managers would advise exposing themselves, rhetorically unarmed, against such a crowd (see Heierbacher 2009; Weigel 2017). Even a sympathetic audience can dismiss civility as an unwelcome distraction from strategic planning. Simply put, politeness has no place behind the barricades.

Even if civility did a modicum of good, the opportunity cost remains too high for those already drained by their daily political struggle. If done correctly, civility requires "emotional labor," akin to the gracious smiles required in the service industry, even when enduring shouts from a customer returning a broken toaster without a receipt. That labor can lead to emotional exhaustion, particularly for those in an "out-group" exposed to more verbal aggression (Lim et al. 2008). Civility that goes beyond respectful listening also requires reflective rhetoric. Effective persuasive appeals to one's opponents require forethought. A sufficiently complex audience analysis takes time, testing, and patience—all of which could have been spent on rallying one's sympathetic base, or at least peeling away the undecided middle in a dispute (Herbst 2010).

The third charge against civility gets to the heart of the problem for many activists: a group requiring itself to behave in a civil manner undermines its own cause. In this view, the requirement to sit down together for a deliberative exchange effectively silences voices that need to be heard in all their emotional color. Civility constrains speakers who need to speak forcefully, dampens fires when passions need to be inflamed, and quells revolutionary messages (Lee 2014; Levine and Nierras 2007; Sanders 1997; Tracy 2010). Civility favors the status quo, implicitly, because it asks enemies adhere to discourse rules they had no hand in setting (Young 2001). In the present day, the stakes are too high and the needs too urgent to pause for polite discourse, lest the opposition use the opportunity to commit one more outrage that otherwise might have been forestalled. Indeed, the evidence suggests that the rate of social change has accelerated, such that "time is of the essence" rings truer today than ever before (Fine 2006).

Civility as Strategic Pacifism

I have sympathy for those criticisms of civility, which have a truth to them. When I served as a campaign manager for congressional, state, and local candidates from 1992 to 1997, I aimed to win votes by any (legal) means necessary. Looking back, I can see that even in that context, however, I exercised a kind of pacifist restraint.

The toughest ethical test came in 1992, when the campaign I managed received an anonymous hand-written letter alleging real estate fraud by our opponent, an incumbent congressman. The letter had rich details, told by someone who claimed to be a long-time supporter who belonged to the same church as the congressman and had learned of this incident during a private conversation on a hunting trip they took together. Releasing that letter to the public without any verification seemed unfair even to our enemy, though we gladly gave it to an investigative reporter from the *San Diego Union-Tribune*, but he operated under the same code. After failing to corroborate its details or even identify the source, he had no story to report.

That congressman won the toughest reelection battle of his career and went on to fight against every cause I support, yet I have no regrets about our campaign's decision. Perhaps it was no coincidence that the candidate, my mother, belonged to the Religious Society of Friends. For her, the Quaker conviction to "speak truth to power" came with a commitment to nonviolence, in the broadest sense of the word. Disobedience had to be civil, even in politics.

Raised in that tradition, I had attended a college founded by Quakers. I read original documents in the Friends' Peace Library archive to write an essay on the "Peace Testimony" for a Quaker journal (Gastil 1992). In the course of that research, I found an *Atlantic Monthly* essay from World War II that sought to explain Quaker pacifism in the midst of a true war against Nazi Germany and the Axis powers.

I returned to that essay this year, when trying to account for my renewed commitment to political civility. After the Charlottesville violence, I had reposted to my Facebook page the clever political meme "Your first name + your last name = Your Nazi-fighting name."

The post expressed my opposition to all things bigoted, but its "fight" metaphor tweaked my Quaker sensibilities. (In the interest of full disclosure, I had left the Religious Society of Friends years earlier, only to discover that I remained "culturally" Quaker.) The metaphoric comparison of actual war with partisan warfare unnerved me, but it helped me recognize the connection between my pacifism and a self-imposed political civility.

Revisiting the Quaker case for *nonviolence* during World War II helped me appreciate the principled—and pragmatic—case for *civility* in contemporary American politics. Thus, I turn now to the dilemma Quakers faced during the war against the Axis powers.

The Quaker Dilemma

By December 1940, Germany, Italy, and Japan had signed the Tripartite Pact, which signaled to the U.S. that its continued support of France and England would draw it into a global war. With the Japanese attack on Pearl Harbor still a year away, intellectuals debated the proper role of the U.S. in World War II. In that context, American "pacifists" came in many varieties, including isolationists, cynical realists, and those sympathizing with Communists or Nazis—with their mutual Nonaggression Pact still in force. By comparison, a precious few opposed war based on a moral or religious conviction, and *Atlantic Monthly* published an "open letter to American undergraduates" that argued against even the most well-conceived pacifism (Whitridge 1940).

It is at this juncture that D. Elton Trueblood—a man with a name as Quaker as one will ever find—stepped forward to publish his response, "The Quaker Way" (Trueblood 1940). Trueblood recognized that *Atlantic Monthly* readers knew little about Quaker tenets, aside from their status as the foremost member of the historic "peace churches," which included the Church of the Brethren and Mennonites. Thanks to Ohio's Quaker Mill Company, his people were most commonly associated with a thick-boned man in a wide-brimmed hat, which further conflated Quakers with the Amish in the public imagination.

"If Quakers were merely opposed to war," Trueblood (1940) explains, the problem posed by Hitler and his allies "would be comparatively simple. . . . Men would refuse military service and would go courageously to prison or to death at the hands of firing squads. . . . The Christian can follow the martyrs' course without inner turmoil, no matter how great the physical pain" (740–741). The problem for Quakers, however, was that an unequivocal anti-war stance could involve ethical trade-offs. As Quaker faith and practice evolved, their "opposition to all oppression" became as important as "opposition to war." This creates a problem when "faithfulness" to one Quaker "testimony" requires "unfaithfulness to another" (741).

Trueblood (1940, 741) asks his American readers to "consider the moral predicament of a Friend in England." He may have taken in Jewish refugees fleeing Europe but now

> sees his own land bombed by day and night and recognizes the imminence of actual invasion. . . . The oppression which he so hates, and which he has had more opportunity to see than have most of his countrymen, will increase its hold on the world unless England makes war effectively.

As much as he opposed war, he recognizes that "peace at this time would break faith with thousands whose only protections from the Gestapo is the British army" (741).

Real British conscientious objectors had earned derision already, with one Scottish critic calling them "parasites of sin" (Trueblood 1940, 741). Even principled pacifists might fear that their actions evaded a grave responsibility. "If we hold that war is sinful," Trueblood asks, "how can we keep our self-respect when we profit by the protection which the armed forces give, but in which we will not share?" To this moral dilemma, Trueblood admits, "We have no perfect solution, in the sense of something that can be neatly put in a sentence" (741–742).

There *is* a solution—but only one that requires a more nuanced explanation. Trueblood asks readers to step back to the Civil War. Abraham Lincoln himself appreciated that the war presented American Quakers with a formidable dilemma. The president held Friends in high esteem. On the day of his assassination, his coat pocket held a letter from Eliza Gurney, who had corresponded with him for two years since first offering him counsel at the White House (Carter 2009). In 1864, Lincoln wrote to Gurley,

> Your people, the Friends, have had and are having a very great trial. On principle and faith opposed to both war and oppression, they can only practically oppose oppression by war. In this hard dilemma some have chosen one horn and some the other.
>
> *(Trueblood 1940, 742)*[3]

Though Lincoln recognized the dilemma, even he could not see that its reso-lution lay in the possibility of taking action simultaneously against the war and the oppression it concerned. As Trueblood explains, Quakers insisted "that they are able to avoid both horns," rather than allowing themselves to "choose between the moral ends involved. Opposed on principle to both war and oppression, they have continued to oppose both in actual practice" (Trueblood 1940, 743).

In the case of the Civil War, Quakers continued to fight slavery even while objecting conscientiously to military conscription:

> Friends went on doing all they could in encouraging the escape of slaves, as they had long done in the conduct of the underground railroad. They felt great sympathy for fellow idealists in the Federal army and were honest enough to recognize that a Federal victory was more helpful to the cause they cherished than a Secessionist victory could have been.
>
> *(Trueblood 1940, 743)*

In the context of World War II, Trueblood says that the same reasoning leads Quakers to aid the oppressed and name the oppressor, even while rejecting vio-lence. Just as the Religious Society of Friends was among the first American reli-gious organizations to take a principled stand against slavery, so were Trueblood and other American Quakers insisting their fellow citizens recognize the Nazi menace for what it was—a "conception of life" that is "the complete antithesis of the Quaker conception" (Trueblood 1940, 743). The Friends' "renunciation of war has not destroyed their powers of moral judgment." Their pacifism could not be mistaken for indifference, "for the Quaker tradition of good will is as far removed from isolationism as it is from militarism" (744).

This marks a key juncture in the development of Trueblood's argument. Though opposition to oppression and violence flows from a spiritual source for Quakers, many Friends include secular evidence and logic in their testimonies. In 1947, the Nobel Peace Prize went to the American Friends' Service Committee (AFSC) for its work during and after the war. In its 1955 pamphlet, *Speak Truth to Power*, the Committee explained, "We believe it is *practical, and politically relevant*, for men and women to move the world toward peace by individually practicing peace themselves" (AFSC 1955, italics added).

It will surprise many to learn that, as Trueblood explains, "the objection to war is almost incidental" in early Friends' writings. The Quaker way of life "seeks to overcome evil with good, not in isolated cases, but as a consistent and enduring policy," in times of peace and war alike. In the case of international strife, this means "active goodwill," such as feeding children, housing refugees, and "inter-visitation" between nations (Trueblood 1940, 744–745). Though led by individual conscience, enlightened through silent worship together, the Quakers' way of life also amounts to a practical political strategy for naming and working against oppression's many forms.

If that way of life seems quaint, or even treasonous, in the midst of World War II, Trueblood asks readers to consider what might have occurred had the Quaker approach prevailed after the misnamed "war to end all wars."

> If this way had been adopted in 1919 by the victorious nations, and if money had been spent lavishly on it, as men spend money lavishly on war when war comes, there never would have been another war. We believe in putting as much intelligence and effort, as well as money, into the technique of peacemaking as people ever put into the technique of military defense or aggression, and we are willing to risk our chances in that kind of world.
>
> *(Trueblood 1940, 745)*

Trueblood recognizes the Quaker method as a *plausible* strategy—one that involves risk and requires favorable circumstance to be practiced effectively on a national scale. In the case of the war against the Nazis, Trueblood acknowledges that by 1932, there was no longer an "open door" toward peace, "but finally it was allowed to go shut." Seven years before Hitler and Stalin put the German invasion of Poland into motion, even Trueblood could see the chance for peaceful resolution had passed (Trueblood 1940, 745).

Such realism does not disrupt the Quaker way of life, but it does require taking a self-aware approach to pacifism that Trueblood (1940, 745) calls "the principle of vocation." He explains, "It may be the vocation of a special group to adhere loyally and sacrificially to a position which even the members of the group recognize is not yet possible for the nation" (745). Thus, many prominent Quakers refused to pressure their own governments to lay down arms during World War II. Trueblood could see that his government had backed itself into a corner: "Since they let the door go shut, they have now no single good choice" (745). Such was the view of the seventeenth-century Quaker author Robert Barclay, who

> found that, in honesty, he had to consider the situation of statesmen who must make decisions about the conduct of nations which do not follow the Quaker way. He found that he could not condemn them for taking the least of possible evils.
>
> *(Trueblood 1940, 745)*[4]

Speaking on behalf of twentieth-century Quakers, Trueblood (1940) stressed that the viability of his strategy depended on careful timing:

> Friends, to be logical, need not maintain that the sudden adoption of non-resistance after war has started will succeed. . . . We do not suppose that our love for an aviator, though we have never done anything to make him know

it, will keep him from dropping bombs on us. In other words, we do not believe in magic. Love must be tangible to make a difference, and in most cases it cannot be tangible unless it is part of a long-time program.

(Trueblood 1940, 745)

That last phrase is the key. For Quaker nonviolence to be effective as a means of opposing oppression, it has to be a "long-time program" safeguarded by people who understand its practice as their chief vocation. What Trueblood asks of his detractors is that they give to such principled pacifists the same tolerance that Quakers give when their governments are forced by circumstances (often of their own making) to take up arms against an invader or oppressor. "We do not condemn them for their failure to change programs overnight, but at the same time we hold that they ought not to condemn us or ask us to abandon our way. . . . We plead for a *mutuality of tolerance* in these difficult matters" (Trueblood 1940, 746).

In other words, if Friends can uphold their testimony against oppression and violence even while tolerating governments forced to act violently, those same governments can tolerate the Friends' insistence on continuing their ways even during times of war. For Trueblood, this mutuality of tolerance requires realism on the part of both parties. Taking up arms must have a clear strategic justification, on its own terms, but so must Quakers be realists. As Trueblood (1940, 746) writes of the Quaker way, "If we have followed it before, and if we have had some measure of success, why should we not continue to follow it?"

At times, the Quakers have, indeed, had a "measure of success." They made powerful contributions to prison reform, abolitionism, and many social movements right up through the end of the twentieth century. Quaker George Lakey, for example, wrote several guides read by organizers, such as the 1965 *Manual for Direct Action: Strategy and Tactics for Civil Rights and All Other Nonviolent Protest Movements* (e.g., Oppenheimer and Lakey 1965; also see Barbour and Frost 1988).

The efficacy of Quaker nonviolence has earned them the tolerance Trueblood requested, but in truth, Friends want more. The detractor who penned the *Atlantic Monthly* "open letter" that compelled Trueblood's reply held Quakers in esteem, but not their beliefs. As Trueblood (1940, 740) wrote, "Though he respects the Quaker stand, he does not believe that it can be reasonably defended."

Civility in the Present Conflict

As Trueblood (1940) showed, the Quaker stance *can* be defended. Moreover, I can summarize his argument by reference to the present day, in which Americans find themselves not (yet) in the midst of a full-scale global or civil war. Though no war is in motion, detractors of those who call for civility in American politics face a similar dilemma to that of Trueblood—and must mount a similar defense. In this case, a partisan struggle is underway for control of every level of American government—or perhaps society itself. Some argue, with good reason, that this involves a struggle for democracy itself, with a president who threatens independent media organizations and federal judges, encourages police brutality against the accused, incites supporters to violence against protestors, and gives encouragement to white supremacists previously presumed to operate outside the boundaries of American political debate (e.g., Klaas 2017).

Renewing one's commitment to civility and deliberative engagement at such times risks the same kind of rebuke Quakers endure during war: the approach, however virtuous out of context, amounts to a hazardous misplacement of one's energy when the only clear path forward is winning the daily propaganda war and every pending legal battle, and, ultimately, securing victory in each and every election from this day forward. If this requires shutting out and shouting down opponents, fighting online flaming with fire by reply, then so be it. Civility can wait for a better day, when democracy's institutions have been secured and normal political life can resume.[5]

A Trueblood defense of civility even in this time begins with tolerance for those committed to unfettered partisan battle. In effect, I can accept that there may be contexts in which campaigns and movements need to inflame political passions in a way that makes a more sober deliberation, momentarily, impossible. A mutuality of tolerance requires me to be realistic about the time and place for civil exchange and to not begrudge skilled practitioners who have no other recourse in the midst of a political battle. I may question whether their approach is as useful as they claim, even in the short term. Provided that they can show the necessity and efficacy of their means of engagement, however, I can accept them.

What I ask in return is for a *mutuality* of that tolerance. Detractors should recognize, when presented with appropriate evidence, the viability of civility as what Trueblood would call a "long-time program." More importantly, critics need to recognize the social utility of having *a group of people vocationally committed* to civil engagement with even those who advocate and practice various forms of oppression. That group goes by no recognized name, though it counts among its numbers many professionals in the civic sector, such as many members in the National Coalition for Dialogue and Deliberation and those signed on to umbrella organizations, such as the Bridge Alliance or the National Institute for Civil Discourse, which brought this book into existence. (For examples and context, see Nabatchi and Leigninger 2015.)

Evidence of a Civility Strategy's Political Efficacy

This brings me to the affirmative case for civil engagement even during hyper-partisan strife and imperiled democratic institutions. Trueblood (1940) asked of his critics, "If we have had some measure of success, why should we not continue to follow it?" Can those promoting civility point to evidence supporting their conviction that their chosen strategy can yield results?

To answer that question first requires a clarification. In parallel to Trueblood's observation about the Quaker peace testimony, a commitment to civility must mean more than a rejection of incivility. Rather, it must affirm an ongoing program of *active engagement*. A more descriptive term for such engagement is "deliberative civic engagement," which denotes an effort to elevate the quality of public discourse on matters of public concern. This approach encourages the exchange of evidence, reasons, and dialogue about experiences in a setting that promotes mutual respect and due consideration (Nabatchi, Gastil, Weiksner, and Leighninger 2012).

On the micro level, considerable evidence suggests the value of civility as a component of civic education. Speech and debate programs in high school and college can (but don't always) teach these skills. One recent idea for revitalizing such programs stresses incorporating more deliberative and dialogic elements of argumentation into the rules that structure debate competitions, lest students learn *only* to contest rival ideas (Hogan, Kurr, Bergmaier, and Johnson 2017). A century ago, well-attended and lively public debates and discussions served as effective means for adult civic education; the fact that Chautauqua assemblies and the like have fallen out of use is no indictment of their efficacy (Keith 2007; Shaffer 2016; also see Shaffer's chapter in this volume). Those who have made a study of deceit and dirty politics still hold out hope for "civil engaged argument" because of the beneficial effect it has on public judgment (Jamieson and Hardy 2012; also see Herbst 2010).

In everyday political discussions online, users can tell the difference between civil and uncivil discourse. In those online settings where the most verbally aggressive engage in unchecked anonymous "flaming," a cascade can occur that degrades the norms of the discussion (Hmielowski, Hutchens, and Cicchirillo 2014; Rowe 2015). People often flee such spaces and show a preference for participating in moderated forums, including those that give users themselves the ability to flag incivility directly (Lampe et al. 2014). Drawn to such spaces partly out of a desire to express themselves and influence their peers (Hoffman, Jones, and Young 2013), positive experiences online can have civic educational effects on younger users that predict future political engagement (Yamamoto, Kushin, and Dalisay 2015).

In the past two decades, an entire public engagement and consultation industry has formed in parallel with an international movement for "deliberative democracy." Across the U.S., one can find public discussion processes with names such as citizens' juries, consensus conferences, deliberative polls, national issues forums, and more, and their collective track record is impressive. Each of these processes has a variation on a strong code of civility, and participating in them can have salutary effects on the participants and, at times, a direct impact on public policy decisions (Gastil and Levine 2005; Johnson and Gastil 2015; Pincock 2012).

Taken together, evidence such as this shows that principled civility, as part of a program of ongoing deliberative engagement, has had more than a "measure of success." Such results contrast sharply with the corrosive long-term effects of incivility on public participation in politics and public institutions themselves

(Maisel 2012; Wolf, Strachan, and Shea 2012). More than that, civility may provide the glue that holds together a sharply divided society and crafts effective policy agreements in the midst of even the worst partisan conflicts (Gutmann and Thompson 2014).

That said, I choose to reserve respect for colleagues who might make less civil choices on the front lines of a partisan battle when their opponent has shown a commitment to an uncivil campaign. The ends of political victory cannot justify all means of engagement, but candidates and their staff can, like nations at war, find themselves left with no good options as Election Day approaches. In return, I trust that even in the midst of a partisan contest, they can retain a mutual respect for a civility ethic even in their darkest hours. After the last ballot is counted or the policy debate resolved, they might have much to gain by seeking out more civil forms of engagement.

Notes

1 Thanks to Eugene P. Deess, John Rountree, Tim Shaffer, Cynthia Simmons, and anonymous reviewers for feedback on an earlier draft of this essay.
2 Google's "n-gram viewer" provides a glimpse of what's in its corpus of American English texts over the past three centuries.[1] By way of a baseline for public life, "government" peaked in 1777, when it appeared once for every 2,000 words published. The use of that term declined until the frequency of "public" overtook it in the 1820s. The Great Depression began a resurgence for "government," which regained its top spot until 1971, when it went back in decline, while "public" remained static. Though "politics" will likely never catch the multipurpose word "public," it has been on the rise in earnest since the early 1800s. The 1970 and 2000 election cycles brought it to its peak use (appearing approximately once in every 16,000 words), but it has settled back into rates last seen in the early 1980s. Against this backdrop, the terms "civility" and "incivility" provide a stark contrast. Both appear in specialized contexts and have correspondingly low frequency scores, with each appearing less than once in a million words. Peak usage for "civility" was in the 1750s, then again at the time of the Declaration of Independence (1776). Since then, the word has dropped to the point where it appears only a tenth as often as it used to. "Incivility" peaked at the time of the Constitutional Convention (1787), but it also declined thereafter. Viewed in the timescale of the last century, however, both words are resurgent in their usage—at peak use rates that have resulted from a climb beginning at the end of the Reagan years (1980–1988). Google finds the word "incivility" in American English texts only a tenth as often as "civility," but the latter often warns of the former. For more analysis along these lines, see Shea and Sproveri (2012).
3 In 1956, the film *Friendly Persuasion*, starring Gary Cooper, brought to a mass audience the dilemma faced by Quaker pacifists during the American Civil War. The film received many Oscar nominations, but its screenwriter was barred from that year's ballot, having been blacklisted for refusing to testify before the U.S. Congress during the McCarthy era. See Rob Nixon's entry, "Friendly Persuasion (1956)," at *Turner Classic Movies* online (www.tcm.com).
4 Many individual Quakers struggled to maintain their peace testimony during the Revolutionary War, the Civil War, and both World Wars. Initially, such Friends who took up arms were "read out of the Meeting"—removed entirely from the membership rolls of the Religious Society of Friends. This resulted in such a catastrophic loss of membership

that by the twentieth century, Friends ended that practice. On the history of Quakers and their demanding testimonies, see Barbour and Frost (1988).

5 John Rountree, an astute reader of a previous draft of this essay, observed that partisans also welcome civility once they have seized the reins of power. Only once their enemies are defeated might they call for civil discourse. This, of course, is the kind of insincere civility designed to reinforce the ruling group's power, rather than open space for genuine deliberation that includes the voices of those who have fallen out of power.

Bibliography

American Friends' Service Committee. 1955. *Speak Truth to Power: A Quaker Search for an Alternative to Violence*. Retrieved January 20, 2018, from www.quaker.org/sttp.html.

AP-NORC. 2016, April. "Rude Behavior in Everyday Life and on the Campaign Trail." Retrieved January 20, 2018, from www.apnorc.org/projects/Pages/rude-behavior-in-everyday-life-and-on-the-campaign-trail.aspx.

Barbour, Hugh, and J. William Frost. 1988. *The Quakers*. Westport, CT: Greenwood Press.

Beinart, Peter. 2017. "The Rise of the Violent Left." *Atlantic Monthly*, September.

Bennett, W. Lance. 2011. "What's Wrong With Incivility? Civility as the New Censorship in American Politics." *Center for Communication and Civic Engagement Working Paper* 2011-1, University of Washington, Seattle.

Benson, Thomas W. 2011. "The Rhetoric of Civility: Power, Authenticity, and Democracy." *Journal of Contemporary Rhetoric* 1 (1): 22–30.

Carter, Max L. 2009. "Elizabeth Kirkbride Gurney's Correspondence With Abraham Lincoln: The Quaker Dilemma." *Pennsylvania Magazine of History and Biography* 133 (4): 389–396.

Fine, Allison. 2006. *Momentum: Igniting Social Change in the Connected Age*. New York: John Wiley and Sons.

Gastil, John. 1992. "Queries on the Quaker Peace Testimony." *Friends' Journal*, August 14–15.

Gastil, John, and Peter Levine, eds. 2005. *The Deliberative Democracy Handbook: Strategies for Effective Civic Engagement in the Twenty-First Century*. San Francisco: Jossey-Bass.

Grabar, Henry. 2017. "Run Them Down." *Slate*, August 14.

Grossman, Matthew, and David A. Hopkins. 2016. *Asymmetric Politics: Ideological Republicans and Group Interest Democrats*. New York: Oxford University Press.

Gutmann, Amy, and Dennis F. Thompson. 2014. *The Spirit of Compromise: Why Governing Demands It and Campaigning Undermines It*. Princeton, NJ: Princeton University Press.

Heierbacher, Sandy. 2009. "Upgrading the Way We Do Politics." *YES! Magazine*, August 21.

Heim, Joe. 2017. "Recounting a Day of Rage, Hate, Violence and Death." *Washington Post*, August 14.

Herbst, Susan. 2010. *Rude Democracy: Civility and Incivility in American Politics*. Philadelphia: Temple University Press.

Hmielowski, Jay D., Myiah J. Hutchens, and Vincent J. Cicchirillo. 2014. "Living in an Age of Online Incivility: Examining the Conditional Indirect Effects of Online Discussion on Political Flaming." *Information, Communication and Society* 17 (10): 1196–1211.

Hoffman, Lindsay H., Philip Edward Jones, and Dannagal Goldthwaite Young. 2013. "Does My Comment Count? Perceptions of Political Participation in an Online Environment." *Computers in Human Behavior* 29 (6): 2248–2256.

Hogan, J. Michael, Jessica A. Kurr, Michael J. Bergmaier, and Jeremy D. Johnson, eds. 2017. *Speech and Debate as Civic Education*. University Park, PA: Pennsylvania State University Press.

Jamieson, Kathleen Hall, and Bruce Hardy. 2012. "What Is Civil Engaged Argument and Why Does Aspiring to It Matter?" *PS: Political Science and Politics* 45 (2): 412–415.

Johnson, Carolina, and John Gastil. 2015. "Variations of Institutional Design for Empowered Deliberation." *Journal of Public Deliberation* 11 (1).

Keith, William. 2007. *Democracy as Discussion: Civic Education and the American Forum Movement*. Lanham, MD: Lexington Books.

King, Elizabeth. 2016. "Stressed? Blame the 2016 Election." *Time*, April 26.

Klaas, Brian. 2017. "The Threat Donald Trump Poses to Democracy Is Not Overblown." *Chicago Tribune*, May 3.

Lampe, Cliff, Paul Zube, Jusil Lee, Chul Hyun Park, and Erik Johnston. 2014. "Crowdsourcing Civility: A Natural Experiment Examining the Effects of Distributed Moderation in Online Forums." *Government Information Quarterly* 312: 317–326.

Lee, Caroline W. 2014. *Do-it-yourself Democracy: The Rise of the Public Engagement Industry*. New York: Oxford University Press.

Levine, Peter, and Rose Marie Nierras. 2007. "Activists' Views of Deliberation." *Journal of Public Deliberation* 3 (1): 1–14.

Lim, Sandy, Lilia M. Cortina, and Vickie J. Magley. 2008. "Personal and Workgroup Incivility: Impact on Work and Health Outcomes." *Journal of Applied Psychology* 93 (1): 95–107.

Maisel, L. Sandy. 2012. "The Negative Consequences of Uncivil Political Discourse." *PS: Political Science and Politics* 45 (3): 405–411.

Marcetic, Branco. 2016. "The Hillary Clinton vs. Bernie Sanders Fight Has Gotten Nasty But It's Not Nearly as Bad as 2008." *In These Times*, June 10.

McCarthy, Tom. 2017. "How Russia Used Social Media to Divide Americans." *The Guardian*, October 14. Retrieved July 25, 2018, from www.theguardian.com.

Nabatchi, Tina, John Gastil, Matt. Weiksner, and G. Michael Leighninger, eds. 2012. *Democracy in Motion: Evaluating the Practice and Impact of Deliberative Civic Engagement*. New York: Oxford University Press.

Nabatchi, Tina, and G. Michael Leighninger. 2015. *Public Participation for 21st Century Democracy*. Hoboken, NJ: Jossey-Bass.

Olson, Kathryn M. 2017. "The Refutational Power of Ad Personam and Tu Quoque Attacks in Advancing Trump's 'Change' Counter-Narrative During the 2016 General Election Presidential Debates." In Robert E. Denton (Ed.), *Political Campaign Communication: Theory, Method and Practice*. Lanham, MD: Lexington Books, 283–302.

Oppenheimer, Martin, and George Lakey. 1965. *A Manual for Direct Action: Strategy and Tactics for Civil Rights and All Other Nonviolent Protest Movements*. Chicago: Quadrangle Books.

Pincock, Heather. 2012. "Does Deliberation Make Better Citizens?" In Tina Nabatchi, John Gastil, Matt Weiksner, and G. Michael Leighninger (Eds.), *Democracy in Motion: Evaluating the Practice and Impact of Deliberative Civic Engagement*. Oxford University Press, 135–162.

Rasmussen. 2018. "31% Think U.S. Civil War Likely Soon." *Rasmussen Reports*, June 27. Retrieved July 25, 2018, from www.rasmussenreports.com.

Rowe, Ian. 2015. "Civility 2.0: A Comparative Analysis of Incivility in Online Political Discussion." *Information, Communication and Society* 18 (2): 121–138.

Sanders, Lynn M. 1997. "Against Deliberation." *Political Theory* 25 (2): 347–376.

Shaffer, Timothy J. 2016. "Looking Beyond Our Recent Past." *National Civic Review* 105 (3): 3–10.

Shea, Daniel M., and Alex Sproveri. 2012. "The Rise and Fall of Nasty Politics in America." *PS: Political Science and Politics* 45 (2): 416–421.

Silver, Nate. 2016. "Why FiveThirtyEight Gave Trump a Better Chance Than Almost Anyone Else." *FiveThirtyEight*, November 11.

Taylor, Jessica. 2017. "Bannon: 'It's A Season of War Against the GOP Establishment.'" *National Public Radio*, October 14. Retrieved January 20, 2018, from www.npr.org.

Thomas, Cal. 2017. "Trump as Insulter-in-Chief." *Sailsbury Post*, July 5. Retrieved July 25, 2018, from www.salisburypost.com.

Tracy, Karen. 2010. *Challenges of Ordinary Democracy: A Case Study in Deliberation and Dissent.* University Park, PA: Pennsylvania State University Press.

Trueblood, D. Elton. 1940. "The Quaker Way." *Atlantic Monthly*, 740–746.

von Clausewitz, Carl. 2008. *On War*. Princeton, NJ: Princeton University Press.

Weber Shandwick, Powell Tate, and KRC Research. 2017. *Civility in America VII: The State of Civility* 2017. Retrieved January 20, 2018, from www.webershandwick.com.

Weigel, David. 2017. "At Raucous Town Halls, Republicans Have Faced Another Round of Anger Over Health Care." *Washington Post*, August 11.

Whitridge, Arnold. 1940. "Where Do You Stand? An Open Letter to American Undergraduates." *Atlantic Monthly*, 133–137.

Wilkie, Christina. 2017. "George W. Bush Assails Trumpism Without Naming Trump." *CNBC.com*, October 19. Retrieved July 25, 2018, from www.cnbc.com.

Wolf, Michael R., J. Cherie Strachan, and Daniel M. Shea. 2012. "Incivility and Standing Firm: A Second Layer of Partisan Division." *PS: Political Science and Politics* 45 (3): 428–434.

Wright, Robin. 2017. "Is America Headed for a New Kind of Civil War? *New Yorker*, August 14.

Yamamoto, Masahiro, Matthew J. Kushin, and Francis Dalisay. 2015. "Social Media and Mobiles as Political Mobilization Forces for Young Adults: Examining the Moderating Role of Online Political Expression in Political Participation." *New Media and Society* 17 (6): 880–898.

Young, Iris Marion. 2001. "Activist Challenges to Deliberative Democracy." *Political Theory* 29: 670–690.

10

THE PATRON SAINT OF CIVILITY?

Benjamin Franklin and the Problems of Civil Discourse

Steven C. Bullock

On September 17, 1787, the final day of the American constitutional convention, Benjamin Franklin addressed the delegates. It was a solemn occasion. Franklin was the group's elder statesman, not only by virtue of his age (at 81 he was too weak to read the piece himself) but also as America's first world-class scientist, its first international celebrity, and its most important Revolutionary diplomat (Beeman 2009, 360–364).

Franklin's speech began unexpectedly. The proposed constitution, he admitted, was not perfect. He disliked some of its provisions. But experience had taught him the importance of not being too sure of himself. "The older I grow," he noted, "the more apt I am . . . to pay more Respect to the Judgment of others." Franklin encouraged delegates to exhibit similar humility, supporting the new constitution as the best possible under the circumstances (Franklin 1787b).[1]

Franklin's words offered an eloquent reminder of the spirit of consultation and compromise that helped create a remarkably durable document. But his arguments were also deeply rooted in his personal concerns. Franklin had not always been, as Thomas Jefferson later judged him, "the most amiable of men in society" (Jefferson 1808). Franklin came of age in a deeply troubled time, working on a Boston newspaper whose harsh criticism and mockery troubled the province's already difficult public life. Not surprisingly, he became a contentious youth who delighted in arguing. As a young man in Philadelphia, however, he learned to curb this combativeness in both his private and public lives, allowing him to develop both a successful printing business and a remarkable series of civic projects (Franklin 1986, 11). In later adulthood, he took these lessons into larger political arenas, helping win the war against the British and shape the new nation.

At a time when maintaining civil discourse again seems particularly problematic, it may be helpful to examine both Franklin's early difficulties in the public realm and his developing approach to nurturing social and political relationships. If we seek a patron saint of civil discourse, a reminder that public life has also been difficult in the past and that more productive pathways may still be possible, we could do worse than look to Benjamin Franklin.

When Benjamin Franklin's name first appeared as publisher of a newspaper, the opening article repudiated "Party Pamphlets malicious Scribbles, and Billingsgate Ribaldry." Such "hateful" pieces only created "Rancour and bitterness." Franklin's newspaper promised something different. It would instead help quiet "harsh Disorders" and "restless Resentments" (Franklin 1723).

The statement was surprising—not because of its sentiment, but its source. In the year and a half before the February 1723 pronouncement, Boston's *New-England Courant* had developed a well-deserved reputation for inflaming rather than quieting resentments. It had mocked its opponents in ways that further encouraged what an observer called the "Quarrels and Divisions" of Massachusetts public life (*Boston News-Letter*, August 28, 1721, 4). Perhaps not surprisingly, the paper's promises of peace remained unfulfilled.

The situation was even more complex for Franklin himself. As his role in the paper seemingly expanded, Franklin became known about town for "Libelling and Satyr" (Franklin 1986, 16). His name on the newspaper, however, was only a legal fiction. The 17-year-old had served as an apprentice to the actual publisher until only a few days before. Furthermore, secret documents signed at the time reaffirmed that status, leaving him bound, to his increasing distress, to James Franklin, a young man who was not only his master but also his brother. Six months later, this ambiguous legal standing allowed Benjamin to escape not only his brother but also his example.

Franklin's adolescent experiences with James and his newspaper offered first-hand experience of the dangers of incivility. Rather than the openness and respect Franklin later recommended, his brother's *Courant* exhibited unquestioned certainty about its positions and angry attacks on its opponents. The troubling effects of the paper on Boston's problematic public sphere began in 1721, when the *Courant* started, and lasted through 1723, when Franklin finally escaped its printing office.

The *New-England Courant* grew particularly harsh at the end of October 1721, when Cotton Mather, perhaps the city's most influential minister, reported on Boston's experience inoculating residents during its smallpox epidemic. James Franklin's newspaper, then almost three months old, had made inoculation its chief topic—and Mather its main target. The minister had learned of the largely unfamiliar practice of inoculation and had prevailed on the town's clergy to support it. Although they in turn had convinced only one Boston physician, he had been actively inoculating people for months. This work would later be recognized as a major advance in medicine and public health, winning the doctor membership in Britain's preeminent scientific society (alongside Mather, who was already a member).

Most Bostonians, however, remained unconvinced. Deliberately infecting people with a deadly disease during a major epidemic seemed reckless, perhaps even criminal. As the *Courant* noted in its first issue, Mather had pushed for inoculation "*in Contradiction* to the declared Opinion" of local doctors and in "Opposition to the Selectmen" (*New-England Courant*, August 7, 1721, 1). The paper further charged (less correctly) that Mather was "*profoundly ignorant of the Matter*" and had been deceived by "Turk[s]" and "Greek old Women" (*New-England Courant*, August 7, 1721, 1–2). The *Courant* was even harsher when one of Mather's relatives, himself a minister, criticized the new paper. Its third issue accused the critical cleric of drunkenness and sexual immorality, even claiming that he and a friend had spent hours in bed with a pair of sisters (*New-England Courant*, August 21, 1721, 2–3).

The issue of *Courant* that followed Mather's late October report attacked Boston's clergy as a whole for even presuming to deal with public issues. Quoting an English book, the author declared that a minister become a devil when he acted beyond the sphere of religion, "a sooty Coal in The blackest Hell" (*New-England Courant*, November 6, 1721, 3–4). Arthur Tourtellot, a leading scholar of Benjamin Franklin's early life (and an admirer of the *Courant*), judges the statement "gratuitous" and "undeserved"—even "irrational" (Tourtellot 1977, 261).

Soon afterward Cotton Mather confronted James Franklin in the street about these attacks. "Banter[ing] and Abus[ing] the Ministers of God," the minister warned, could provoke divine punishment. Franklin called the statement a "curse" (*New-England Courant*, December 4, 1721, 1). Mather also felt under assault. Even before the *Courant* item, he had complained in his diary that Bostonians treated him in "a most … murderous Manner," a comment that in different circumstances might have seemed a characteristic overreaction (Mather 1912, 655). But the night after he approached Franklin, someone threw a firebomb into the room where Mather normally slept. Even the heavy ball itself, Mather judged, would have been deadly if it had landed on someone. Fortunately the bomb hit the floor, and the impact shook loose the lit fuse before the powder ignited. The paper with the grenade read, "Cotton Mather, You Dog, Dam you: I'll inoculate you with this" (Mather 1912, 657–658).

The *Courant* responded with further contempt. Its report on the attack appeared on the same page as a piece mocking Mather's elaborate writing style, a favorite game among the newspaper's authors (*New-England Courant*, November 20, 1721, 2). James Franklin answered Mather's public admonition the following week. The printer admitted that the paper should not have attacked the earlier clergyman's private life, but claimed ministers had not been criticized before they advocated inoculation. Franklin's lengthy essay failed to mention the bombing. Yet it reprinted in full the item about ministers becoming devils. Further refusing any quarter to opponents who found it offensive, Franklin responded to Mather's assertion that the clergy had not been treated as badly anywhere else by reprinting an English poem the editor deemed even more insulting (*New-England Courant*, December 4, 1721, 1–2).

Such anti-clericalism remained a central theme of the *Courant*. An early 1722 article called the clergy "instruments of Mischief and Trouble both in Church and State, from Witchcraft to Inoculation" (*New-England Courant*, January 22, 1722, 3). Another piece applied a biblical passage to Boston's ministers: "*the Prophet is a Fool, and the Spiritual Man is mad*" (*New-England Courant*, January 8, 1722, 2).

Admittedly Mather was a difficult man to get along with, prone to incessant moralizing and almost as incessant condemnation. Besides careful analysis, his report on inoculation also suggested that God might hold the town liable for considering the blessing of inoculation "*the Work of the devil*" (*Boston Gazette*, October 30, 1721, 2–3). But Mather at least understood the danger of harsh words. In a statement released in January 1722 on behalf of Boston's clergy, he urged that "we should not *Unchristianly* Censure and Condemn one another [over the matter], but preserve a due *Esteem* and Veneration for each other." Bostonians should instead "*Unite* in all those things which tend to promote the *Common Good*." Calling for "*Civil* Conversation," he wrote plaintively that he believed people could disagree about inoculation "without declaring themselves *Open* Enemies to one another" (Mather 1722, 14).

As the smallpox epidemic slowed in early 1722, the *Courant* grew less combative. Ironically, however, the public's white-hot anger over inoculation that spurred the paper's harshness had also protected it from official oversight. As tempers cooled over the next year, Massachusetts legislators twice turned on James Franklin. The first of these incidents came in June 1722 over a seemingly innocuous news item. Legislators held Franklin in jail until the end of the legislative session almost a month later.

Not surprisingly the second, more serious, intervention also came during a time of particular difficulties. By the end of 1722, Massachusetts governor Samuel Shute had grown so weary of the province's political problems (including dealing with a lower house led by a man who considered him a "blockhead") that the executive left the colony without warning to carry his complaints directly to London (Lustig 1999, 910).

Once again, crisis energized the *Courant*. Its January 14, 1723, issue began with an essay condemning religious hypocrisy. Strong religious principles, it warned, should be suspected. They often served as mere covers for immoral behavior. The piece grudgingly conceded that religion was "the *principal thing*"—but also declared "too much of it is worse than none at all." What seems an imitation of Mather's writing style mocking the minister's earlier praise for the governor followed, an item seemingly calling the people of Massachusetts foolish. A third piece criticized the legislature's appointment of an English agent to defend the colony, one of the few times that the newspaper directly addressed public policy outside the inoculation controversy (*New-England Courant*, January 14, 1723, 1–2).

Already on the defensive after the governor's shocking departure, legislators responded harshly. The two houses created a joint committee on the very day the paper appeared. After discussion, the legislators forbade Franklin from publishing any piece without the express consent of the secretary of the province. The final pronouncement particularly focused on religious issues, declaring,

> That the tendency of the said Paper is to Mock Religion. . . . That the Reverend and Faithful Ministers of the Gospel are injuriously reflected on: His Majesty's Government Affronted: The Peace and good Order of His Majesty's Subjects of this Province disturbed.
>
> (Journals, *1919–1990, 4: 205, 208–209*)

Massachusetts leaders still saw the province as a family, a corporate entity in which internal criticism must be controlled. Yet most legislators also opposed requiring permission for publication. The lower house in 1721 had rejected Governor Shute's request for just such a plan of licensing for all Massachusetts publications. It is a sign of the *Courant's* problematic standing that that so many provincial leaders became convinced such a remedy was needed.

Not surprisingly, Franklin remained defiant. He continued to prepare his issue for the following Monday. On Sunday morning, Chief Justice Samuel Sewall, a member of the legislative committee that had considered the *Courant*, awoke to find a note in his doorway he considered a "Virulent libel" (Sewall 1973, 2: 1004–1005). The next day the *Courant* placed two psalms condemning unjust judges on its front page. It was a clear expression of contempt. Not surprisingly, Sewall considered the paper libel and the libelous newspaper intertwined. Franklin went into hiding.

Less than three weeks later, Benjamin Franklin's name first appeared as publisher of the *New-England Courant*. It was a transparent ruse, asking people to believe that the 16-year-old young brother of the publisher, someone who still lived with him, and who had been apprenticed to him until a few days before, now controlled the newspaper. But the ploy was seemingly sufficient to dissuade legislators from further action, a decision perhaps aided by the calming message of the first issue under Benjamin's name. The very next day James Franklin turned himself in and posted bail. The grand jury that considered the case in May refused to indict.

The "Rancour and bitterness" the *Courant* decried (and helped encourage) within the community at large increasingly extended into James Franklin's household as well. Harsh words, even beatings, soured his relationship with his apprentice. The younger man's success in pleading his case before their father only made things worse. Benjamin fled Boston in September 1723 (Franklin 1723).

With these early experiences, both public and private, it is not surprising that Benjamin Franklin became an argumentative young man, someone who, as his famously combative English contemporary Dr. Samuel Johnson noted of himself, "talked for victory" (Boswell 1936, 7). Franklin's adolescent debates with his friend John Collins encouraged what the *Autobiography* called his "disputatious turn." The "abrupt Contradiction and positive Argumentation" he began with, however, went only so far. Franklin soon added a new conversational technique. His Socratic method used clever questioning and people's own words to trick them into contradicting their own arguments. Although the approach did not immediately seem as dogmatic and harsh as his earlier tactics, it continued, as Franklin later noted, to seek conversational "Victories" (Franklin 1986, 11, 13).

As he grew older, however, Franklin reconsidered. Deciding that argument had no place in conversation, he rejected contradicting people in public. The air of "modest Diffidence" he had developed for his Socratic questioning became central to his adult self-presentation (Franklin 1986, 13).

This rethinking reinforced a broader shift in Franklin's relationships. As an adolescent he had shunned sociable activities. He turned to vegetarianism in part so he could eat by himself, avoiding interactions with both his co-workers and the host family James paid to feed his household. Benjamin similarly skipped church services in part so he could enjoy solitude in the printing office. Even after moving to London a year after running away to Philadelphia, Franklin continued to resist other people's expectations. Beginning work in the composing room of a printing office, he discovered that the new man on the job was expected to contribute to a round of drinks. Franklin refused to pay the relatively small sum, arguing that he had already worked elsewhere in the print shop. He persisted for two or three weeks even as co-workers sabotaged his work. Franklin finally gave in and he became a popular figure in the room. He later commented that he had become "convinc'd of the Folly of being on ill Terms with those one is to live with continually" (Franklin 1986, 37). It was a lesson he and his brother never learned while they were together.

Franklin had perhaps not yet begun to see accepting his co-workers' demands as much more than a means of easing hostility. As he moved back to Philadelphia in 1726 and became an independent artisan with his own print shop in 1728, however, he applied the principle of attending to other people's concerns more systematically. The apprentice had struggled to expand his freedom from his brother and the limitations of his status. Franklin had then "found delight" in "entangling" people in arguments. But such triumphs offered little help in a broader world where success required continuing connections (Franklin 1986, 13).

Franklin clearly considered the lessons he had learned about conversation very important. His account of this shift in the *Autobiography* (1986, 13–14) carefully instructs readers in civility, conversation, and influence. Franklin encourages people to speak in "Terms of modest diffidence" and avoid the "Air of Positiveness." He advises against terms such as "*Certainly*" and "*undoubtedly*," instead suggesting formulations such as "It appears to me, or I should think it so or so for such and such Reasons, or I imagine it to be so." This "Habit" of expressing opinions cautiously, he notes, "has been of great Advantage to me."

By contrast, Franklin warns, a bold assertion "seldom fails to disgust." It "tends to create Opposition," discouraging people from listening carefully and provoking other people (other young Franklins) to offer "Contradictions." Even worse, it led "modest sensible Men, who do not love Disputation" to avoid sharing their own wisdom. Dogmatism, he declares, fulfills none of the goals of conversation. It did not serve "to *inform*, or to be *informed*, to *please* or to *persuade*" (Franklin 1986, 14).

Franklin's growing awareness of the need to build connections and influence shaped his early experiences as an independent publisher. In London he had published a philosophical piece denying free will and the existence of virtue, a work of such unsparing logic and inattention to public concerns that he later labeled it one of the major errors of his life. His 1729 case for expanding Pennsylvania's paper currency, published less than a year after starting his own business, followed a new pattern. Franklin cautiously titled his new work a "modest enquiry" and began by stating that he "sincerely desire[d] to be acquainted with the Truth" if he was wrong (Franklin 1729). As with his new conversational practices, the goal was to be not just correct but also convincing.

Franklin also adopted a new attitude toward personal attacks. The *Courant's* authors regularly traded in grievance and mockery. The *Pennsylvania Gazette* rejected such reflection on individuals. When Franklin returned from a long journey in 1733, he discovered that a piece published in his absence had mocked the author and publisher of an item in a rival paper. Franklin announced that he had not approved the article. Franklin's alter ego Poor Richard explicitly rejects divisive loyalties later in the issue: "I'm not High-Church, nor Low-Church, nor Tory, nor Whig" ("*To all, whom it may concern*," 1733, 6). The elder Franklin's newspaper had helped open up the American press to different perspectives and sometimes to early English defenses of a free press. But the younger's enterprises, including his Junto, the club of young aspiring Philadelphians, better represent the ideal of a public sphere where policy matters and government actions are discussed rationally and apart from relationships of power (Habermas 1989).

The differences between the two Franklins also appear in their responses to more established printers. James's newspaper mocked rival newspaper publisher and postmaster Philip Musgrave as "*butter-headed*" (*New-England Courant*, January 22, 1722, 3). Benjamin took a different and more productive approach in his quest to become the government's official printer. When Franklin noticed that his rival had printed an address from the assembly to the governor in "a coarse blundering manner," the young artisan quickly prepared a new version "elegantly and correctly," distributing one to each legislator. Franklin received his first significant government contract as a result—and was better positioned to become official printer the following year (Franklin 1986, 51).

But Franklin wanted more than business success. He also aspired to shape policy—and even to improve society itself. As he wrote to Cotton Mather's son in the 1780s, "I have always set a greater Value on the Character of a Doer of Good, than on any other kind of Reputation," an attitude he attributed largely to his early reading of Mather's piece subtitled "Essays [that is, attempts or plans] to Do Good" (Franklin 1784). Franklin may have seen his letter as an implicit apology for the harshness of the *Courant* (including perhaps his own adolescent "Silence Dogood" essays), a matter of doing justice to the main target of his brother's paper. He had in any case long since repudiated James's view of inoculation, supporting the practice strongly in his Philadelphia newspaper.

Like Mather, Franklin became what was then called a "projector" (and today might be termed a "social entrepreneur"). Beginning in the 1730s he proposed and brought to fruition an extraordinary series of attempts to improve life in Philadelphia, in Pennsylvania, and in America as a whole. He helped address local problems, such as crime, fire, and dirty streets. He helped create institutions, such as a library, a hospital, a college, and a scientific society, that extended across all of British America. Franklin even took the lead in creating Pennsylvania's first military organization, at a time when its government was still run by pacifist Quakers.

Franklin's own "Essays to Do Good" relied heavily on the lessons he had learned about social interactions. As he noted in his *Autobiography*, the modesty he had adopted as a young man served him well in the public realm. It helped "persuade Men into Measures" he had "engag'd in promoting." The passage goes on to quote the poet Alexander Pope's recommendation that people "speak, tho' sure, with seeming Diffidence" (Franklin 1986, 14).

Franklin's reference was particularly appropriate. Pope was the preeminent poet of the culture of politeness that had developed around the turn of the eighteenth century. The *Essay on Criticism* that Franklin quoted appeared in 1711, only six years after his birth. Pope's relevance came not only in his meticulously crafted couplets but also in his celebration of these emerging ideals. The term "polite" had long meant smooth or polished. It now came to refer to humans themselves and to their relationships—to interactions in which participants treated each other thoughtfully and respectfully (Bullock 2017). In the same passage, Pope (1711) also observed that truth itself was often "disapprov'd" if it was not presented properly: "Blunt truths" caused "more mischief than nice falsehoods."

As the son of a soap-boiler, Franklin lacked the extended training in proper behavior and self-presentation given proper English gentlemen and increasingly some American colonials. Franklin was born in 1705, just after his fellow-Bostonian Jonathan Belcher, son of a council member, returned from an extended trip to continental Europe with a journal declaring that "A man without travelling is not altogether unlike a Rough diamond": "Unpolisht and without beauty." The young Franklin had to make do without travel to German courts or the dancing and fencing instruction Belcher later provided for his son (Bullock 2017, 2).

But being "well-bred" was not limited solely to the wealthy. The term then spoke of training rather than bloodlines. Franklin learned these values as an adolescent through intensive study of the *Spectator*, the influential London periodical from 1711 and 1712 whose essays conveyed polite ideals in elegantly casual prose. In his *Autobiography* Franklin (1986, 11–12) describes this painstaking process of taking apart and rewriting these pieces primarily as an exercise in writing. But imitating essays necessarily required attention to their ideals as well—to the "good-nature, compassion, and humanity" they embodied as well as taught. Franklin may even have studied and rewritten the 1711 essay that not only celebrated these values but also warned about the "dreadful spirit of division" that had in recent years made Britons "furious zealots," or "barbarians toward one another," difficulties he might have recognized in Boston as well (Addison and Steele 1891, July 24, 1711, 1: 441). In the new life he developed in Philadelphia he increasingly attempted to avoid such behavior himself and discourage it in others.

In 1749, only two years after he retired from his printing business and began his political career, Franklin expressed these lessons in a pamphlet advocating an improved college curriculum. After addressing such learned topics as the relative value of ancient versus modern languages, Franklin concluded by suggesting the whole should be presented with continual attention to "the Foundation of what is called Good Breeding": a broader benevolence "which shows itself in *searching for* and *seizing* every Opportunity *to serve* and *to oblige*" (Franklin 1749). "The polite Man," he noted more succinctly the following year, "aims at pleasing *others*" (Franklin 1750).

As Franklin matured, he encouraged civil discourse in even larger spheres, not only in one of the world's great centers of culture and politeness but also in one of the most significant series of meetings in American political history. In each he deliberately drew on and shared the lessons of polite interactions that he had learned in his young adulthood.

Of course, neither Franklin nor American society as a whole lived up to these high ideals. Even at its most influential, politeness remained an aspirational ideal. In an essay published in 1755 Franklin complained about "*Palatine Boors*" "swarm[ing]" into Pennsylvania, a term perhaps meant merely to refer to German peasants, a common usage in the period (Franklin 1755). But the word by that time also implied the lack of refinement and polite manners. Franklin removed the passage from later printings of the piece, but the incautious insult still stung. His political opponents used the words against him in the Pennsylvania's harsh 1764 election (Gleason 1961, 78–81).

In May 1775 Franklin returned to Philadelphia after nearly two decades spent primarily in England. By the end of the following year, he was on his way to France, seeking to nurture its support for the Revolution—and turning its secret aid into formal alliance. Operating in Paris itself, whose inhabitants were widely viewed as the most polite on earth, would have been daunting. Yet, despite his shaky French, Franklin's long attention to politeness proved ideally suited for such an assignment.

Franklin's social acumen—what might be called his emotional intelligence—encouraged his enormous popularity in the capital city and beyond. He charmed the leading figures of Parisian society, including the women whose salons encouraged refined and high-minded conversation. These social interactions were particularly important because influencing France's absolutist monarchy, with no tradition of a strong legislature, required strong relationships with major figures in the aristocracy and the government. Franklin's careful management culminated first in a formal treaty of alliance and then in the French acceptance of a peace treaty favoring American over French interests. His work remains arguably the greatest series of diplomatic successes in American history.

John Adams, however, was less impressed. Serving alongside Franklin in Paris, he chided the senior diplomat for not representing American interests forcefully enough. Expressions of gratitude to the French were all well and good, even necessary. But (as Franklin summarized Adams's position) "a little apparent Stoutness and greater Air of Independence & Boldness in our Demands" were also required. French officials needed to understand that supporting America was in their interest, a benefit rather than a sacrifice (Franklin 1780).

Franklin disagreed. Talk of self-interest, he contended, diminished the sense of virtuous benevolence that the French believed underlay their relationship with America, the generosity of friendship rather than narrow calculations of advantage. Franklin told the president of the Continental Congress that he too sought "to procure what Advantages I can for our Country," but he would do so "by endeavoring to please this Court" (Franklin 1780). Adams and at least one American legislator took this phrase amiss. But Franklin undoubtedly saw himself as displaying what he had called a central characteristic of politeness, concern for "pleasing *others*" (Franklin 1750). As he had taught in *Poor Richard*, "a Person of good Breeding . . . should make it his chief Aim to be well with all" (Franklin 1757).

Though Franklin was clearly slowing down by the time he served as a member of the Constitutional Convention in 1787, his support for civil discourse remained undiminished. Two of the four formal remarks he prepared for delivery directly address the issue. His concluding call for unity not only warned against claiming "infallibility" but also advocated greater "Respect" for other people. Delegates should not be as oblivious as the French woman who wondered why "I meet with no body but myself that's *always* in the right" (Franklin 1787b). Franklin's fullest attention to the subject, however, came several months earlier as the convention addressed its most divisive issue, the question of representation by states or population that nearly upended the convention.

Franklin's proposed solution to the problem attracted no support, but he offered a compelling case for working together—and a clear statement of the main lessons he had learned in a lifetime of seeking civil discourse. Not surprisingly he warned against "Positiveness and Warmth" (i.e., anger): "Declaration of a fix'd Opinion" would "neither enlighten nor convince us." Instead, he declared, "Harmony and Union are extremely necessary for "promoting and securing the common Good." Delegates were there, he reminded them, "to *consult*," rather than "to *contend*" (Franklin 1787a).

Note

1 Franklin's writings, including the *Autobiography*, are available in easily searchable form at http://franklinpapers.org/franklin. All citations of Franklin's writings, unless otherwise noted, are from that site, which does not provide page numbers.

Bibliography

Addison, Joseph, and Richard Steele. 1891. *The Spectator: A New Edition, Reproducing the Original Text*, Vol. 3. Edited by Henry Morley. London: G. Routledge & Sons.

Beeman, Richard R. 2009. *Plain, Honest Men: The Making of the American Constitution*. New York: Random House.

Boston News-Letter, August 28, 1721

Boswell, James. 1936. *Boswell's Journal of a Tour to the Hebrides with Samuel Johnson, LL.D.* Edited by Frederick A. Pottle and Charles H. Bennett. New York: The Viking Press.

Bullock, Steven C. 2017. *Tea Sets and Tyranny: The Politics of Politeness in Early America*. Philadelphia: University of Pennsylvania Press.

Franklin, Benjamin. 1723. "The Printer to the Reader." February 11, 1723.

Franklin, Benjamin. 1729. *A Modest Inquiry into the Nature and Necessity of a Paper-Currency*. Philadelphia: Printed and Sold at the New Printing-Office, near the Market.

Franklin, Benjamin. 1749. *Proposals Relating to the Education of Youth in Pennsylvania*. Philadelphia.

Franklin, Benjamin. 1750. "Rules for Making Oneself a Disagreeable Companion," *Pennsylvania Gazette*, November 15, 1750.

Franklin, Benjamin. 1755. "Observations Concerning the Increase of Mankind." Printed in [William Clarke], *Observations On the Late and Present Conduct of the French, With Regard to Their Encroachments Upon the British Colonies in North America. . . . To Which Is Added, Wrote by Another Hand; Observations Concerning the Increase of Mankind, Peopling of Countries, &c.* Boston, MA: S. Kneeland.

Franklin, Benjamin. 1757. *Poor Richard Improved: Being an Almanack and Ephemeris . . . for the Year of Our Lord 1757*. Philadelphia: Franklin and David Hall.

Franklin, Benjamin. 1780. To Samuel Huntington, August 9, 1780.

Franklin, Benjamin. 1784. To Samuel Mather, May 12, 1784.

Franklin, Benjamin. 1787a. "Convention Speech on Proportionate Representation," June 11, 1787.

Franklin, Benjamin. 1787b. "Speech in the Convention on the Constitution," [September 17, 1787].

Franklin, Benjamin. 1986. *Benjamin Franklin's Autobiography*. Edited by J. A. Leo Lemay and P. M. Zall. New York: W. W. Norton.

Gleason, J. Philip. 1961. "A Scurrilous Colonial Election and Franklin's Reputation." *William and Mary Quarterly* 18 (1): 68–84.

Habermas, Jurgen. 1989. *The Structural Transformation of the Public Sphere: An Inquiry Into a Category of Bourgeois Society*. Translated by Thomas Burger with Frederick Lawrence. Cambridge, MA: The MIT Press.

Jefferson, Thomas. 1808. To Thomas Jefferson Randolph, November 24, 1808. Retrieved from founders.archive.gov.

Journals of the House of Representatives of Massachusetts. 1923. v.4 (1722–1723). Boston, MA: Massachusetts Historical Society.

Lustig, Mary Lou. 1999. "Shute, Samuel." In *American National Biography*, Vol. 19. New York: Oxford University Press, 909–911.

[Mather, Cotton]. 1721. "A Faithful Account of What Has Occur'd Under the Late Experiments of Small-Pox Managed and Governed in the Way of Inoculation." *Boston Gazette*, October 30, 1721, 2–3.

[Mather, Cotton]. 1722. *A Vindication of the Ministers of Boston, From the Abuses & Scandals, Lately Cast Upon Them, in Diverse Printed Papers. By Some of Their People.* Boston, MA: B. Green, for Samuel Gerrish.

Mather, Cotton. 1912, "Diary of Cotton Mather, 1709–1724." *Massachusetts Historical Society Collections*, 7th series, Vol. 8. Boston, MA: for the Society.

Pope, Alexander. 1711. *Essay on Criticism* (1711), Part III.

Sewall, Samuel. 1973. *The Diary of Samuel Sewall, 1674–1729.* Edited by M. Halsey Thomas. New York: Farrar, Straus and Giroux.

The Spectator, no. 125, July 24, 1711.

"*To All, Whom It May Concern to Know R. S.*" 1733. *Pennsylvania Gazette*, November 16, 1733.

Tourtellot, Arthur. B. 1977. *Benjamin Franklin, the Shaping of Genius: The Boston Years.* Garden City, NY: Doubleday.

11

ENABLING CIVIL DISCOURSE

Creating Civic Space and Resources for Democratic Discussion

Timothy J. Shaffer

In another edited volume on civility, published 15 years ago, Christine Sistare wrote that

> Civility, civic virtue, tolerance, and sociological unity have been the subjects of considerable discussion in recent years, and their purported demise has been the subject of much lament. In both popular media and academic publications, social commentators of varied political persuasions have argued over the extent to which these social goods have declined in modern liberal societies, the causes of their decline, and the very meaning of the terms.
>
> *(2004, vii)*

Sistare's concern about the deterioration of civility and the decline of public life rings true today—arguably even more than was the case at that time. As has been noted throughout the chapters in this book, our contemporary climate highlights the ways in which we are challenged to engage perspectives, experiences, and, fundamentally, persons different from our own. With a civil war and other deep fissures in our past, we ought to acknowledge the long history of discourse and action, sometimes civil and sometimes not.

At the heart of civil discourse, and civil *discord*, is an essential wrestling with civic identity. In Western societies such as the United States, this conflict reflects a tension between two deeply held competing public philosophies that can be described in simplistic terms as individualism and communitarianism. E. J. Dionne captured these dueling sentiments well: "American history is defined by an irrepressible and ongoing tension between two core values: our love of individualism and our reverence for community" (Dionne 2012, 4). Scholars and popular commentators alike have highlighted the presence of this pulling at the heart of democratic life and the challenges to preserving or developing it (Dionne 2012; Ehrenberg 1999; Marcus and Hanson 1993; Palmer 2011; Sandel 1996; Sullivan 1982). Interrogating this tension is important because the way we speak of ourselves as citizens and as part of a larger civic identity shapes how we live and engage with others (e.g., Charland 1987). Further, as Russell L. Hanson put it, "when ideas about democracy change, so do the practices of democracy" (1985, 7). The relationship between the way we speak about democracy and the way we engage each other as democratic citizens is of critical importance, especially when we are exploring processes and approaches to civil discourse that shape our collective existence through public discussion.

As I shall seek to demonstrate, discussion about civil society and its aims has long been an essential part of addressing the problems in shared democratic life. The focus of this chapter is on the resources and materials developed around *how to have civil discussions* that were central to an effort of cultivating democratic life starting in the mid-1930s and continuing into the 1940s, a period when many changes were occurring and people were deeply divided about how to address economic failures, environmental degradation, and uncertainty about the continuation of democratic governance (Shaffer 2013, 2014, 2017c, 2018, 2017d). Much of what we know about historical attempts at encouraging civil discourse comes from the writings of organizers and/or commentators on those efforts. However, rarely do we look to the source materials that shaped these discussions.

Civil discourse does not just happen; it is cultivated and encouraged, often relying on institutions and models that afford people opportunities to discuss public issues that tap into the deeper philosophical views that ask people to consider how they see themselves as political actors in relationship with others. We know that civil society has deep roots, with popular and scholarly narratives tracing back to places such as ancient Athens and its agora and the (relatively) more recent New England town halls where one's identity was wrapped up in a collective identity rather than primarily a private one (Bryan 2004; Ehrenberg 1999; Fullinwider 1999; Hall 1998; Qvortrup 2007; Woodruff 2005). For example, writing about the influences on the National Issues Forums Institute and its work convening democratic discussions since the early 1980s, David Mathews notes the influence of the town meeting and the idea that citizens engaging one another about shared public problems should be at the center of American democratic life. As Mathews noted, this is because democracy in the United States is a story that "begins in 1633, not 1787" in large part because citizen-centered political life predated the formalized institutions of American democracy that would come later (Mathews 1988, 1). At the heart of such a civic identity is the actual interaction and engagement of people with one another. The fundamental act of democratic communication speaks to the need to consider public discourse at the center of civil society (Escobar 2011).

But communication shaped by civil discourse is not something that is inherent in the practice of civic life. It is important to recall that

> Civil society is not a panacea. Modernity is strewn with the detritus of civil societies, shipwrecks, such as the Third Republic in France and the Weimar Republic in Germany, whose carcasses came near to suffocating the twentieth century. The discourse of civil society can be as repressive as liberating, legitimating not only inclusion but exclusion.
>
> *(Alexander 2006, 4)*

The challenge we face lies not only in considering the existence of civil society or public discourse but also in thinking about whether those political, cultural, and communicative aspects of public life allow a more civil expression of society to be formed.

The terms used to describe the practices of a civil society have changed over time, however. While we may think of "civility" being a constitutive element of how we ought to engage one another in public life, explicit mention of the term has not always been part of our discussions. For example, Andy Blunden's study of the origins of collective decision making never uses the term "civility" (2016). While other terms such as "deliberation," "discourse," and "discussion" appear, it is a helpful reminder that civility has not been the preferred expression in various times and contexts. Even when we think of civility being analogous to politeness, we find few examples (Bejan 2017; Carter 1998; Davetian 2009; Herbst 2010; Washington 1926; see also Anthony Simon Laden's chapter in this volume). It is a more nuanced and complex term and concept.

For example, attempts in the 1920s to the 1940s to "clean up" how people spoke in public came under the mantle of mental and social hygiene. In both urban and rural contexts, social hygiene was of great importance, especially among youth (Rosenberg 2016, 88–118). Speaking and acting appropriately in public were of great consequence. It was believed that the ability to shape or mold how someone spoke could have broader impacts on how they functioned in society. Many members of the field of speech communication saw the classroom as "not so much a place for improvement in communication as an arena for the remodeling or 'adjustment' of personality" (Cohen 1994, xii). Education was playing a crucial role in preparing people, particularly youth, for public life.

The centrality of mental hygiene was built on the notion that through proper management, one could maintain and/or improve mental health as was done with physical health. As Cohen (1994) put it,

> The responsibility for maintaining mental health, however, was not limited to the ministrations of physicians. Rather, many elements of society were involved in the search for mental health. The schools and the family

bore special responsibility for insuring that we had healthy minds as well as healthy bodies.

(119)

A critical element to this view of a healthy person was how they communicated. More than simply being able to speak, communication was increasingly viewed through the lens of group discussion (Shaffer 2017a).

With this as a backdrop, the emergence of the discussion movement within the fields of communication and adult education strikes an intriguing balance between the idea of having an appropriate disposition and way of being in the world and the idea that a healthy society is shaped by the opportunity for people to engage in robust discourse in order to understand and address shared problems (Shaffer 2017a). John Dewey proclaimed that "democracy has to be born anew every generation, and education is its midwife" ([1916] 2008, 139). He spoke to the actionable steps necessary to ensure that democratic practices and institutions would continue to exist and, ideally, flourish. Dewey's proclamation serves as the impetus for this chapter. In the following pages, I present three different examples of how discussion-based adult education cultivated in people the democratic practices and habits that created the space for civil discourse and public problem solving. These examples are drawn from the 1930s and the New Deal—a period not often associated with local efforts to cultivate civil discourse among citizens because of the government's attempt to provide expert-driven responses to public problems (Shaffer 2018, 316).

Civil Discourse at the Request of the Federal Government

The election of Franklin D. Roosevelt in 1932 brought about a new vision for American society, which would become known as the "New Deal" (Sloan 2008). The lasting effects of that time include the growth of the federal bureaucracy and its presence in personal and public dimensions of citizens' lives (Conkin 1955; Moreno 2017; Sanders 1982). In particular, the relationship between the government and citizens was dramatically altered in rural America, where farmers faced severe challenges. Many, though not all, farmers looked to the federal government to intervene on their behalf in order to improve their lives economically (Gilbert 2015; Loss 2013; Shaffer 2018).

While the New Deal is commonly viewed as a period in which the government played an outsized role in the lives of ordinary people, one aspect of the Roosevelt administration's efforts to reach people was not a top-down approach but rather an attempt to foster citizen-centered discussion.[1] As part of a larger effort to engage rural people in planning processes about which land should be used for farming and which was submarginal and thus not appropriate for farming, the United States Department of Agriculture (USDA) created a program, initially housed within the Agricultural Adjustment Administration and later within the Bureau of Agricultural Economics, that emphasized the use of small-group discussion to help citizens understand the economic and social issues facing rural communities (Shaffer 2013, 2016, 2017c, 2018a, 2017d, 2018b). The voice of citizens and the role of group discussion were to be "one of the major pillars of national agricultural policy" (Gilbert 2015, 146).

There had been significant interest in the idea that public discussion was central to democratic life during the first decades of the twentieth century. This interest was embodied most notably in the work of John Studebaker through the Des Moines forums and later the Federal Forum Project (Hilton 1981; Keith 2007; Mattson 1998). His championing of local discussion in neighborhood schools created "opportunities for public discussion and . . . education for and in citizenship" (Studebaker and Cartwright 1936, 19). Studebaker went on to state that

> I feel that a democracy must provide for open and free discussion of all public problems, stimulate the counselling of the citizens in group discussions, encourage the clash of opinion in the open market, and thus prepare the people for intelligent exercise of power.
>
> *(Studebaker and Cartwright 1936, 19)*

His experiments in Des Moines and later work as commissioner of education in the Department of the Interior stand as signposts in the development of public forums and discussion in democracy (Keith 2007).

New Deal–era writers and USDA administrators emphasized that what they were doing was nothing new; in a fundamental way, there had always been groups of people engaging in public discussion (Judson and Judson 1937; Shaffer 2017a, 2017b). As Lyman and Ellen Judson noted, "Group discussion is not new. Essentially, it is as old as the councils of the cavemen. However, in the development of its technics and the applications of its methods, it is a product of our present century" (1937, 9). Since the turn of the twentieth century, public discussion received great interest from many parts of the country, in both urban and rural settings (Coleman 1915; Keith 2007; Keith and Cossart 2012; Meyers 2012; Overstreet and Overstreet 1938). Shifting populations from a rural majority to an "urban nation" alongside the "rise of the new mass-production-consumption economy," as George Mowry put it, helped inspire interest among farmers and urban dwellers alike regarding their futures and what role they would play in the transformations of the American economy as well as culture and life (Mowry 1965, 3). There was a broader public discussion taking place about how best to address and respond to changes in the economic, social, and political realms that raised questions and fears about the future of democracy in the face of fascism and other forms of political association (Katznelson 2013; Rosen 1937; Toynbee 1932). Economics and politics were changing, and one response was to encourage civic adult education and public discussion about the problems *of* and *in* democracy.[2]

Beginning in late 1934, the USDA set out to build on the energy of Studebaker as well as interest in the group discussion method in general. The Program Study and Discussion (PSD) Section (and later Division) within the USDA created opportunities for primarily rural people to engage in discussion about a range of topics, including taxes, farm ownership, soil conservation, imports, and exports, as well as tensions between urban and rural communities.[3] What distinguished the USDA's efforts from other discussion models was that government administrators shaping this effort saw discussion being an essential element of creating an "entirely new structure of decision making that would involve ordinary citizens in the day-to-day business" of governance (Jewett 2013, 405).

Guides to Discussion: Training Materials for Civil Discourse

Following the lead of the USDA regarding the development of discussion programs across the United States, land-grant universities through the Cooperative Extension Service brought to life a nationwide experiment of democratic group discussion. Universities dedicated Extension positions to organize these efforts, utilizing an established network to encourage democratic discussion among citizens, especially in rural areas. In addition to developing discussion guides on a range of topics, the USDA produced methodological resources for those seeking to convene group discussions in their communities.

Used by Extension agents and others who wanted to organize discussion groups in rural communities, the USDA produced *Discussion: A Brief Guide to Methods* as an introduction to the idea of group discussion. It was created through a collaborative process that saw many revisions, involving discussion experts, government administrators, and on-the-ground practitioners using the guides. As the guide noted, the USDA saw this document as a "response to an increasing number of requests for guidance of this character" (United States Department of Agriculture, the Extension Service, and Agricultural Adjustment Administration 1935, i). Presented in non-technical language, the publication outlined three distinct ways that people could organize and facilitate discussion—forums, panels, and discussion groups—with an emphasis on discussion groups. Additional materials would be produced, pointing to very practical matters of how to organize and conduct forums (United States Department of Agriculture, the Extension Service, and Agricultural Adjustment Administration 1936). These different approaches to engaging people in public discussion were addressed in multiple resources from the period (Ely 1937; Judson and Judson 1937), in addition to resources highlighting the benefits of both debate and discussion while noting distinct differences between them (Bureau of Agricultural Economics 1942).

Discussion: A Brief Guide to Methods offered "advantages" for the use of public discussion in contrast to other methods for presenting information to groups. As

the guide noted, discussion methods offered several advantages for the consideration of fundamental issues and policies. The guide suggested two major advantages
inherent in the discussion approach.

1. They give opportunity to the individual to think and to express his thoughts.
    Through the give and take of what is said in a discussion group, the individual
    acquires the ability:

    a. to look behind familiar phrases and see if they have meaning.
    b. to analyze policies as stated by the groups or interests putting them
        forward.
    c. to formulate and express his own point of view on issues and policies.

2. At the same time, the discussion method contributes to the enlightenment of
    the public and to the civic vitality of the community:

    a. by affording an opportunity to its citizens to become active participants
        in public affairs instead of being mere passive recipients of radio pro-
        grams, speeches, lectures, newspaper articles, and the like.
    b. by opening national problems to serious public consideration. This
        grounding of local, regional, and national issues and policies in the minds
        of the people is indispensable to the functioning of a democracy (United
        States Department of Agriculture et al. 1935, 1–2).

The guide emphasized the importance of being able to get beyond the superficial understanding of issues. As it noted, "The primary consideration in the development of discussion is to obtain from members of groups the expression of a
variety of genuine differences of viewpoint" (United States Department of Agriculture et al. 1935, 2). To get groups to have enough diversity, it was essential to
convene a group large enough (fewer than ten was looked down upon) but not so
large (less than 30 to 35 people was preferred) that people could not have an open
discussion. One of the state publications that was produced as part of this national
effort by the USDA put the ideal number for a group discussion at 18 people (Taff
1935, 9). In some circumstances, there were questions about how diverse a group
must be in order to be useful, or even if it was helpful to have a range of ages (e.g.,
including youth and adults in the same discussion) (Gemmell 1935). There were
instances when discussion groups would be classified as enclave discussions rather
than being composed of diverse perspectives and/or experiences. The tensions
and trade-offs of having diverse groups and like-minded groups talking about
issues were present in this work.

In the following years, the USDA created additional resources in response
to the developing interest in group discussion in both urban and rural settings
(Bureau of Agricultural Economics 1942; Gould 1942; United States Department
of Agriculture, the Extension Service, and Agricultural Adjustment Administration 1937). The need for resources and training regarding discussion methods,

and not simply relying on the Extension agent who was a content specialist for the particular issue(s) being discussed, was realized by those attempting to train individuals and communities in these methods (Wileden 1935, 3). In 1937, the USDA published *What Is the Discussion Leader's Job?* Superseding the earlier publications that offered introductions to discussion methods and how to organize forums, this third USDA discussion resource outlined further practical matters about how to plan for civil discussions and, among other benefits, how to create opportunities for people to learn to "listen to and think through divergent views and cooperat[e] in finding common ground between them" (United States Department of Agriculture, The Extension Service, and Agricultural Adjustment Administration 1937, 4). The benefit of a discussion leader making people feel at ease in order to discuss public issues should not be simplified. As the guide noted, "The wording of topics is important. . . . The question form is often desirable, particularly if the question is so phrased that it cannot be quickly disposed of by a 'Yes' or 'No' answer, or a list" (United States Department of Agriculture, The Extension Service, and Agricultural Adjustment Administration 1937, 9). This document would continue to be revised over the next decade of the PSD's existence, pointing to the important role of having someone organize and lead public discussion in order to accomplish the desired impact of civil discourse.

The desire to retrieve aspects of the town meeting or county cracker barrel greatly influenced the discussion movement efforts, especially those within the USDA trying to help organize study and discussion groups in rural communities (Hill 1935; Wilson 1937). Carl F. Taeusch, head of the PSD, talked about a loss of the "art of conversation" and the unfortunate reality that "the individual farmer no longer has time to stop between corn rows to think about public questions." Taeusch posited, "Can we restore this lost art or find a good substitute for it?" (Taeusch 1940, 43). By developing materials that helped people understand different methods for engaging in public discussion, the USDA played a critical role in fostering discussion and providing additional resources to those who were already using discussion methods (e.g., as was the case in Wisconsin). A bibliography was included in the USDA's guide, thus "enabl[ing] leaders of public discussion to go into the question of methods at greater length" (United States Department of Agriculture et al. 1935, 9). Through the partnership with land-grant universities and Extension, training opportunities flourished for Extension agents and other community leaders to become familiar with discussion methods and to determine how best to integrate discussion into existing organizational meetings. Farm organizations as well as informal community clubs became sites for civil discourse through the use of discussion methods.

In addition to what the USDA produced, universities across the country created similar materials to encourage civil discussion. New Mexico College of Agriculture and Mechanic Arts (now New Mexico State University) published Extension Circular No. 144 with the title "Discussion Methods," explaining the value of group discussion, the role of a discussion leader, how to organize such discussions, and challenges—namely, how to ensure that leaders do not take over a group's own discussion (Hollinger and Hawk 1936). The publication began by noting that "It takes more study and thought to plan to be a good citizen than it does in many cases to make a good living" (Hollinger and Hawk 1936, 2). By developing a resource for 4-H clubs and other youth organizations in addition to adult groups, such as rural women's clubs and farmers' organizations, the guide for discussion methods from New Mexico Extension helped to create a culture of open and frank discussion. Rules for discussion offered a framework for engaging others in a way that stimulated individual thinking while cultivating an openness among members. The rules offer a sense of how group discussion was approached (Hollinger and Hawk 1936, 6):

1. All discussion is informal. Greetings, personal remarks and jokes are in order as long as they are brief and incidental.
2. Responsibility should be placed on the group in that they as a group are doing whatever is done.
3. Questions which lead to discussion should be asked.
4. Everyone should be encouraged to participate in the discussion.
5. The progress of the discussion should be pointed out at desirable places in order to lead to the next logical step.
6. Group discussion is not an attempt to come to hard and fast conclusions. It is more an attempt to make problems more understandable and thus furnish a basis for individuals to come to their own conclusions.
7. Discussion should suggest lines of follow-up activity. It should encourage reading and discussion between meetings.
8. As discussion groups progress there will be more need for additional information either from books, magazines, or an expert on the subject to be discussed.
9. Regular attendance at discussion meetings is important for the steady growth of the individual.

The regular and routine meeting of discussion groups allowed each discussion to build on previous discussions, creating opportunities for participants to explore issues in greater depth, especially if the topic being discussed required further background reading and preparation.

Similarly, in Iowa, Paul C. Taff of Extension organized discussion groups across the state with the goal of bringing together people with different experiences and views. As he put it in a report on experiments in group discussion, "it is thought advisable to have a variety of opinions and interests represented in each group. A group with the same background, same training and same general interests often will have about the same ideas to contribute" (Taff, n.d., 7). The desire for diverse voices was essential to discussion groups, making the discussion of national, statewide, and local issues something that should be done with a group representative of a range of perspectives. The selection of the discussion leader, according to Taff, was to be carefully done to ensure fairness and equity. As he put it, "care should be used to have leaders who are not prejudiced or biased in favor of any certain policies or view points" (Taff, n.d., 12). With a leader shepherding the conversation, the discussion could include all perspectives. As he stated in an article in the *Iowa Farm Economist*, "Close observation leads one to believe that there is no reason why any fair-minded group cannot be brought together for discussion, no matter what difference of opinion may exist among individuals" (Taff 1935, 9–10). If people were at least open to discussion, the experiences from Iowa and elsewhere pointed to a method and approach that afforded opportunities for diverse citizens to speak with and listen to others who might share their views—and to respectfully engage those with whom they didn't.

In addition to training community leaders in discussion methods, Extension agents also introduced young people to discussion methods and sought to give them opportunities to develop the necessary skills to facilitate small-group discussion. Extension agents worked not only to help facilitate discussions among rural people who were established in their social, cultural, and economic ways but also to reach out to young people (who were presumably less set in their ways) with the hope of encouraging and fostering civil discussion about the issues that mattered to them. As it was put by Eugene Merritt, an Extension economist,

> If the majority of young people in any county are to be reached, they will have to be trained to handle their own discussion. The extension worker, therefore, must know not only how to lead a discussion but how to teach others so they can become leaders. Where the term "leader" is used in this circular it refers to a member of the farm young people's group. If young people are to develop skill in the use of the discussion method they should be given every opportunity to participate in all its phases.
>
> *(Merritt 1937, 6)*

Familiarity with discussion methods was a critical first step to encouraging people to participate in civil discussions with friends and neighbors. Additionally, being trained as a leader opened up the possibility that more individuals—young and old—could take up the important role of organizing discussions on a range of topics. Knowing how to organize and facilitate a group was one thing. Being able to utilize resources for discussion that allowed diverse groups and individuals to talk with one each other was another.

Discussion Group Pamphlets: Topical Resources for Civil Discourse

In addition to materials used for preparing people to engage in civil discourse, it is helpful to look at the actual discussion materials used by citizens in these discussions. As part of the USDA's effort to encourage small-group discussion, the Farmer Discussion Group Pamphlet series was composed of guides on a range of topics for discussion (Gilbert 2015, 261–263). Each year, especially in the winter months, when farmers had more time to engage in such activities because of the offseason, the USDA disseminated discussion materials through Extension agents. The federal government freely produced and distributed tens of thousands of discussion guides. Groups also created their own materials or drew on locally created resources, but many utilized the well-researched and polished guides from the USDA.

Guides presented different perspectives on common issues facing rural communities. While not true for every discussion guide, materials often presented "either/or" framing of issues. Yet, this open approach to the most significant challenges facing farmers and others was not welcomed by everyone. Some farm groups objected to the USDA materials because, as an article in *Wallace's Farmer* stated, "there [wasn't] any answer in the back of the book" offering the approved position by the government.

> Nowhere do these pamphlets try to say what the "right" answer to each question is. . . . Instead, they merely say that there are half a dozen answers, supported by certain evidence. It is up to the farm groups to go over the various arguments and try to figure out how much sense there is in each of them.
>
> *("No Answers in the Back of the Book,*
> Wallaces' Farmer, *April 13 1935," 1935)*

In a variety of contexts, people had grown accustomed to doing what experts suggested, especially during the New Deal, when the federal government was shaping so much of what was taking place in rural America; civil group discussion offered an alternative to people so that they might come to their own conclusions about the public matters impacting them.

As part of the 1936–1937 season for discussion, the guide "How Do Farm People Live in Comparison with City People?" explored issues that dealt with the differences between rural and urban populations, teasing out the distinctions—and disparities—among citizens. The guide began with the statement, "It is not intended to direct attention to any particular point of view or conclusion, and no statement contained herein should be construed as an official expression of the Department of Agriculture" ("How Do Farm People Live in Comparison With City People?," 1936). M. L. Wilson wrote about the objective of discussion groups being the opportunity for people to make informed decisions. As he put it,

> The object would not be propaganda, not aimed in the direction of bringing people to any specific or "right" conclusions, but rather through an adult educational process to provide them with means of getting facts,

information and opinions which would assist them in reaching intelligent, considered decisions.

(Wilson n.d.)

The goal was to produce materials that could be utilized by people across the country in order to help them think about the growing divide between urban and rural communities, especially as rural communities were experiencing a drain in population to urban centers.

The guide was framed around the issue of standards of living. "How Do Farm People Live in Comparison With City People?" began with a number of questions in response to the issue of disparity in the standard of living for Americans. These included the following:

1. What do you consider the greatest advantage of country life? The greatest disadvantage? Why?
2. What reasons would you give for the great range of living standards in the city? In the country? Are city slums any worse than rural submarginal areas?
3. How do rural schools compare with city schools?
4. How do rural and city medical facilities compare? How many people can afford to use present facilities as much as they need?
5. How can lowest living standards be improved?
6. How closely does the unemployment problem touch city works? Farmers?
7. Where do you think today's farm boys and girls will find jobs? Why?
8. In how many ways are city workers and country workers dependent on one another?

The rest of the 13-page document was structured as a conversational narrative, encouraging discussion participants to reflect on the aforementioned questions by reading about and considering different perspectives as embodied in the voice of fellow citizens. Many guides would evoke an image of farmers chatting with one another over a fence, listening to another viewpoint while also offering one's own voice to the conversation. While the guide was written for an intended audience of rural people, the document took great care to ensure that bias was tempered. In addition to including sections on the appeals of the urban or rural communities, the "brown spots" on both sides of the fence were discussed—making clear the challenges facing both urban and rural people. The guides sought to present the various perspectives on the given issues as plainly as possible and without preference, and "How Do Farm People Live in Comparison With City People?" was no different. This guide took on serious challenges facing citizens, exploring issues of the quality of public schools, housing, employment opportunities, return on production (in factories or on farms), and medical care. The scope of the elements shaping both rural and urban life was found within the document's pages.

For the 1937–1938 discussion season, topics included taxes, insurance, farm finance, and soil conservation. On the heels of the Dust Bowl, issues about the depletion and conservation of soil were of great public interest. The beginning of the guide "Soil Conservation: Who Gains by It?" put the issue this way:

> What do we mean when we say soil conservation? Some people mean stopping soil erosion. They mean keeping the soil where it is, keeping gullies from forming and growing larger, halting wind erosion, or checking the run-off of water; they even advocate, in extreme cases, changing the use of the land from cultivation to grazing, forestry, or recreation.
>
> To other people, soil conservation means stopping soil depletion or leaching, and restoring or building up fertility. They call attention to the fact that crops may deplete the soil by extracting valuable elements. They say that while the soil of some farms may be carried off by wind or water, the readily available plant food in the best soil of some farms may be carried off by the farmers' own trucks in the form of shipments of wheat or potatoes. To them, soil conservation means restoring the elements that past crops have taken out, and planning future farming to cause less wear and tear on the farm.
>
> Still other people say, "It's not a case of either-or, but a case of both-and."
> ("Soil Conservation: Who Gains By It?," 1937, 1)

At the end of the guide a number of questions were posed to the reader. During a time when there was deep division in rural communities about whether and how people were receiving government aid to keep family farms afloat, it was significant that the federal government encouraged vigorous discussion about its work. The questions posed in the guide were as follows:

- Do you think that what a man does with his farm is his own business and nobody else's?
- Do you think that the community, through the Government, should offer farmers:
  - Information on scientific ways to prevent blowing, washing, and leaching of their soil?
  - Benefit payments for following improved practices?
  - Powers to set up a soil conservation district in their neighborhood and vote legally enforceable regulations on themselves?

("Soil Conservation: Who Gains By It?" 1937, 12)

All of the discussion guides presented questions rather than answers. There were often graphs that offered essential factual information for informed discussion, but those convened in grange halls and front rooms of farm houses had to make sense of the information; there were no easy answers, only further questions. The federal government partnered with universities, entities that typically provided expert knowledge to farmers. In this light, the USDA's work with Extension through the PSD was a deviation from the norm for these public institutions—as well as the expectation for citizens involved in the discussion project. Part of the discussion project's demise occurred because of this sense that Extension was to provide expertise on a range of issues rather than simply convene people for discussion.

The Wisconsin Extension Program: Shaping Democratic and Civil Culture

As the federal government partnered with land-grant universities across the country to make the discussion project possible, it tapped into efforts already in existence. One of the most robust examples of public discussion taking place through Extension was in Wisconsin. Starting in the summer of 1932 and continuing through the late 1940s, public discussion became a central element of the University of Wisconsin–Madison Extension program for rural communities. Partnering with the Department of Debating and Public Discussion for the loaning of background materials to people so they could understand an issue as thoroughly as possible, the Rural Sociology Extension staff supported discussion about topics such as taxation in rural areas, marketing of farm products, farm credit, and rural government. Additionally, training people in discussion techniques was of great interest across the state, utilizing the resources made available by the USDA as well as producing many documents for their own localized needs. The investment in staff and other resources makes the University of Wisconsin–Madison an exemplar when it comes to understanding how discussion was spread across the state and then eventually embedded in numerous other programs. One of the people involved with that work eventually wrote a 678-page dissertation on this work, offering an extensive look into the development of a democratic culture based on the idea that people can and should engage one another in meaningful discussion (Andersen 1947).

Capturing the view of those leading this discussion work in Wisconsin, the May 1938 publication of the University of Wisconsin's newsletter from Rural Sociology staff and Extension presented the benefits of participation in public discussion ("The Place of Discussion in Rural Life," 1938, 11):

1. Increases the individuals' understanding of problems discussed.
2. Facilitates the correlation of new knowledge and past learning and experience.
3. Stimulates further study and independent investigation.
4. Develops a critical attitude which demands validation of claims.

5. Promotes tolerance and open-mindedness.
6. Stimulates sense of public responsibility.
7. Develops logical thinking and improves the speaking ability of the average man.
8. Reduces power of emotionalism and prejudice.
9. Trains people in methods of analysis and testing of facts.
10. Builds community spirit and fosters neighborliness.

The understanding that discussion fosters understanding of content as well as of one's neighbors is important, but the process by which that occurs is of critical significance. As the newsletter noted, "tolerance and open-mindedness" and the reduction of "emotionalism and prejudice" were essential elements. People needed to be open to diverse voices and viewpoints, especially if the future prospects for one's community or industry were reliant on people being able to work together on shared concerns.

Clara Lindsley, a librarian at the Waupun Public Library in Waupun, Wisconsin, offers an extended narrative about the experiences of one such discussion group. In her relative straightforward description of a discussion group, she offers insight into how we might attempt to bridge differences and foster civil discourse with those who disagree. To quote her at length (Lindsley 1937),

> Four or five years ago when the depression was at its worst, I saw around me a number of my young friends with more than average mentality, but being unable to find jobs or start or finish college courses, they had too little to do.
>
> To furnish some worthwhile mental occupation for these young people I conceived the idea of starting a little informal discussion group for persons ranging in age from about eighteen to twenty-five. This group met every two weeks throughout two winters, discussing with considerable thought and intelligence various controversial questions.
>
> As times become somewhat better the members of this group either went away to school or found jobs here or elsewhere. The few remaining members of this earlier group with additional men and women constitute the present discussion group which has met regularly and constantly winter and summer, since its inception.
>
> It is, of course, public and open to anyone interested in the discussion of important, public controversial questions, but about the same people come rather regularly which makes us feel better acquainted and more "outspoken." The people who come represent all adult ages and are about equally divided as to sex. We have an average attendance of about eighteen to twenty. Both "conservative" and "liberal" thought are represented.
>
> In the winter the meetings are held in the library club room with those attending seated in a semi-circle around a grate fire and in the summer

we have picnic suppers around a fire followed by discussion. An attempt is made to make all the meetings friendly, informal, spontaneous, and to encourage everyone to express opinions. In this, I feel, we are successful; we are not so successful in restraining one or two people who talk too long or too often. This is the most serious problem we have encountered.

The topics for discussion are sometimes chosen ahead of the meeting, sometimes not. There is not particular leadership. At the beginning of the meeting I announce a subject for discussion or ask the group if they have one to suggest, and we are off. It seems better to know beforehand what we are to discuss so that we may have an opportunity to read and become better informed on any particular questions. This is, of course, one of the main objects of holding the meetings. On the other hand some of the devotees say that they wish to discuss, sometimes at least, what is at that time of great current interest, as a strike when it is taking place or the Supreme Court when the President throws a bomb shell at it.

Some of the questions we have discussed are: payment of the soldiers' bonus; government ownership of public utilities; currency question; old age pensions; unemployment insurance; limitation of wealth; the different economic systems: communism, socialism, fascism, capitalism; state and socialized medicine; crime, its prevalence, causes, cost cure; war, causes and cure; tariffs; capital punishment; use of leisure time; race equality; cooperatives; neutrality legislation; right to free speech; freedom of the press; strikes, the right to organize industry; power of the Supreme Court; collective bargaining, etc.

I believe that it should be kept constantly in mind that the sole purpose of a project of this sort is for people to try to learn something from each other from open discussion, and not to try to take group action on anything as a few people mistakenly believe.

Conclusion

Civil society can be understood as something that is shaped primarily or exclusively by those in elected office. However, civil society can (and should) be thought about as something that is shaped by ordinary people who have perspectives and positions that merit public consideration. Deliberative democracy has put into practice some of these concepts (Dryzek 2000; Gastil and Levine 2005), but it is useful to look to historical examples to see how efforts to cultivate a robust and engaged civil society were predicated on the idea that citizen-centered discussion was of great importance. The focus of this chapter has been on some of the materials utilized in such an effort, in part because we have often overlooked the practical aspects of political philosophies. Rather than simply say we ought to have civil discourse, it is useful to consider examples of how it has been put into practice—whether during the 1930s or today. Insights gained from looking at a time not our own can be instructive on multiple levels.

First, civic discourse, as embodied by the discussion project of the PSD and Extension, highlighted an intensely practical way to engage the deeply held views of Americans about the tension between self and community. Each of the topical discussion guides pointed to shared concerns and problems—such as taxes, farm ownership, soil conservation, and differences between urban and rural communities—that began with the invitation for citizens to consider their own views and experiences. It was through honest discussion about one's own views alongside the views of others that considerations about a larger social identity could emerge. While some discussions took place within community enclaves, others brought together diverse individuals who strongly opposed one another. Discussions about soil conservation addressed immediate and personal responses to the issue, but they also invited and encouraged discussion about collective action. For those with a disposition to see themselves as autonomous farmers, such discussions challenged mindsets regarding action. Discussion was both philosophical and deeply grounded in reality; while someone could focus only on their own interests, those interests were interconnected with markets, communities, and the environment. Sitting and discussing with others brought this to the surface. For groups that met over a number of weeks or months, this sense of connection to others grew with time (Shaffer 2014, 95–128).

Second, having the necessary resources aided in accomplishing the intended goal of informed democratic discussion on the part of the federal government. It was extremely important to have resources available that could be utilized both for understanding group discussion as an approach and methodology for engagement and for having topical materials to use once the organizer is comfortable convening people to participate in such discussions. For Extension educators who were not necessarily trained in organizing discussion groups, the supportive infrastructure of materials and personnel made a significant difference (Shaffer, 2018b). Additionally, the flexibility of the PSD with how materials were used enabled states to create resources that could more closely align with the interests and needs of particular communities. Having Iowa farmers be able to discuss their localized concerns while places such as New Mexico and Wisconsin could do the same enabled the top-down nature of a USDA to become more homegrown. The ability to connect concerns with possible policy decisions as well as better understanding of issues helped inculcate the democratic discussion idea within an institution (Extension) and communities (composed largely of independent farmers) that were not inherently inclined to engage in such a way.

Third, democratic discussion in the 1930s grew out of, but was distinct from, earlier forms of public discussion. The open forum movement and lecture circuits that dominated the late nineteenth century and first decades of the twentieth century helped create an environment in which democracy could be "born anew" in the New Deal (Shaffer 2017b). Yet, transformation was occurring that led people away from convening for public discussions. The adoption of radio as entertainment took away some of the interest and intrigue of gathering in such public ways (Shaffer 2017b, 37–39). New technologies altered the ways people communicated and socialized. Panel discussions moved from lecture halls and auditoriums to recording studios. Energy and interest in civil discourse waned as pressing challenges of the Great Depression gave way to World War II and, later, the booming post-war economy.

The discussion program of the USDA during the New Deal sheds light on the possibilities that exist for cultivating democratic discussion, the resources essential to making that possible, and some of the challenges of doing so. Public institutions have the opportunity to encourage civil discourse among citizens. The USDA committed to a project that took small-group discussion among rural people to nearly every state, with one of the PSD staff members writing in 1941 about this work engaging 3 million farm people in discussion groups as a "conservative estimate" (Jones 1941, 122). As this staff member noted, "families of rural America have been discovering that collective effort among themselves can result in a mutual sharing of opinion which turns their old world of ideas into a new universe of problems filled with challenge and optimism" (Jones 1941, 123). Civil discourse can lead to informed action. As we consider the impact of what such a chapter in the democratic narrative of American life has on an audience today, we do well to remember that the garden of democracy requires some tending and we can utilize tools to cultivate that fertile soil.

Notes

1 The Agricultural Adjustment Act, passed in 1933, incentivized farmers to cut their acreage and, by doing so, provided compensation through the Agricultural Adjustment Administration. This action, and subsequent alterations to this original approach, set a course for how the federal government would shape agricultural production.
2 On this difference between the systemic and circumstantial difficulties within democracy, see Mathews (2014).
3 For a full list, see Gilbert (2015, 261–263).

Bibliography

Alexander, Jeffrey C. 2006. *The Civil Sphere*. New York: Oxford University Press.
Andersen, Martin P. 1947. *A Study of Discussion in Selected Wisconsin Adult Organizations and Public Agencies* (Doctoral Dissertation), The University of Wisconsin–Madison, Madison, WI.
Bejan, Teresa M. 2017. *Mere Civility: Disagreement and the Limits of Toleration*. Cambridge, MA: Harvard University Press.
Blunden, Andy. 2016. *The Origins of Collective Decision Making*. Boston, MA: Brill.
Bryan, Frank M. 2004. *Real Democracy: The New England Town Meeting and How It Works*. Chicago: University of Chicago Press.
Bureau of Agricultural Economics. 1942. *Group Discussion and Its Techniques: A Bibliographical Review*. Washington, DC: US Government Printing Office.

Carter, Stephen L. 1998. *Civility: Manners, Morals, and the Etiquette of Democracy.* New York: Basic Books.

Charland, Maurice. 1987. "Constitutive Rhetoric: The Case of the Peuple Québécois." *Quarterly Journal of Speech* 73 (2): 133–150.

Cohen, Herman. 1994. *The History of Speech Communication: The Emergence of a Discipline, 1914–1945.* Washington, DC: National Communication Association.

Coleman, George W., ed. 1915. *Democracy in the Making: Ford Hall and the Open Forum Movement.* Boston: Little, Brown, and Company.

Conkin, Paul Keith. 1955. *Franklin D. Roosevelt and the Origins of the Welfare State.* New York: Harper.

Davetian, Benet. 2009. *Civility: A Cultural History.* Toronto: University of Toronto Press.

Dewey, John. [1916]2008. "The Need of an Industrial Education in an Industrial Democracy." In Jo Ann Boydston (Ed.), *John Dewey: The Middle Works, 1899–1924,* Vol. 10: 1916–1917. Carbondale: Southern Illinois University Press, 137–143.

Dionne, E. J., Jr. 2012. *Our Divided Political Heart: The Battle for the American Idea in an Age of Discontent.* New York: Bloomsbury.

Dryzek, John S. 2000. *Deliberative Democracy and Beyond: Liberals, Critics, Contestations.* New York: Oxford University Press.

Ehrenberg, John R. 1999. *Civil Society: The Critical History of an Idea.* New York: New York University Press.

Ely, Mary L. 1937. *Why Forums?* New York: American Association for Adult Education; George Grady Press.

Escobar, Oliver. 2011. *Public Dialogue and Deliberation: A Communication Perspective for Public Engagement Practitioners.* Edinburgh: Edinburgh Beltane.

Fullinwider, Robert K., ed. 1999. *Civil Society, Democracy, and Civic Renewal.* Lanham, MD: Rowman and Littlefield.

Gastil, John, and Levine, Peter, eds. 2005. *The Deliberative Democracy Handbook: Strategies for Effective Civic Engagement in the Twenty-First Century.* 1st ed. San Francisco: Jossey-Bass.

Gemmell, George A. 1935. Brief Summary of Discussion Group Experiments in Kansas *Office of the President: Francis D. Farrell.* 9D Home Study Department George Gemmell.

Gilbert, Jess. 2015. *Planning Democracy: Agrarian Intellectuals and the Intended New Deal.* New Haven, CT: Yale University Press.

Gould, Marie L. 1942. *Material on Group Discussion and Conference Methods Available in Portland Branch Library.* U. S. Department of Agriculture. Portland, OR.

Hall, John A. 1998. "Geneologies of Civility." In Robert W. Hefner (Ed.), *Democratic Civility: The History and Cross-Cultural Possibility of a Modern Political Ideal.* New Brunswick, NJ: Transaction Publishers, 53–77.

Hanson, Russell L. 1985. *The Democratic Imagination in America: Conversations With Our Past.* Princeton, NJ: Princeton University Press.

Herbst, Susan. 2010. *Rude Democracy: Civility and Incivility in American Politics.* Philadelphia: Temple University Press.

Hill, Frank Ernest. 1935. "Back to 'Town Meetings.'" *New York Times Magazine,* September 15, SM9.

Hilton, Ronald J. 1981. *The Short Happy Life of a Learning Society: Adult Education in America, 1930–39.* (Ph.D. Doctoral Dissertation), Syracuse University, Syracuse, NY.

Hollinger, E. C., and Emma Hawk. 1936. *Discussion Methods.* State College, NM: New Mexico College of Agriculture and Mechanic Arts Agricultural Extension Service.

How Do Farm People Live In Comparison With City People? 1936. *Farmer Discussion Group Pamphlet*, Vol. DS-2. Washington, DC: U.S. Department of Agriculture; The Extension Service; Agricultural Adjustment Administration.

Jewett, Andrew. 2013. "The Social Sciences, Philosophy, and the Cultural Turn in the 1930s USDA." *Journal of the History of the Behavioral Sciences* 49 (4): 396–427.

Jones, A. D. 1941. "Farmer Discussion Is Adult Education." *Adult Education Bulletin* 5 (4): 121–125.

Judson, Lyman, and Judson, Ellen. 1937. *Modern Group Discussion: Public and Private*. New York: The H. W. Wilson Company.

Katznelson, Ira. 2013. *Fear Itself: The New Deal and the Origins of Our Time*. New York: Liveright Publishing Corporation.

Keith, William M. 2007. *Democracy as Discussion: Civic Education and the American Forum Movement*. Lanham, MD: Lexington Books.

Keith, William M., and Paula Cossart. 2012. "The Search for 'Real' Democracy: Rhetorical Citizenship and Public Deliberation in France and the United States, 1870–1940." In Christian Kock and Lisa S. Villadsen (Eds.), *Rhetorical Citizenship and Public Deliberation*. University Park, PA: Pennsylvania State University Press, 46–60.

Lindsley, Clara. 1937. *The Experiences of Our Discussion Group Wisconsin Rural Organizations News*, Vol. 9, pp. 9. Madison, WI: College of Agriculture, University of Wisconsin and U. S. Department of Agriculture.

Loss, Christopher P. 2013. "The Land-Grant Colleges, Cooperative Extension, and the New Deal." In Roger L. Geiger and Nathan M. Sorber (Eds.), *The Land-Grant Colleges and the Reshaping of American Higher Education*. New Brunswick, NJ: Transaction Publishers, 285–310.

Marcus, George E., and Russell L. Hanson, eds. 1993. *Reconsidering the Democratic Public*. University Park, PA: Pennsylvania State University Press.

Mathews, David. 1988. *The Promise of Democracy: A Source Book for Use With National Issues Forums*. Dayton, OH: Kettering Foundation.

Mathews, D. 2014. *The Ecology of Democracy: Finding Ways to Have a Stronger Hand in Shaping Our Future*. Dayton, OH: Kettering Foundation Press.

Mattson, Kevin. 1998. *Creating a Democratic Public: The Struggle for Urban Participatory Democracy During the Progressive Era*. University Park, PA: Pennsylvania State University Press.

Merritt, Eugene. 1937. "Group Discussion and the Problems of Farm Young People." *Extension Service Circular* 263.

Meyers, Arthur S. 2012. *Democracy in the Making: The Open Forum Lecture Movement*. Lanham, MD: University Press of America.

Moreno, Paul D. 2017. *The Bureaucrat Kings: The Origins and Underpinnings of America's Bureaucratic State*. Santa Barbara, CA: Praeger.

Mowry, George E. 1965. *The Urban Nation, 1920–1960*. New York: Hill and Wang.

No Answers in the Back of the Book, *Wallaces' Farmer*, April 13, 1935. *Record Group 16*, Vol. The Records of the Office of the Secretary of Agriculture. Box 4: Entry 34, Folder "Iowa".

Overstreet, Harry A., and Bonaro W. Overstreet. 1938. *Town Meeting Comes to Town*. New York: Harper.

Palmer, Parker J. 2011. *Healing the Heart of Democracy: The Courage to Create a Politics Worthy of the Human Spirit*. San Francisco: Jossey-Bass.

Qvortrup, Matt. 2007. *The Politics of Participation: From Athens to E-democracy*. New York: Manchester University Press.

Rosen, S. McKee. 1937. *Modern Individualism: The Development of Political Thought and Its Present Crisis*. New York: Harper.

Rosenberg, Gabriel N. 2016. *The 4-H Harvest: Sexuality and the State in Rural America*. Philadelphia: University of Pennsylvania Press.

Sandel, Michael J. 1996. *Democracy's Discontent: America in Search of a Public Philosophy*. Cambridge, MA: Belknap Press of Harvard University Press.

Sanders, Elizabeth. 1982. "Business, Bureaucracy, and the Bourgeoisie: The New Deal Legacy." In Alan Stone and Edward J. Harpham (Eds.), *The Political Economy of Public Policy*. Beverly Hills, CA: Sage Publications, 115–140.

Shaffer, Timothy J. 2013. "What Should You and I Do? Lessons for Civic Studies From Deliberative Politics in the New Deal." *The Good Society* 22 (2): 137–150.

Shaffer, Timothy J. 2014. *Cultivating Deliberative Democracy Through Adult Civic Education: The Ideas and Work That Shaped Farmer Discussion Groups and Schools of Philosophy in the New Deal Department of Agriculture, Land-Grant Universities, and Cooperative Extension Service* (Doctoral Dissertation), Cornell University, Ithaca, NY.

Shaffer, Timothy J. 2016. "Looking Beyond Our Recent Past." *National Civic Review* 105 (3): 3–10.

Shaffer, Timothy J. 2017a. "Democracy and Education: Historical Roots of Deliberative Pedagogy." In Timothy J. Shaffer, Nicholas V. Longo, Idit Manosevitch, and Maxine S. Thomas (Eds.), *Deliberative Pedagogy: Teaching and Learning for Democratic Engagement*. East Lansing: Michigan State University Press, 21–36.

Shaffer, Timothy J. 2017b. "Institutions Supporting Democratic Communication Among Citizens." *National Civic Review* 106 (1): 32–41.

Shaffer, Timothy J. 2017c. "Supporting the 'Archstone of Democracy': Cooperative Extension's Experiment With Deliberative Group Discussion." *Journal of Extension*, 55 (5), Article 5FEA1. Retrieved from https://joe.org/joe/2017october/a2011.php.

Shaffer, T. J. (2017d). Democracy as Group Discussion and Collective Action: Facts, Values, and Strategies in Canadian and American Rural Landscapes. *The Good Society*, 26 (2–3), 255–273.

Shaffer, Timothy J. 2018a. "Thinking Beyond Food and Fiber: Public Dialogue and Deliberation in the New Deal Department of Agriculture." In A. Bryce Hoflund, John Jones, and Michelle C. Pautz (Eds.), *The Intersection of Food and Public Health: Examining Current Challenges and Solutions in Policy and Politics*. New York: Routledge, 307–326.

Shaffer, Timothy J. 2018b. A Historical Note: Farmer Discussion Groups, Citizen-Centered Politics, and Cooperative Extension. In S. J. Peters, T. R. Alter, & T. J. Shaffer (Eds.), *Jumping into Civic Life: Stories of Public Work from Extension Professionals* (pp. 191–212). Dayton, OH: Kettering Foundation Press.

Sistare, Christine T. 2004. "Preface." In Christine T. Sistare (Ed.), *Civility and Its Discontents: Essays on Civic Virtue, Toleration, and Cultural Fragmentation*. Lawrence: University Press of Kansas, vii–x.

Sloan, John W. 2008. *FDR and Reagan: Transformative Presidents With Clashing Visions*. Lawrence: University Press of Kansas.

Soil Conservation: Who Gains By It? 1937. *Farmer Discussion Group Pamphlet* (DS-11). Washington, DC: U.S. Department of Agriculture; The Extension Service; Agricultural Adjustment Administration.

Studebaker, John W., and Morse A. Cartwright. 1936. *Plain Talk*. Washington, DC: National Home Library Foundation.

Sullivan, William M. 1982. *Reconstructing Public Philosophy*. Berkeley: University of California Press.

Taeusch, Carl F. 1940. "Discussing Public Policies." *Adult Education Bulletin* 4 (1): 43–47.

Taff, Paul Clifford. 1935. "Iowa Farm People Talk Things over." *Iowa Farm Economist* 1 (4): 8–10.

Taff, Paul Clifford. n.d. Rural Discussion Groups for Iowa, 1935–1936 Taff Papers, Rural Discussion Groups for Iowa, 1935–1936, Box 17: Folder 7, Plan Rural Discussion Groups in Iowa 1935–1936. Iowa State University Special Collections.

The Place of Discussion in Rural Life. 1938. *Wisconsin Rural Organizations News* 10 (1): 11–15.

Toynbee, Arnold. 1932. *Survey of International Affairs, 1931*. London: Oxford University Press.

United States Department of Agriculture, The Extension Service, and Agricultural Adjustment Administration. 1935. *Discussion: A Brief Guide to Methods D-1*. Washington, DC: U. S. Government Printing Office.

United States Department of Agriculture, the Extension Service, and Agricultural Adjustment Administration. 1936. *How to Organize and Conduct County Forums D-2*. Revised ed. Washington, DC: U.S. Government Printing Office.

United States Department of Agriculture, the Extension Service, and Agricultural Adjustment Administration. 1937. *What Is the Discussion Leader's Job? D-3*. Washington, DC: U. S. Government Printing Office.

Washington, George. 1926. *Rules of Civility and Decent Behaviour in Company and Conversation: A Book of Etiquette*. Edited by Charles Moore. Boston, MA: Houghton Mifflin.

Wileden, A. F. 1935. "Five Years of Public Discussion in Rural Wisconsin." *Stencil Circular* 163. Madison, WI: Extension Service of the College of Agriculture, University of Wisconsin.

Wilson, M. L. 1937. "Crackerbarrels 1937 Model." *The Nation's Agriculture* 12 (4), 7–9, 14.

Wilson, M. L. n.d. National Project Discussion Groups and County Forums on National Agricultural Policy *M. L. Wilson Papers, 1913–1970, Merrill G. Burlingame Special Collections, Montana State University*. Box 57, File 14, Discussion Group Notes.

Woodruff, Paul. 2005. *First Democracy: The Challenge of an Ancient Idea*. New York: Oxford University Press.

12

CONCLUSION

The Real Morality of Public Discourse: Civility as an Orienting Attitude[1]

Deborah S. Mower

As the previous chapters in this book show, the United States has experienced many periods of political and cultural conflict before. Yet civility does seem to be in rapid decline today. The culture wars of the 1990s led to the strong group identities fostered by the rise of populist politics in the 2000s and the echo chambers within the radio, print, television, and online media of the 2010s. This development has elicited conditions conducive to incivility and the loss of the careful, considered evaluation of ideas within public life. The 2016 U.S. presidential election was unlike anything most of us have ever seen. While there are doubtless many social, structural, economic, and political factors leading to such a decline, there are psychological forces as well. These forces include (1) our capacity to engage in careful reasoning, (2) our identity or the self-concept we hold of ourselves, our abilities, and our knowledge, and (3) the attitudes that we take toward our fellow citizens as interlocutors, and the evaluation of belief itself. Each of these psychological capacities and foibles affect the assumptions we make about ourselves, about others, and about how we should treat others.

Philosophers and psychologists have long known that our reasoning is subject to influence and error. The tension between reason and emotion—first appearing in Plato's famous division of the human psyche into three parts—is commonly felt.[2] Many times our decisions are irrationally swayed by impulses, overridden by desires, or clouded by emotion. Arguments are often the expression of our anger rather than a real attempt to resolve a problem, as any party in a discussion about public policy (or a long-term relationship) well knows.

We also hold inaccurate and inflated views of ourselves and our capacities. In a study of positive illusion—illusions we hold for the sake of protecting our ego or concept of the self—psychologists Alicke and Govorun (2005) describe the "better-than-average effect": using data from the 1976 College Board Exams for students who took the SAT (approximately 1 million that year), they show that 70% of students rated themselves above the median for leadership, 60% ranked themselves as higher in athletic prowess, and 85% of students reported they had a higher-than-average ability to get along well with others. Our cognitive illusions also extend to morality and our beliefs. Tappin and McKay (2016) published a study in 2016 in which 270 subjects were asked to evaluate their own traits as compared to others. Nearly all individuals in the study considered themselves more moral than others and ranked themselves most highly for the category of morality over the collection of 30 traits.

We not only have cognitive illusions about ourselves but also assume the reliability and accuracy of the views we hold. Study after study demonstrates confirmation bias, our tendency to seek out and uncritically accept evidence that supports our existing views (Lord, Ross, and Lepper 1979). Worse still, we are increasingly unwilling to engage with others or to have our ideas challenged to any degree. Beginning in 2008 there was a sharp increase in the number of individuals who reported displeasure at the very idea of their son or daughter marrying a member of the opposing political party (Iyengar, Sood, and Lelkes 2012). And the recent well-publicized spate of student protests against speakers on college campuses speaks volumes.[3] Clearly, we want to avoid talking about politics at family dinners and to surround ourselves with those who affirm our views, not those who challenge them.

While there is nothing new about the polarizing nature of contentious issues, this very recent spike in incivility, polarization, political sorting, and the loss of public discourse portends a dark future for the American people. Constant calls for civility in the media, on the campaign trail, and on college campuses have come to naught because, as a collective body of reasoners, we are past the point where vague appeals will be effective. Conceptual confusion between politeness and civility abounds, introducing confounds in what researchers on public discourse study as well as blurred lines for acceptable behavior within public discourse. Most problematically, some assume free speech to be normatively boundless and treat calls for civility as an immoral imposition.

We need a better conception of civility and why it matters—one that accurately reflects our psychological capacities and foibles—and concrete proposals for how civility can be developed, maintained, and increased within the American people. John Stuart Mill's classic text *On Liberty* is renowned for its passionate defense of liberty and free speech, yet his demands for the normative constraints on public discourse are little known. To some, it might seem counterintuitive to mine an analysis on liberty to develop an account of civility. If civility—as commonly assumed—requires holding one's tongue, placing restrictions on ideas, adhering to social conventions, or restricting free speech in any way, then it seems like an uneasy marriage, at best, and antithetical, at worst, to the nature of liberty. However, Mill wrote extensively on the liberty of thought and discussion, and his insights can help us to understand what civility is, what its relationship is to politeness, and why it does not restrict free speech when such speech is in the service of inquiry and analysis. Further, the metaphor of the marketplace of ideas—commonly but mistakenly believed to capture Mill's position—has wide appeal, but it falsely assumes that human reasoners are purely rational.[4] A careful examination of Mill's account provides a psychologically realistic model of reasoners in the midst of our irrationality, conviction, and illusions. Using Mill's insights, I develop a robust account of civility that capitalizes on our psychological foibles to provide a normative guide for public discourse. Given the concept of civility as an orienting attitude, I ultimately offer an empirical proposal for researchers, an educational policy proposal, and an appeal to all citizens.

Public Discourse and the Freedom of Thought

Most of us believe we are free as long as we are able to engage in various pursuits unfettered physically, socially, or politically (e.g., political occupation). But for Mill, such freedoms, although legitimate, do not exhaust the nature of liberty: true liberty consists in the freedom of thought. Unfortunately, freedom of thought is everywhere chained by our parochialism, contingent on our individual experience, social groups, institutions, culture, and history as well as on the prejudice created by our unquestioning acceptance of beliefs. Mill provides many examples of such parochialism, but in particular he offers an extended discussion of the nature of Christian belief in his day (Mill 1965, 291–301). He points out that although many individuals have a deep respect for and adhere to Christian doctrines, they do not believe the doctrines because they chose them after a process of selection, had a doctrinal preference, or had a deep historical and theological understanding. Rather, they inherited the doctrines from their families, neighbors, and culture. Religious belief continues as an example in our time as well, although it might be easier for us to recognize the inherited beliefs surrounding race given the highly publicized nature of confederate heritage and monuments.[5] For Mill, even if inherited beliefs are true (think, for example, of the legacy of knowledge in science), unless they are believed *because* one understands the reasons and evidence in support of them—and has chosen and assented to them thereby—one is merely trapped by the received narrow-mindedness of one's family, neighbors, country, culture, or period of time in history.[6]

Even worse than the chains and weights of parochialism on the freedom of thought is the fact that inherited and passively accepted beliefs (what Mill calls "dead beliefs") can become so cemented that they prejudice us both against new ideas and against the active process of evaluating ideas. Mill explains the effect of dead belief on free thought:

> Encrusting and petrifying it against all other influences addressed to the higher parts of our nature; manifesting its power not by suffering any

fresh and living conviction to get in, but itself doing nothing for the
mind or heart, except standing sentinel over them to keep them vacant.
(Mill 1965, 290–291).

Again, Mill (1965, 285–286) notes that inherited dead beliefs may, as a matter of luck, be true—but their truth is no guard against their destructive power
as gatekeepers. He asserts that "this is not the way in which truth ought to be
held by a rational being. This is not knowing the truth. Truth, thus held, is but
one superstition the more, accidentally clinging to the words which enunciate a
truth." Legitimate (as opposed to dead) belief not only requires active assent, but
also requires assent as a consequence of evaluation of reasons and evidence.

Mill (1965, 289) refers to ignorance of the reasons and evidence in support of
one's belief as more than a mere intellectual or epistemic problem; rather, he calls
such ignorance a "moral evil." For Mill, freedom of thought requires both (1) the
active subjection of opinion to evaluation as widespread and accepted practice
and (2) the development of minds. Individuals must have the mental capacity
to fairly and impartially subject opinion to scrutiny, see the relevance of reasons,
comprehend the quality of evidence, believe only on the basis of evidence, and
suspend judgment otherwise—recognizing our fallibility and the limits of knowledge.[7] He notes (286) that "if the cultivation of the understanding consists in one
thing more than in another, it is surely in learning the grounds of one's own opinions." And because both our own beliefs and those of others are equally fallible,
given the contingencies of inheritance and the threat of prejudice, Mill insists that
the practice of evaluating beliefs must be widespread, ongoing, and engaged in by
all.[8] If the conditions of society are such that they exclude either of the foregoing
two necessary conditions, then a people cannot be free. He explains:

> No one can be a great thinker who does not recognise, that as a thinker it
> is his first duty to follow his intellect to whatever conclusions it may lead.
> Truth gains more even by the errors of one who, with due study and prepa-
> ration, thinks for himself, than by the true opinions of those who only hold
> them because they do not suffer themselves to think. Not that it is solely,
> or chiefly, to form great thinkers, that freedom of thinking is required. On
> the contrary, it is as much, and even more indispensable to enable average
> human beings to attain the mental stature which they are capable of. There
> have been, and may again be, great individual thinkers in a general atmos-
> phere of mental slavery. But there never has been, nor ever will be, in that
> atmosphere an intellectually active people.
>
> *(284)*

Mill does not mince words: the loss of freedom of thought is mental slavery—a moral
evil—perhaps most insidious because it escapes identification in our very thoughts.

Given Mill's defense of the freedom of thought, he devotes a great deal of attention to how individuals both can and should engage in evaluating belief. The importance of securing freedom of thought, while essential to each individual, increases with both time and numbers. We are not isolated, individual thinkers; rather, we are engaged in a collective human enterprise in which we pass information and build on knowledge from generation to generation. As many thinkers have expressed (most famously, Isaac Newton), each individual is miniscule, but we see farther and accomplish more by standing on the shoulders of giants, the amalgam of human knowledge through history.[9] Much like Newton, Mill notes that the vast majority of human beliefs contain partial truths.[10] The history of human progress is marked by jettisoning false or partially true beliefs in favor of those which are better—those either true or closer to the truth as we advance our knowledge.[11] Mill (272) explains that "wrong opinions and practices gradually yield to fact and argument; but facts and arguments, to produce any effect on the mind, must be brought before it." We have the opportunity to seek freedom of thought and advance our knowledge, both collectively and individually, only when we can replace false or partially true beliefs with better beliefs.

This emphasis on attaining true beliefs sets a normative goal, which should guide us in our endeavors, both private and public. Mill proposes that agents should adopt a particular attitude in the interest of truth and justice that entails

> condemning every one, on whichever side of the argument on which he places himself, in whose mode of advocacy either want of candour, or malignity, bigotry, or intolerance of feeling manifest themselves; but not inferring these vices from the side which a person takes, though it be the contrary side of the question to our own: and giving merited honour to every one, whatever opinion he may hold, who has calmness to see and honesty to state what his opponents and their opinions really are, exaggerating nothing to their discredit, keeping back nothing which tells, or can be supposed to tell, in their favour. This is the *real morality of public discussion*.
>
> *(303–304, my emphasis).*

For Mill, this attitude toward public discussion is not one merely of politeness or expediency, but a matter of *morality*. It is a moral matter because the conditions of public discussion and the evaluation of belief affect the opportunity for both ourselves and others to seek freedom of thought and advance knowledge. As a moral matter, this attitude is one we should take not toward specific persons but toward the enterprise of evaluating belief itself.

Civility as an Orienting Attitude

Mill's description of the morality within public discussion provides us with a normative goal for seeking the truth and developing knowledge along with a normative justification of the attitude we should take toward the enterprise of evaluating belief. I argue that such an attitude can best be understood as an *orienting attitude*.[12] One can take an attitude, or mental stance, toward a variety of objects, states of affairs, or propositions. For instance, one can take the attitude of *hope* toward a plan or be *apathetic*; one can *despise* a nosy neighbor, *love* a thoughtful partner, *fear* losing a job, or *wish* that one had a crack at that upcoming promotion. Similarly, one can *believe* a proposition like "George W. Bush weighs less than an elephant," or believe that the proposition that "Donald Trump won the popular election" is false (taking the attitude of *disbelief*). Like a regular attitude, an *orienting attitude* is a mental stance one takes. Unlike a regular attitude, an orienting attitude is not linked to specific objects, states of affairs, or propositions but is instead a general stance one takes. As a general stance, an orienting attitude directs one as to what attitude should be taken across a range of objects, states of affairs, or propositions. And just as the concept of "orienting" connotes direction, alignment, or positioning relative to specified criteria, the notion of an orienting attitude connotes direction, alignment, or positioning relative to specified goals, thereby providing both constraints and guidance for actions.

The metaphor of a compass is helpful in explicating the notion of an orienting attitude. As a device or tool for orientation, a compass makes traveling through familiar terrain easier and is invaluable in helping one navigate unfamiliar terrain. But, of course, a compass is useful only if one has the ability to use the tool properly. If one holds the compass upside down, one cannot see the dial; if one holds it vertically, the dial will not move—either way, the compass provides the user with no information. But if one holds the compass flat in the palm of his hand, the dial reliably aligns with the magnetic north pole, providing the user with moment-by-moment updates of the slightest alteration in direction. Given one's goal—let's say one is in Pittsburgh and has a hankering to travel east to New York—the magnetic compass dial will track north, which allows one to travel due east, marked by 90 degrees to the right of north on the dial. Further, one can use the cardinal directions of north, south, east, and west as well as the notational directions embedded in the compass housing (N, S, E, W) to evaluate both whether the device is functioning properly and whether one should stay the course or alter the path at any given moment. For instance, if the magnetic compass dial does not rotate as one turns but is "stuck" irrespective of the direction in which one moves, then the device is jammed or broken. But in cases where the magnetic dial spins freely as one moves, consistently tracking the magnetic north, it is functioning properly and is a reliable mechanism. In these cases, the notational directions marked on the compass housing provide the standards one relies on to identify the current direction of travel and whether any adjustments are needed. Lastly, as an orienting device, one need not check the compass prior to taking each step; rather, one can use the tool to provide general direction, and one needs only to glance at it for either a quick confirmation or realignment.

With the metaphor of the compass in place, we can turn again to the notion of an orienting attitude and its connection with civility. Just as a compass is a device that orients one toward a selected destination, civility as an orienting attitude directs the activity or enterprise of evaluating belief. Just as a compass is an orienting device that guides one's travel, civility is an orienting attitude that guides not only how we should engage in evaluating beliefs but also how we should interact with each other when doing so. And just as a compass limits or excludes alternative travel routes given one's desired destination, given our desires for freedom of thought and the advancement of knowledge, civility limits, constrains, and guides our actions. There is clearly nothing stopping one from changing travel destinations: one is always free to abandon the goal of trekking to New York in favor of, say, hiking southeast to intersect with the Appalachian Trail. Similarly, one is always free to abandon the foundational goals of liberty in thought and gaining true knowledge in favor of, say, maintaining a political group identity and rejecting any potential problematic evidence out of hand. However, unlike the case of selecting travel destinations, abandoning these epistemic and normative goals yields a moral harm to both oneself and others, losing the current conditions of and the opportunity for complete liberty for a people. As an orienting attitude then, civility aligns our pursuits with these goals, directs the activity or enterprise of evaluating belief, and guides our actions and interactions—simultaneously imposing constraints on unacceptable practices while promoting those that are acceptable in light of our goals. As an orienting attitude, civility is action-guiding in the fullest sense.

For a deeper analysis of how civility is an orienting attitude, let's return to Mill's description of the real morality of discussion, as quoted on page 214:

The first thing to note is that such an attitude carries within it goals and values, standards or crit ria for how to evaluate belief, and parameters for the acceptable behavior of oneself and others. By emphasizing the fact that there are various sides to an argument and that one evaluates what counts as being in favor of or discrediting an opinion, Mill reaffirms that the *goal* of public discussion is the evaluation and selection of beliefs that increasingly edge nearer the truth. He also offers us some specific *standards* or *criteria* to use regarding how to evaluate beliefs: first, every side of an argument must be considered; second, our evaluative efforts must be honest (i.e., one must not exaggerate details, distort facts, or deflect challenges for the sake of "saving" a cherished belief)[13]; third, we must consider the entirety of evidence (i.e., one cannot withhold crucial information because its presentation would weaken one's position); and fourth, we cannot discredit a position because it is held or stated by another with whom we disagree (i.e., we cannot reject arguments based on their origins, but only in virtue of evaluating their content and quality).[14] Lastly, he provides *parameters* for the acceptable behavior of oneself and others. There are two such parameters: first, he details what individuals should avoid doing (i.e., maligning others, being intolerant, presenting bigoted views, or lacking frankness); and second, he recommends what individuals should do (i.e., attempt to consider all sides of an opinion calmly, and to be impartial, fairly stating and evaluating positions). These parameters not only provide each individual with behavioral guidance but also offer a standard of assessment. As he notes, anyone—including oneself—who violates these parameters should be condemned, and those who adhere to them should be praised and treated with honor.

Mill does not end his account with a mere recommendation for assessment, but provides a powerful tool for the development and reinforcement of *values*. Although individuals can attempt to discover the grounds of their beliefs privately, the very nature of public discourse makes the process of belief evaluation a public matter. And as a public matter, we can assess how successfully others (as well as ourselves) adhere to the standards for evaluating belief and how they follow the parameters for acceptable behavior in interacting with others while doing so. The very public nature of such assessment capitalizes on the power of models, social censure or praise, and peer pressure. Whenever any individual evaluates beliefs well and behaves appropriately in the process of doing so, she provides a model to others that serves as a form of social education. For example, think of a young child watching his father discuss the DACA initiative (the Deferred Action for Child Arrivals, otherwise known as the failed DREAMer Act) with a next-door neighbor. The child will learn whatever standards and behaviors the father demonstrates as he interacts with the neighbor, even if he is unaware that he is providing an educational model. As the child observes others engaging in conversation in the neighborhood, at church, at school, or on the news, the model he previously learned will either be challenged or reinforced.

Suppose that by the time he becomes a teenager the child (let's call him Ted) fully absorbs a model that endorses the distortion of facts and maligning the character of others the moment they appear to disagree with his stated position. Mill recommends that his interlocutors make liberal use of social censure or praise: in this case, those around him should criticize him for his treatment of facts and others— his mode of advocacy—not for the position he holds. Such social censure need not take a negative or combative turn, for one can demonstrate disapproval merely by withholding attention from one and while giving it to another.[15] For instance, if Sarah presents her arguments without attacking others—even if her position is poorly explained, unclear, lacking good support, or involves outlandish claims—others should continue to engage in conversation: pressing her on various claims, asking questions for clarification, presenting worrisome scenarios she must explain, and so forth. And if young Ted persists in twisting facts and attacking the character of others—even if he has a well-thought-out position and interesting claims—others should redirect their attention to Sarah for she, and only she, is attempting to engage in the enterprise of evaluating belief within a public discussion. Ted will get the message that he needs to alter his approach when he is sidelined each and every time he violates the standards and parameters of civility. He may be quite stubborn or not the brightest, but he will eventually understand and update his model accordingly.[16]

This adjustment of action and the aligning of a model with public expectations inculcate value for the behavioral parameters, evaluative standards, and the goal of evaluating belief. In caring about whether others listen to him, whether they think he said something valuable, or whether he can persuade others to adopt his opinion, Ted eventually realizes that there are better and worse ways of engaging with facts and others and comes to understand the value of civility. Even though he started out with a poor model, the social and psychological power of public discussion and interaction induces him to value civility. He sees the value it holds for others, recognizes the value for himself, and then adopts, implements, and guides his actions accordingly. And for those individuals fortunate enough to start out with an excellent model, the public enforcement of civility—through the behaviors exhibited and modeled by others, social praise, and peer encouragement—serves to reinforce the value of civility. The social nature of public discourse inculcates value for civility, and civility—as an orienting attitude—serves to reinforce the standards used to evaluate beliefs and how we interact with others while doing so.[17] To return to our metaphor earlier, one may not initially see the value of the compass (perhaps one thinks it a silly and useless tool), but one comes to understand its value by watching how others use it, learning how it functions, having others correct one's use of it (as needed), and witnessing how it successfully directs travel and progress toward one's destination. The compass is no longer seen as a useless gadget. Instead, it becomes an indispensable device for hiking and orienteering, functioning to guide and direct one's own travel. Similarly, once one recognizes that there are better and worse ways of evaluating belief and interacting with others, civility functions as an orienting attitude. It aligns our pursuits with the selection of better belief, directs the activity or enterprise of evaluating belief through standards, and guides our actions and interactions through parameters of acceptable behavior.

Orienting attitudes align, direct, and guide the actions of individuals, but the practice of civility is not a solitary affair: civility is strengthened through social support. As we all know, it is easy to see the faults and failings of others but it is monumentally difficult to see them in ourselves. It is even more difficult to scrutinize the grounds of chosen beliefs or to attempt to break the concrete framing of our inherited beliefs. Mill grants that very few individuals have the capacity of high logical reasoning, capable of honestly evaluating both sides of a position with absolute impartiality.[18] We may have civility as an orienting attitude and honestly and forthrightly attempt to align our reasoning to the standards for evaluating belief. Yet we may manage to do so only part of the time or to a certain degree: civility guides our attitudes, but our thoughts themselves are not yet free. Civility becomes easier when others share the same orienting attitude and serve as a "check" on the opinions we hold and the ways in which we evaluate them. To return to our metaphor, suppose that one amateur hiker reliably reads the compass accurately but tends to veer slightly to the left with every step, while another is capable of maintaining a straight course but tends to read the compass quickly and make sloppy measurements. They both are orienting via the compass, but their various liabilities and skills affect their travel. When corrected by the other, each is a more effective orienteer.

Correspondingly, civility is strengthened and becomes more effective when others hold the same orienting attitude toward the enterprise of belief evaluation. For instance, one individual may consistently default to a particular interpretation of events, while another can evaluate events impartially yet, when feeling pressed, tends to blow up in anger or to malign characters rather than to evaluate claims. Because it is psychologically easier for us to evaluate how successfully others adhere to the foregoing standards for evaluating belief and follow the parameters for acceptable behavior (blind to our own faults, we tend to protect our tender egos but can be ruthless with others), we each serve as a means of correction or "check" in the enterprise of belief evaluation. In an odd twist, our psychological limitations become a form of support for others in the process of belief evaluation. As Mill explains, "the steady habit of correcting and completing his own opinion by collating it with those of others, so far from causing doubt and hesitation in carrying it into practice, is the only stable foundation for a just reliance on it" (272). The social nature of public discourse means that we each serve as such checks, yet nothing about our interaction requires active cooperation. As an orienting attitude, civility requires only that each individual maintain a commitment to the parameters, standards, and goal of belief evaluation: a commitment to the enterprise itself. As long as individuals have such an orienting attitude, their commitment guides their own actions and places others under their watchful eye. Given the strong role others play in sustaining civility, in the next section I explain the implications of civility as an orienting attitude for engagement, tolerance, and free speech.

Implications for Engagement, Tolerance, and Free Speech

We previously considered the example of Sarah and Ted and how the standards for belief evaluation and behavioral parameters both develop and reinforce the value of civility. Rather than providing a set of guidelines, an account of civility as an orienting attitude serves to develop a general approach, stance, or attitude that one should take toward the evaluation of belief across all situations and in all contexts. And as an orienting attitude, civility carries some interesting—and perhaps unexpected—implications for our attitudes toward engagement, tolerance, and free speech. One might assume that civility would require three things: (1) our engagement with others must always be polite, (2) extreme emotion or conviction would be considered unacceptable, or (3) one must avoid treating interlocutors as adversaries. On the contrary, Mill's behavioral parameters are narrowly focused on the activity and process of belief evaluation. They impose no additional limitations as long as such behaviors do not negatively affect the process. To understand why, let's take a closer look at each of these.

Let us first consider politeness. Although many people assume that civility and politeness are synonyms, politeness is merely a potential marker for civil behavior. For example, seeing a colleague carry an umbrella is a good marker or clue that it is raining outside, but the clue does not mean that it is in fact raining: on this sunny day, your colleague might merely be returning the umbrella to her office. Much like the statistical regularity between rainy days and umbrellas, there are statistical regularities between occurrences of civility and politeness. Markers merely provide valuable information about the relationship or occurrence. Politeness serves to regulate our action in conformity with commonly held social expectations: the social niceties of phrases surrounding arrival and departure, gift giving and acts of kindness, group gatherings and family events, professional interactions, and ceremonies or rituals. In short, politeness is the standard of proper manners in social contexts. But of course, manners also include speech, and this is the crucial point of intersection between these two concepts. Regarding polite speech, former U.S. ambassador to the United Nations Adlai Stevenson II perhaps defined politeness best when he quipped, "Politeness is the art of choosing among one's real thoughts."[19] In the midst of conversation—particularly, heated conversation over contentious topics—one may be tempted to say many things, but politeness is the learned art that helps us to reduce inflamed feelings, tame our tongues, and select our thoughts with an eye toward maintaining the niceties of social convention.

Politeness serves as a potentially valuable marker or clue that another is civil, or that one is guiding one's actions by the orienting attitude of civility. Suppose that one is engaged in a highly emotional argument about kneeling during the national anthem with Sarah. Because tempers have flared on all sides, when one observes Sarah pause, mull over her thoughts, and then say something in a calmer fashion than she had previously, her newly polite speech provides a valuable clue that she is now attempting to engage civilly and to guide her actions accordingly—despite failing mightily when she lashed out in anger earlier in the conversation. Suppose Ted is also a member of this heated debate and previously flung personal insults and mocked everyone who disagreed with him. When one observes him refrain from making such comments when he speaks next, this marked change toward polite behavior is again a valuable clue that he is now attempting to engage civilly. But politeness is merely a marker and not definitive proof of civility, for one can artfully select words that are perfectly polite yet say them in a tone dripping with contempt or poorly concealed anger. Although the formal niceties of social convention may be maintained, contempt and anger are especially valuable clues that one's interlocutor is unlikely to evaluate one's argument impartially.

Such clues provide valuable information about the attitude held by others, and they allow us to know how to respond. Suppose that Ted calmly presents a view about black football players and appears to be earnest and frank in presenting his belief, yet the view he presents is highly bigoted. Mill insists that all must present opinions calmly, evaluate claims and positions impartially, and refrain from

maligning others, being intolerant, presenting bigoted views, or being disingenuous. So how should one respond in this case? Ted has violated the criteria for
evaluating belief, yet meets the behavioral parameters. Is he being inflammatory?
Up to his old tricks? Does he honestly believe the bigoted view he just presented?
Does he even realize that it is a bigoted view? Should one engage him or simply
give up on the attempt? If Ted has adjusted his previous behavior, his increased
politeness is a valuable clue that he now is engaging civilly; hence, one should
continue to engage him. However, if Ted had not adjusted his previous behavior, standards of polite discourse provide no markers of a civil attitude; hence,
continued attempts at engagement accomplish nothing beyond providing him a
soapbox. Polite speech merely serves as a possible marker for a civil orientation,
but civility does not require politeness.

Second, let us consider the role of emotion in our discourse. Suppose Ted
presents his bigoted views without maligning or attacking others, but it is clear
that he is very passionate about the views he presents and cannot hide his anger
in response to Sarah's arguments. Civil engagement also does not prohibit the
presence and expression of extreme emotion or strong conviction, as long as it
does not negatively affect the enterprise of evaluating belief. Because issues that
dominate public discourse are typically highly contentious, prohibiting extreme
emotion and conviction would be impractical: few of us have the desire and none
of us have the ability to engage as passionless Vulcans.[20] How, then, should we
interpret Mill's behavioral parameters to consider all sides of an opinion calmly,
and to be impartial, fairly stating and evaluating positions? The solution here is
to note that emotions come in types and degrees. Some emotions will be more
disruptive to our reasoning than others. A momentary flash of anger at something
another says may pose no lasting harm to our interactive enterprise of belief
evaluation, but flying into a blind rage surely does. Feeling righteous indignation
at the misinterpretation of one's claim poses no harm as long as one is able to
explain the evidence and reasons for one's position clearly, but refusing to engage
further because of the (mistaken) slight surely does. Similarly, feeling strong conviction that drives one to engage in vigorous debate poses no harm. Mill (275)
notes, "I must be permitted to observe, that it is not the feeling sure of a doctrine
(be what it may) which I call an assumption of infallibility. It is the undertaking
to decide that question *for others*, without allowing them to hear what can be said
on the contrary side."

Strong conviction that motivates the attempt to restrict the free thought of
others—an abuse of power and the destruction of an opportunity—is surely harmful. Consequently, whether extreme emotions or strong convictions are acceptable
depends entirely on whether they are curtailed to function appropriately within
our interactions and public discourse: aligned, guided, and directed by civility as
an orienting attitude.[21]

And third, let us consider the potential adversarial nature of some forms of
discourse. As we noted earlier, civility is sustained and strengthened under the

watchful eye of others, but such a watchful eye does not require active cooperation and may even take the air of a careful guard. In fact, Mill argues that the
stakes of belief evaluation are so high that human knowledge and progress toward
the truth "has to be made by the rough process of a struggle between combatants
fighting under hostile banners" (Mill 1965, 297). Fighting under hostile banners—
opposing forces—does not entail that one should behave with hostility toward
another. It merely suggests that one's interlocutor is a competitor. To civilly engage
with another as a competitor, one constantly challenges the beliefs of others: testing them for weaknesses, posing objections, raising additional sources of evidence,
evaluating the quality of the evidence presented, considering whether facts have
been presented fairly, and rooting out the bias and prejudice of hidden, inherited,
dead beliefs. Although such a constant and direct challenge to the views of others
violates norms of politeness, such engagement is civil because it is guided by a
commitment to the foregoing behavioral parameters and standards of belief evaluation. In an interesting twist, civil engagement allows treating one's interlocutor
as a competitor and engaging in aggressive debate as long as one is guided and
limited by civility as an orienting attitude.[22]

What do these details surrounding civil engagement mean for tolerance?
Because the term "tolerance" is used in various ways, how we answer this question depends on how we think of the concept of tolerance: tolerance for actions,
other persons, or ideas. Our previous discussion of engagement offers insights
for tolerance of action. In the context of belief evaluation,[23] actions that violate
the evaluative standards and behavioral parameters of civil engagement need not
be tolerated. If another is slinging insults, spouting prejudiced, dead beliefs, and
refusing to consider facts and sources of evidence fairly then there is no point
in attempting to engage. But if there is any indication that the other is honestly
interested in engagement, even if he is quite poor at doing so or presents a bigoted view, then one should tolerate his actions, attempt to engage, and guide the
process of belief evaluation given one's own commitment to civility. In making
this determination, Mill (302) demands careful analysis of one's motives for, most
often, the appeal to temperance or toleration "is given whenever the attack is
telling and powerful, and that every opponent who pushes them hard, and whom
they find it difficult to answer, appears to them, if she shows any strong feeling on
the subject, an intemperate opponent." We cannot make calls for temperance and
we cannot charge another with incivility in the self-serving support of our position. Doing so would itself violate the evaluative standards of belief required by a
civil orientation. Consequently, as long as another is attempting to engage civilly,
we must continue as well, tolerating him and his ideas.

Note that true tolerance in the context of civil engagement is not silence,
but the active discussion of ideas, however abhorrent they may be. As he notes,
an agent "is capable of rectifying his mistakes, by discussion and experience. Not
by experience alone. There must be discussion, to show how experience is to be
interpreted" (272). Tolerance of ideas is not acceptance, but the submission of an

idea—like any other—to the same process of belief evaluation. Tolerance of one who holds abhorrent ideas is not silent exclusion, but active engagement with a competitor, a competitor that one happens to believe holds a false belief, a poorly formed opinion, or an inherited bigoted view. In fact, Mill urges gratitude at the opportunity to challenge one's own position: "let us thank them for it, open our minds to listen to them, and rejoice that there is some one to do for us what we otherwise ought, if we have any regard for either the certainty or the vitality of our convictions, to do with much greater labour for ourselves" (285). True tolerance in civil discourse is not silence, exclusion, or avoidance but the active engagement with those with whom one disagrees and the subjection of their beliefs to scrutiny.

Lastly, we can examine the implications for free speech. Given Mill's analysis of the nature of liberty, freedom of thought, and insistence on the consideration of all ideas, free speech is of supreme—although not absolute—value. In our culture, appeals to free speech are often made to justify statements intended to harm, such as slurs, labels that marginalize, attacks on character, or public ridicule. As we have seen, such statements would violate the behavioral parameters of civility and Mill holds that they should be denounced. This bears repeating: the most ardent defender of free speech would deny that such statements have any place in public discourse. One's utterance may have other purposes—to express indignation, demonstrate party loyalty or partisanship, maintain identity with a social group, and so forth—but such an utterance is not the presentation of a belief for the purposes of its evaluation. Of course, one remains physically and politically at liberty to say and do whatever one pleases, but such statements have no moral justification insofar as they do nothing to support or advance conditions for the liberty of thought. Similarly, mere pronouncements of one's view (e.g., "I believe X, I have the right to say so, and I do not care what you think") also fail to claim the moral justification for free speech. Such a close-minded pronouncement may be nothing more than the presentation of an inherited, dead belief, full of bias, once true and full of meaning, but now merely a façade of words for a trapped mind. Again, one remains physically and politically at liberty to make such pronouncements, but for Mill such utterances are not forms of free speech. Consequently, whether something qualifies as an instance of free speech—and hence, whether it has moral justification for its expression—depends on whether one is actively engaged with others in the enterprise of evaluating belief. For Mill, the difference between mere utterances and free speech is the nature of the activity and the orienting attitude we hold.

Proposals: Empirical, Educational, and Personal

We began this chapter with the hunt for a better conception of civility and how it was related to the notions of politeness, free speech, and toleration for difference. A second motivating question for the chapter was to discover how civility can be developed, maintained, and increased within the American people. How the second question is answered depends on our answer to the first as well as our goals, which are either descriptive or normative.

As citizens and researchers, we all recognize the problem: a rapid loss of civility and a severe decline in the quality of American public discourse. One approach to studying the problem is descriptive: the goal is to catalog the variety, extent, and interaction of contributing factors. Clearly, before we can take steps to address the problem, we must understand how it came to be. And an essential step in gaining an accurate description is to identify civility as a distinct concept and phenomenon. Much like a physician attempting to diagnose a patient, it is essential to detail all the symptoms and to discriminate between related phenomena. If she confounds two related illnesses or makes the wrong diagnosis, the prescribed treatment plan may accomplish little, be completely ineffective, or make the illness worse.

The account of civility as an orienting attitude allows researchers to tease apart the notions of civility and politeness. By maintaining a focus on civility as norms surrounding the enterprise of belief evaluation and politeness as social convention more broadly, researchers can more accurately describe and diagnose the rapid loss of civility and its effects on reason and evidence in the public square. The account of civility offered here also allows researchers to tease apart civility and toleration. By maintaining a focus on civility as normative requirements for engagement and toleration (or what typically passes for it) as refusal to engage yet suffering to listen in silence, researchers can more accurately describe and diagnose the rapid loss of civility and how it relates to disengagement and exclusion (and engagement and inclusion, correspondingly). This account of civility also clarifies the relationship between civility and free speech. By maintaining a focus on civility as a normative limit on free speech, researchers can more accurately describe and diagnose when claims to free speech are likely to be inflammatory or receive public support, whether on college campuses, in the media, or in the speech of politicians. Lastly, this account of civility integrates a psychological and a social analysis. By maintaining a focus on the psychological foibles of individual human reasoners and how they function within social contexts, researchers can more accurately describe and diagnose how certain kinds of social interactions either diminish or strengthen civility and our capacity for deliberation within a democracy. Consequently, my first proposal for researchers is to adopt the model of civility as an orienting attitude for myriad empirical benefits.

The second approach in answering the question of how civility can be developed, maintained, and increased within the American people is normative. On this approach, the goal is to explain civility as an achievable ideal. Clearly, before we can take steps to address the problem of the rapid loss of civility and its effect on public discourse we must know what we would like to achieve. The most detailed description of the problem yields no productive proposals without a vision for what we think *should* be the case. A physician may have full access to all information about a patient—weight and blood pressure readings, diet analysis, lists of allergies and medications, bloodwork, genetic tests, x-rays, and MRI scans—but lacking a guiding conception of health and a plan to achieve it, one is merely awash in detail.

The account of civility as an orienting attitude provides precisely such an achievable ideal. Through his discussion of the "real morality" of public discussion, Mill provides us with a normative argument based in freedom of thought. The robust conception of civility developed upon it provides a goal or an aspirational vision for what we can achieve as individuals and collectively in public discourse. The goal is simple and likely to be overlooked by many as being too mundane, for it merely requires the adoption of a particular attitude toward the enterprise of belief evaluation. This account of civility provides researchers with a normative basis on which they can develop their proposals to arrest and reverse the loss of civility and the erosion of public discourse. The marriage of the descriptive and normative approaches provides an analysis that not only accurately describes the current state of the problem but also provides a normative justification for a proposal that can move us toward our goal.

Although Mill provides us with a normative justification for civility, our goal is not an idealistic philosopher's fiction for he also offers practical guidance on how civility can be achieved: training in philosophy, beginning with logic. He notes,

> It is the fashion of the present time to disparage negative logic—that which points out weaknesses in theory or errors in practice, without establishing positive truths. Such negative criticism would indeed be poor enough as an ultimate result; but as a means to attaining any positive knowledge or conviction worthy the name, it cannot be valued too highly; and until people are again systematically trained to it, there will be few great thinkers, and a low general average of intellect" (294–295).

As individuals, we need not become great thinkers. We merely should aspire to become citizens of general and average intellect. This is an attainable goal, reached easily by teaching citizens how to evaluate arguments with the tools of logic.

Beyond the explicit study of logic, general training in philosophy serves to mitigate the psychological foibles of human reasoners, and in particular the cognitive illusions that interfere with the impartial and accurate evaluation of belief. We tend not only to hold ourselves in great esteem, better than average on a host of traits, but we also tend to engage in motivated reasoning to maintain our beliefs. We seek out evidence that confirms the beliefs we currently hold, and we accept supporting evidence without question. It is worse still when all parties to a debate believe that they are more moral than others, that the views they espouse are better supported, and that they have the weight of morality behind them in discounting all attempts to challenge their positions. Philosophy, as a discipline, focuses on the analysis and justification for belief—any belief and all beliefs—regardless of topic. The modes of presenting arguments and subjecting all belief to equal scrutiny, the use of logic to examine the underlying structure or form of an argument, the careful evaluation of evidence, the variety of argument types, and the systems of logic all provide individuals with a common basis: a collective set of concepts, theoretical tools, and strategies for evaluating belief.

This is where civility as an orienting attitude not only gains a foothold but also becomes a fortress. Even though individual thinkers may not have the developed cognitive and logical skills to be fully impartial, civil interlocutors provide sufficient challenge to their beliefs: pressing claims, presenting counterexamples, challenging evidence, questioning the relevance of evidence for a claim, condemning one for a misstep in making an attack on another's character or relying on a fallacy to press a point. This kind of civil engagement is modeled within classes where claims and positions are considered as items of analysis—apart from the loyalties or illusions of who happens to believe them—and jointly scrutinized by members of the class.[24] Such a method teaches students the common tools and strategies with which to evaluate belief, the manner in which they might engage civilly in the midst of scrutinizing highly contentious issues, and the ways in which they can be combatants and defenders of an idea under the guidance and constraint of civility as an orienting attitude.

Mill's endorsement of philosophy, both in terms of the study of logic and as active training in belief analysis, leads me to offer an educational proposal for increasing civility within public discourse. Nationwide, general education programs within colleges and universities require some facility with critical thinking, but unfortunately, much of what passes for critical thinking amounts to a general process of analysis and synthesis from Bloom's taxonomy of learning, not rigorous belief evaluation trained by logic and philosophy. Educators can make general education requirements more stringent, and college and university officials can also impose additional requirements: if our concern is to educate students to be competent reasoners capable of engaging in civil discourse, then few requirements seem as pressing.[25] Further, critical thinking and logic can and should be taught at all levels of the curriculum, adjusting for content, difficulty, and skill from K-12 through college.[26] By teaching students the tools of logic and providing active training in belief analysis, educators teach students norms for belief evaluation and parameters for acceptable behavior when evaluating beliefs with others.

Seen in this light, the project of teaching philosophy is to teach the shared norms of public discourse. And the justification for teaching students these shared norms can only be normative: it necessarily depends upon a goal or aspirational vision for what we can achieve as individuals and collectively in public discourse. As individuals, we can become good thinkers, capable of engaging with others to evaluate personal beliefs and public policy on issues that affect our lives. And collectively, we can become an informed and engaged people, capable of choosing policies that determine the conditions and opportunities of people, including those for discussion and free thought—the only conditions Mill thought made us truly free. In the end, these reflections drive us to think about how we, as citizens, can help to develop, maintain, and increase civility within the American people. In thinking about this second motivation for the chapter, what concrete things can we do to increase civility within our own lives and our interactions with others?

The third and final proposal I offer is ultimately an appeal to each citizen: if we are concerned with increasing civility within public discourse, then we must each attempt to adopt civility as an orienting attitude. Given the length of time it takes to implement new research and educational policies, such a commitment on the part of each citizen may seem insignificant, yet is perhaps the most crucial given the current lack of civility within American public life. In the words of Abraham Lincoln, this is an appeal to "the better angels of our nature" in the pursuit of our vision. We have already seen that our cognitive illusions affect how we think of ourselves and how we treat others. We are each subject to cognitive illusions about the quality of our own reasoning, the self-serving belief that we are more moral than others, and the propensity to engage in motivated reasoning by seeking evidence to support our reasoning and avoiding that which does not. To have these illusions of our cognitive and moral superiority and the quality of our arguments and yet to commit to subjecting one's beliefs to the scrutiny of another—whose morality one suspects is tainted and whose reasoning capacity one believes is low—are difficult.

Adopting civility as an orienting attitude is a significant action on the part of each individual because it is a significant commitment. Such a commitment requires us to make choices, moment by moment, as to how we will treat others: whether we will engage with them and submit our cherished beliefs to scrutiny, attempt to manipulate the outcome through skewing evidence or attacking others, or perhaps refuse to engage at all. These choices are not all made in moments of calm discussion with those who share like positions. The choices that matter most are those in the midst of discussions with those with whom we share the least commonality of experience, assumption, interpretation, and belief.

Perhaps this appeal to adopt civility as an orienting attitude should be recast as a challenge—a challenge to each citizen because it is a challenge in terms of difficulty. If we merely interact with those who share like positions, who hold the same religious beliefs, share our political beliefs, or desire to raise children in the same way, we will doubtless have many polite and pleasurable reaffirmations of commonly shared beliefs. Such interactions primarily involve the exchange of dead beliefs. Rarely do they involve the enterprise of belief evaluation. The challenge for us is to realize that our desire to surround ourselves with like-minded others is an unwillingness to have our identities, moral views, and beliefs challenged. So this is another concrete choice, moment by moment, about our attitudes toward those with whom we choose to engage. We do not need to be bosom friends with others, share a commitment to shared governance, have an attitude of cooperation, agree with any opinion they hold, like them as persons, or even respect others' intellects. All we must do is to commit to engage with others, even if and even when they challenge our beliefs, and to guide and direct our actions and responses by civility. In the end, civility within public discourse depends on each individual holding civility as an orienting attitude.

Conclusion

The primary motivation for this chapter was to develop a better conception of civility combined with a secondary motivation to explore how civility can be developed, maintained, and increased within the American people. John Stuart Mill's account of liberty and the freedom of thought provides the normative basis for public discourse we need to develop a robust conception of civility. The account of civility as an orienting attitude provides researchers with clear distinctions as well as explanations of the relationships between civility and politeness, tolerance, and free speech. Additionally, this account of civility can help us all to navigate our social relations better by providing a new interpretive context for challenges to our beliefs and new criteria to know what tolerance requires of us, when free speech is justified, and when the social norms of politeness are appropriately breached.

As well as shaping our research on civility, this account also yields an educational proposal that we redirect our efforts to teach the shared norms of public discourse. Although there may be many proposals for how to address the problem of declining civility and increasingly dysfunctional public discourse, no proposals will be effective solutions unless they attend to the ways in which individuals either learn or fail to learn the shared norms of public discourse. Similarly, no proposals will be effective solutions unless they attend to the psychological foibles and limitations we have as human reasoners. And in the end, all research and proposals are but theoretical exercises unless we make the choice to engage with others and careful choices about how we treat them when doing do. As Mill puts it, this is the real morality of public discourse. The smallest step forward, yet one that all can take, is for each individual to adopt civility as an orienting attitude. And with one step, we begin.

Notes

1 I am deeply grateful to Robert Boatright and Steven Skultety for helpful comments on an earlier version of this chapter.
2 Although Plato presents an extended metaphor and discussion of the division of the psyche into the charioteer and two horses in his dialog *Phaedrus*, readers will likely be most familiar with *The Republic* in which he marks a tri-partite division of the psyche into reason, spirit (emotions/the passions), and the appetites (instincts). See Plato (2008), Book IV.
3 See for example, details about the protests surrounding political scientist Charles Murray, as described in Svrluga (2017).
4 The metaphor of 'the marketplace of ideas' first appeared in print in Justice William O. Douglas' concurring opinion in the 1953 United States Supreme Court case *United States v. Rumely*. Unfortunately, Mill never used that phrase and the metaphor—hailing from

models of free-market capitalism and idealized purely rational actors from economics—
is woefully inadequate at best and a gross misrepresentation at worst. Mill's arguments
involve a teleological progression toward truth, competition between agents (not ideas),
are fully attentive to all the psychological foibles of real thinkers, and offer an account
of cognitive development.

5 Examples abound surrounding the controversies of declarations of Confederate Heritage Month and the Confederate flag and monuments. In 2016, Mississippi governor
Phil Bryant declared April to be "Confederate Heritage Month" and posted the official
proclamation on his website. The proclamation, issued again 2017 but nowhere to be
found on the governor's website, was found for a time on the Mississippi Division of the
Sons of Confederate Veterans website. The controversies over the use of the Confederate
symbol on the Mississippi state flag persist to this day with groups on both sides forming
protests demanding its maintenance or removal. The issues are best explored in a newspaper article by a local paper in Mississippi: see Dreher 2015.

6 Mill notes that individuals place "unbounded reliance only on such of their opinions
as are shared by all who surround them, or to whom they habitually defer; for in proportion to a man's want of confidence in his own solitary judgment, does he usually
repose, with implicit trust, on the infallibility of 'the world' in general. And the world,
to each individual, means the part of it with which he comes in contact; his party, his
sect, his church, his class of society" (270). This more narrow-minded person he con-
trasts with someone slightly more open-minded, yet still a slave to inherited beliefs:
"the man may be called, by comparison, almost liberal and large-minded to whom it
means anything so comprehensive as his own country or his own age. Nor is his faith
in this collective authority at all shaken by his being aware that other ages, countries,
sects, churches, classes, and parties have thought, and even now think, the exact reverse.
He devolves upon his own world the responsibility of being in the right against the
dissentient worlds of other people; and it never troubles him that mere accident has
decided which of these numerous worlds is the object of his reliance" (270).

7 He notes that an agent's "reasons may be good, and no one may have been able to refute
them. But if he is equally unable to refute the reasons on the opposite side; if he does
not so much as know what they are, he has no ground for preferring either opinion. The
rational position for him would be suspension of judgment" (287).

8 He explains that "the beliefs which we have most warrant for, have no safeguard to
rest on, but a standing invitation to the whole world to prove them unfounded. If the
challenge is not accepted, or is accepted and the attempt fails, we are far enough from
certainty still; but we have done the best that the existing state of human reason admits
of; we have neglected nothing that could give the truth a chance of reaching us: if the
lists are kept open, we may hope that if there be a better truth, it will be found when
the human mind is capable of receiving it; and in the meantime we may rely on having attained such approach to truth, as is possible in our own day. This is the amount
of certainty attainable by a fallible being, and this is the sole way of attaining it" (271).

9 The original quotation by Newton is "If I have seen further it is by standing on ye
sholders [sic] of Giants." *The Correspondence of Isaac Newton, Volume I*, edited by HW
Turnbull, 1959, p. 416.

10 Mill notes, "the conflicting doctrines, instead of being one true and the other false,
share the truth between them; and the nonconforming opinion is needed to supply the
remainder of the truth, of which the received doctrine embodies only a part" (295).

11 Within the history of science, the concept of phlogiston provides the best example
of Mill's point. Early chemists sought to explain why items that burned lost weight,
given that the remaining ash was considerably lighter. They posited phlogiston as a substance inhering in combustible objects, that, when burned, was given off into the air.
Although we now know that phlogiston does not exist, the theory was not completely
wrong-headed. Phlogiston theorists were correct that there was some substance that

was being lost or exchanged in the process of combustion, although they did not have a correct account of the substance. The rejection of phlogiston theory in favor of oxygen illustrates how humanity can move to adopt better beliefs that capture or more closely approximate the truth.

12 Philosophers will recognize in the following discussion many features of a virtue; indeed, I think civility is best understood as an intellectual virtue. There are many fascinating issues as to how civility relates to other intellectual virtues, such as humility, open-mindedness, or prudence, but that discussion is beyond the purpose of this chapter.

13 He charges that the "gravest" problem with argumentation is "to argue sophistically, to suppress facts or arguments, to misstate the elements of the case, or misrepresent the opposite opinion" (302–303).

14 Philosophers refer to the attempt to either accept or reject an argument based on its origin as a "genetic fallacy": the erroneous evaluation of an argument based on factors extraneous to it rather than the content of the argument itself.

15 And of course, social censure may sometimes require more dramatic—and direct— action. Such situations some easily to mind (e.g., a disruptive student in a classroom, a peer making a racist slur in the midst of co-workers), and the types of direct responses are clear (e.g., the professor excusing the student from class or imposing penalties on classroom participation points, informing the peer that such views are unacceptable). My focus in this paragraph is on less direct forms of social censure because such examples and potential responses do not spring easily to mind, although they are no less common and the responses are no less powerful a form of disapproval.

16 As this example makes clear, Mill is not endorsing the modern notion of the "call-out." The public call-out is a recent strategy adopted by some (typically on online platforms and in social media) to draw attention to the views of others considered morally problematic in some way (e.g., an instance of cultural appropriation, such as a photograph posted on Facebook of someone at a party dressed as a Native American), under the assumption that social progress is best made by making particular individuals accountable (and subject to public censure) for the views they hold. Despite the (potentially) laudable goals (i.e., moral progress) behind the notion of the call-out, the trouble is that it has tended to be used merely as a way to malign the character of others, which forestalls all conversation and is itself considered morally unacceptable by Mill (see points earlier). The crucial point is that for Mill, public censure can be used only when individuals are failing to engage civilly within public discourse in how they either approach facts or engage with others, but one cannot censure others merely because of the views they hold. For Mill, there are moral limits on when any form of public censure can be used, either direct or indirect: it must be in the service of advancing public discourse. Consequently, the notion of accountability would not suffice to morally justify a public call-out, even for views that we find morally reprehensible.

17 Moral psychologist Mark Alfano (2013) similarly notes the power of public assessment in his description of virtue labels to describe the behavior of others as a means to inculcate virtue.

18 Mill notes that "there are few mental attributes more rare than that judicial faculty which can sit in intelligent judgment between two sides of a question" (301).

19 Despite the fact that this quotation is widely attributed to Stevenson, I have never been able to track down a precise reference for a particular speech, letter, or text.

20 As noted above, it is because so few of us have the developed ability to engage in truly impartial reasoning that we serve as 'checks' for each other's arguments.

21 Note that this is a claim about how emotion functions within the exchange and not an empirical claim about the possibility or difficulty of curtailing emotion psychologically for specific individuals. Clearly, curtailing emotion is difficult. Within any interaction with another, we may successfully experience extreme emotion and engage civilly at one moment and fail to do so later in the conversation. Similarly, someone who has

a goal to lose weight or to stop smoking may successfully avoid chocolate cake or a tempting cigarette at one moment and not another. Extreme emotion can be but is not always disruptive; nor is it impossible to overcome. Psychologists using cognitive behavioral therapy to treat anxiety, depression, addiction, and anger management provide a great case in point.

22 This feature of civility as an orienting attitude has an important connection with the distinction between competition and melees in the philosophy of sport. Competitions are constrained by background agreement on rules, standards, or norms while melees lack such means of governing or guiding behavior. Note that what is most distinctive about civility as an orienting attitude is that it may begin with only one party conforming to the standards of belief evaluation and parameters of behavior. Over time, one can inculcate value in others for the background rules, standards, or norms via social praise and censure. From this standpoint, what is so problematic about much of what passes for discussion in the public square presently is that it has the character of a melee. And what is so interesting about civility as a orienting attitude in light of the distinction between competitions and melees is that it offers a means to transform current melees into competitions for the analysis of belief and social policy. For more on the distinction between competition and melees and types of competition, see Skultety, Steven. 2011.

23 Tolerance of actions toward others given cultural and global differences is a different topic, far beyond our focus on the conditions of public discourse.

24 This is the basis for taking on the role of a "devil's advocate" in which one must practice the ardent defense of a position, regardless of whether one happens to believe it. The aggressive presentation of arguments is invaluable for learning the grounds of our beliefs, and Mill argues that if we cannot find individuals who actually believe positions to argue for them, then we must ourselves become devil's advocates. We must "know them [the arguments] in their most plausible and persuasive form; he must feel the whole force of the difficulty which the true view of the subject has to encounter and dispose of; else he will never really possess himself of the portion of truth which meets and removes that difficulty.... So essential is this discipline to a real understanding of moral and human subjects, that if opponents of all important truths do not exist, it is indispensable to imagine them, and supply them with the strongest arguments which the most skilful devil's advocate can conjure up" (287–288).

25 The new University of Mississippi Creed includes civility, and faculty, staff, and administration are actively seeking ways to foster and develop it within curricula and extracurricular activities. For more information, see https://olemiss.edu/info/creed.html.

26 In fact, the national organization PLATO (Philosophy Learning and Teaching Organization) focuses on pre-college philosophy learning opportunities. See https://www.plato-philosophy.org/ for more information.

Bibliography

Alfano, Mark. 2013. *Character as Moral Fiction*. New York: Cambridge University Press.

Alicke, Mark and Olesya Govorun. 2005. "The Better than Average Effect." In Mark Alicke, David Dunning, and Joachim Krueger (Ed.), *The Self in Social Judgment*, New York, NY: Psychology Press, 85–108.

Charles Lord, Lee Ross, and Mark Lepper. 1979. "Biased Assimilation and Attitude Polarization: The Effects of Prior Theories on Subsequently Considered Evidence." *Journal of Personality and Social Psychology* 37 (11): 2098–2109.

Dreher, Arielle. 2015. "Mississippi Flag: A Symbol of Hate or Reconciliation." *The Jackson Free Press*. Retrieved September 9, 2015, from http://www.jacksonfreepress.com/news/2015/sep/09/mississippi-flag-symbol-hate-or-reconciliation/.

Iyengar, Shanto, Gaurav Sood, and Yphtach Lelkes. 2012. "Affect, Not Ideology: A Social Identity Perspective on Polarization." *Public Opinion Quarterly* 76 (3): 405–431.

Lincoln, Abraham. 1861. "First Inaugural Address."*Abraham Lincoln Online.* Retrieved March 4,1861,from http://showcase.netins.net/web/creative/lincoln/speeches/1inaug. htm.

Mill, John Stuart. 1965. "On Liberty" (1859). In Lerner (Ed.), *Essential Works of John Stuart Mill.* New York: Bantam Books.

Newton, Isaac. 1959. The Correspondence of Isaac Newton, Vol. I. Edited by H.W. Turnbull.

Plato. 2008. *The Republic,* Benjamin Jowett, translator. Project Guttenberg. http://www. gutenberg.org/files/1497/1497-h/1497-h.htm.

Skultety, Steven. 2011. "Categories of Competition." *Sport, Ethics, and Philosophy* 5 (2): 433–446.

Svrluga, Susan. 2017. "Some Harvard Students Protest Charles Murray Speech." *Washington Post,* Retrieved September 6, 2017, from www.washingtonpost.com/news/grade-point/wp/2017/09/06/some-harvard-students-protest-charles-murray-speech/?utm_ term=.1325b94e0b44.

Tappin, Ben, and Ryan McKay. 2016. "The Illusion of Moral Superiority." *Social Psychological and Personality Science* 8 (6): 623–631.

INDEX

Note: Page numbers in *italics* and **bold** denote references to figures and tables, respectively.

action as choice: as affair of the moment 16; changing behavior and 27; classifying 17–18; as exercise of various skills 15–16; as intellectual act 17; obscuring civility as responsiveness 19–21; for quantitative work 18–19; surface features of 17–18

action as exercise of skill 11, 15–19, 21, 23, 27–28

active engagement 170–171

Adams, John 185

ad hominem attacks 148–149, 163

aggressive strategic game framing: contributing to candidate incivility 89–90; impact of 91; shaping election hostility and incivility 91; strategic game frames vs. 85–86; war-like language in 86–87; *see also* strategic game frames

Agricultural Adjustment Act (1933) 205n1

Ahmed, Farham "Ronny" 98, 105

Alicke, Mark 210–211

American Friends' Service Committee 167

anti-political correctness 127–129

Artan, Abdul Razak Ali 98

aspersions 50–52

authoritarians: characteristics of 117–118; motivations of 117–118; opposition to political correctness 132; reactions to threats of out-groups 115; as

Republicans 131; threat perception of 116–117; worldview of 117

avatars 78

bandwagon effect 98

Bannon, Steve 162

Barclay, Robert 168

behaviors 39, 48

Belcher, Jonathan 183

Bennett, W. Lance 162

Bin Laden effect 119

bipartisanship and government 14

Brooks, Deborah Jordan 47, 56, 62

Buck, Ken 64–65

campus shootings: civility in FSU tweets **105**; civility in OSU tweets **108**; data and methods 98–100; FSU crisis narratives 109; FSU discourse *100*; FSU shooting 102–106; FSU tweets content **103**; misinformation of 106–107; OSU crisis narratives 109; OSU discourse *101*; OSU shooting 106–108; OSU tweets content **106**; overview 100–102; social media discourse on 104–105

Chafe, William 63

Charlottesville, Virginia rally 162

citizen-centric frames 88–89, 90

citizens' trust in government 73–74, 76

civic controls 52–53